ADOPTION LITERATURE
FOR CHILDREN
AND YOUNG ADULTS

Recent Titles in
Bibliographies and Indexes in Sociology

Housing and Racial/Ethnic Minority Status in the United States: An Annotated
Bibliography with a Review Essay
Jamshid A. Momeni

Homicide: A Bibliography
Ernest Abel, compiler

Youth Information Sources: An Annotated Guide for Parents, Professionals,
Students, Researchers, and Concerned Citizens
Marda Woodbury, compiler
With a chapter on data bases compiled by Donna L. Richardson

Work and Alcohol Abuse: An Annotated Bibliography
John J. Miletich, compiler

Violence and Terror in the Mass Media: An Annotated Bibliography
Nancy Signorielli and George Gerbner, compilers

Latin America, 1983-1987: A Social Science Bibliography
Robert L. Delorme, compiler

Social Support Networks: A Bibliography, 1983-1987
*David E. Biegel, Kathleen J. Farkas, Neil Abell, Jacqueline Goodin, and
Bruce Friedman, compilers*

Diffusion of Innovations: A Select Bibliography
Klaus Musmann and William H. Kennedy, compilers

Native American Youth and Alcohol: An Annotated Bibliography
Michael L. Lobb and Thomas D. Watts

The Homosexual and Society: An Annotated Bibliography
Robert B. Marks Ridinger, compiler

Pro-Choice/Pro-Life: An Annotated, Selected Bibliography (1972-1989)
Richard Fitzsimmons and Joan P. Diana, compilers

Sikhs in North America: An Annotated Bibliography
Darshan Singh Tatla

ADOPTION LITERATURE FOR CHILDREN AND YOUNG ADULTS

An Annotated Bibliography

SUSAN G. MILES

Foreword by John T. Pardeck

BIBLIOGRAPHIES AND INDEXES IN SOCIOLOGY, NUMBER 21

Greenwood Press
New York • Westport, Connecticut • London

Library of Congress Cataloging-in-Publication Data

Miles, Susan Goodrich.
   Adoption literature for children and young adults : an annotated
bibliography / Susan G. Miles ; foreword by John T. Pardeck.
     p.   cm.—(Bibliographies and indexes in sociology, ISSN
0742-6895 ; no. 21)
   Includes indexes.
   ISBN 0-313-27606-4 (alk. paper)
   1. Adoption—Juvenile literature—Bibliography. 2. Adoption in
literature—Bibliography. 3. Children's literature—Bibliography.
4. Young adult literature—Bibliography.   I. Title.   II. Series.
Z7164.A23M55 1991
[HV875]
016.3627'34—dc20   91-31854

British Library Cataloguing in Publication Data is available.

Library of Congress Catalog Card Number: 91-31854
ISBN: 0-313-27606-4
ISSN: 0742-6895

First published in 1991

Greenwood Press, 88 Post Road West, Westport, CT 06881
An imprint of Greenwood Publishing Group, Inc.

Printed in the United States of America

The paper used in this book complies with the
Permanent Paper Standard issued by the National
Information Standards Organization (Z39.48-1984).

10 9 8 7 6 5 4 3 2 1

To my husband, William,

and to our daughters,
Amy, Jennifer, Lindsay, Emily, Kelsey,
Morgan, Courtney, Julia and Whitney
who taught us much

Contents

Foreword by John T. Pardeck   ix

Acknowledgments   xi

Introduction   xiii

Preschool and Primary Readers   1

Intermediate Readers   33

Junior High Readers   83

High School Readers   111

Appendix A: Selected Resources for Further Reading   169

Appendix B: Directory of Adoption-related Organizations   175

Author and Illustrator Index   181

Title Index   189

Subject Index   197

Foreword

Using books to help people deal with problems has been known by a variety of names including bibliotherapy, bibliocounseling, biblioeducation, bibliopsychology and literatherapy. Regardless of how one defines the use of books in treatment, we know that for centuries books have helped people deal with the problems of everyday life. In recent years, both professionals and laypersons have found books to help not only adult deal with problems, but also children.

Books are especially useful in helping children deal the developmental and adjustment difficulties related to the adoption process. In my practice, I have found that books allow adopted children to read about others who have had problems similar to their own including anxieties and frustrations, hopes and disappointments, failures and successes. Books offer adopted children solutions as well. Adopted children can read about how others have overcome problems related to adoption and then apply this information to their own situation. Books can also serve as a preventative tool; they can help not only adopted children, but also adoptive parents, prevent difficult situations from becoming major problems.

As professionals and experienced adoptive parents realize, there are many critical dynamics that occur when children move into an adoptive home. First, they begin to realize that they will not be returning to their biological families. Even if a child has been in foster care for an extended time period, he or she may continue to harbor the fantasy of returning to the biological family. Adoptive parents must help the child work through this fantasy, as the fantasy will not be given up easily.

Adoptive children also go through a period of mourning once they realize they will not return to their biological family. Throughout this period, the child will need help expressing anger and pain about the past. We now realize that open and truthful discussion of the past is the best approach; denial and secrecy can have negative effects on the child's well-being.

Adoptive children, especially those who were abused or neglected, or are older, may have particular needs. Often they are angry and fearful of adults, and simply see the adoption as another placement that will end in rejection. Even though the first several weeks of adoption may go smoothly, this period of tranquility may be artificial if the child has not yet bonded with his or her new family. This "honeymoon" period often ends when the child begins to feel stirrings of caring and longing. These feelings stimulate earlier unresolved pain and generate fears of again being rejected, and the child's response may be to resist the adoptive parents. The child may even anticipate this rejection and fight it by resisting the adoptive parents to avoid being rejected again.

Through all of these complex emotions and pressures, books can provide tangible support and information for both adoptive parents and their children. Numerous books, both fiction and nonfiction, are presented in Susan Miles' **Adoption Literature For Children and Young Adults**. These books capture the critical dynamics of the adoption process. Miles offers an annotated bibliography of over 500 books focusing on the preschool child to the young adult. The books address a variety of adoption and adoption-related situations that focus on current issues including transracial and intercountry adoption, special needs adoption, and surrogacy and open adoption. Even though the books offered focus on children and young adults, older adults, in particular adoptive parents, will find the work helpful.

Adoption Literature For Children and Young Adults is invaluable as a resource guide for those who need information about adoption. The intended audience--parents, practitioners, teachers, librarians, and especially adopted children--will benefit from this timely work.

John T. Pardeck

Acknowledgments

In thanking those who provided assistance and support I wish to recognize Central Michigan University for granting my sabbatical leave request for the fall 1990 semester and to my colleagues within the University who supported my efforts. As well, I express much appreciation and gratitude to Ruth Helwig, Margaret Dodd and Michael Fitzpatrick of the Central Michigan University Library Interlibrary Loan Office for their precise, well-timed, systematic acquisition of more than 700 books over a year's time for me to read and evaluate. Ever able and willing to respond to my calendar and reading needs, they are largely responsible for the completion of this book.

Likewise, I am indebted to adoptive parents, professionals, agencies and support groups that have assisted and encouraged me to complete this volume because they see it as a useful, valuable and needed resource. Knowing I was working on a project that potential readers were already eager to consult helped me endure the process.

At the same time I am grateful to Mildred Vasan and Lynn Taylor, editors at Greenwood Press, for their advice, editorial assistance and suggestions. Thanks also go to Jennifer and Courtney Miles for their willingness to help evaluate books and assist in the editing process; and to Kim Thornton for assisting with the initial compilation. In addition, Karyn and Wayne Kiefer, of Little Dickens Book Shoppe, were very helpful in suggesting titles and providing information on recent releases.

I am especially appreciative to Carole Beere, Associate Dean of Graduate Studies and Research at Central Michigan University, not only for her technical assistance with word processing and laser printing of the manuscript, but also for her friendship, encouragement and moral support. While not an adoptive parent herself, she is able to listen, empathize and support as if she were.

I express thanks and heartfelt gratitude to my family for their helpfulness, patience and understanding for the year I spent with my nose in a book and my eyes glued to a computer monitor. I wish to thank my husband, Bill, who helped me conceive of the idea and lovingly prodded me when I balked that there might not be enough material for a book. I thank him for his persistence when mine failed. I also want to thank our eight adopted children, some of whom helped me by bringing me titles scribbled on scraps of paper, dog-eared books from the local paperback exchange and books from their own bookshelves and trips to the library. I especially thank them for they are the ones who convinced me, verbally as well as silently, that this book was a needed resource.

Introduction

After we adopted our first child, a preschooler, I went to the local public library hoping to obtain a few books which mirrored our family's adoption experience to read with her. While I found a few books, there were not as many as I expected there to be. As a parent I was rather disappointed, but as a librarian I was bothered that children's adoption books were not more readily available and accessible. Indeed, I was expecting to find a bibliography such as this to help guide me through the literature on the topic.

Similarly, years later, one of our Korean-born young teens plaintively asked me why she could not find books in her school library or the public library about families "just like us." Seeking the reassurance of a shared experience, she wanted to read about other multi-racial families created through adoption, but could not find them with the library skills she had learned. In fact, many of the books included within this bibliography cannot be found in libraries under such seemingly appropriate subjects as "adoption," "multi-racial families" or "Koreans in the United States," because those aspects of the books have not always been determined to be an important enough feature of the book to warrant a subject heading in the card catalog. Rather, the assigned subject headings for such books might be "family life," "school stories" or "friendship" making it nearly impossible for the reader, adult or child, to discover those dealing specifically with adoptive situations.

PREVIOUS BIBLIOGRAPHIES

Although some standard bibliographies on adoption have been published, their scopes have either been too broad or too limited to meet this need. For example, the first recognized bibliography which attempted to bring together adoption literature was **Adoption Bibliography and Multi-Ethnic Sourcebook** compiled and annotated by Elizabeth Wharton Van Why (Hartford: Open Door Society of Connecticut, 1977). In her introduction, Van Why indicated she endeavored "to catalog the writings of adoption regardless of the audience intended." (p. vii) The bibliography is arranged by type of publication, such as periodical articles, non-fiction books, fiction books, children's books, audio-visual materials, periodicals and bibliographies. In addition to the forty-four children's books identified, ten other works of fiction and twenty-nine personal narratives are also listed.

In order not to duplicate Van Why's work, Lois Ruskai Melina began her research in 1974 for the compilation of **Adoption: An Annotated Bibliography and Guide** (New York: Garland, 1987). Each chapter is devoted to a specific aspect of adoption, such as birthparents, infant adoptions, special needs adoptions, intercountry adoptions, psychological issues in adoption, minorities, and search and reunion. One chapter, which lists forty titles, examines children's resources. Although adult fiction is not covered and the scope and arrangement of Melina's bibliography is different from Van Why's, it clearly takes its place as Van Why's logical successor and remains the most recent comprehensive bibliography on the subject.

At approximately the same time, seeking to address the need for a bibliography of reading material on adoption for children and young people, the National Adoption Center produced a fourteen-page booklet by Louisa Berger and Ellen G. Satre entitled **Books on Adoption for Children and Youth** (Philadelphia: National Adoption Center, 1986). Not widely available, this bibliography annotates fifty-nine titles, fiction as well as non-fiction, divided into three broad grade-level categories. Sensing the same need, in her **Making Sense of Adoption** (New York: Perennial Library, 1989), Melina included an appendix entitled "Bibliography of Children's Books" in which she features ninety books, separating fiction and non-fiction and arranging them by broad grade levels. As an additional useful feature, Melina devised a separate subject index to these books.

In addition, within the general literature as well, there are reference volumes which help to identify some books with adoption themes. Resources such as Dryer's **The Bookfinder: A Guide to Children's Literature About the Needs and Problems of Youth Aged Two and Up** (Circle Pines, MN: American Guidance Service, 1977-89); Fassler's **Helping Children Cope: Mastering Stress Through Books and Stories** (New York: The Free Press, 1978); and Bernstein's **Books to Help Children Cope With Separation and Loss** (2nd ed. New York: Bowker, 1983) all refer the reader to a few appropriate titles. None of the titles mentioned here, however, covers the depth of the adoption literature suitable for children and young people nor provides reasonable subject access.

SCOPE OF THIS WORK

To fill the need not met by these previous titles, what follows here is an initial attempt to gather and bring some order to that literature published primarily since 1900, suitable for children and young adults, dealing in some way with the adoption experience. In addition to addressing a variety of adoption and adoption-related situations, these books also take on a diversity of literary forms. Indeed, there are books at all reading and interest levels which deal with a variety of adoption-related issues and themes, such as arrival stories featuring children of varying ages, books concerning different family situations and different types of adoptions. Although most of the books included feature adoption as a main theme, others use adoption as a secondary theme, while others still have characters who just happen to be adopted. Due to the nature of the bibliography, there was no attempt to be qualitatively selective. As a result, the quality of the books identified here varies greatly. The lengthy annotations will allow readers a better opportunity to evaluate each title's usefulness. Although books will often fit into more than one category, the titles mentioned here are representative.

ADOPTION SITUATIONS

Age of Arrival

Arrival stories are recounted for small children in such titles as Koehler's **The Day We Met You** (61) in which the adoptive parents detail the plans that led up to the baby's coming home. Taber's **Adopting Baby Brother** (88) tells about the arrival of a new baby from a sibling's point of view. Titles for older readers regarding infant adoptions are Ryan's **Adoption Story: A Son is Given** (413) which describes an unusual independent adoption and Viguers' **With Child: One Couple's Journey to Their Adopted Children** (430).

Books which feature children adopted at a slightly older age include Turner's **Through Moon and Stars and Night Skies** (91) in which an southeast-Asian-born preschooler boy retells the story of his journey to his new home and parents. Titles for older readers include Carney's **No More Here and There** (354) which describes the adjustment of a five-year-old adoptee, while White's **Journey for Margaret** (435) recounts a father's journey to World War II England to adopt a daughter.

Older child adoptions featuring children between the ages of six and eleven at the time of their arrival include Fredkove's **Advice for Adopted Kids** (106), Talbert's **Dead Birds Singing** (324), and Gates' **Sensible Kate** (163). Books for older readers include Magorian's **Good Night, Mr. Tom** (306) and Palmer's **And Four to Grow On** (395).

Although in the minority, there are some books which feature adolescent (age twelve through eighteen) adoptions. First's **I, Rebekah, Take You, The Lawrences** (160) and Lowe's **The Different Ones** (188) share main characters who are adolescents. These books combine the personal qualities of adolescence with the trust and uncertainty issues associated with an older adoption.

Sibling Adoption

Not always do children arrive in adoptive families one at a time. Several books deal with the adoption of sibling groups. Doss' **The Really Real Family** (105) relates one family's experience adding two sisters to a family that already had children. Fear and distrust are sensitively portrayed in Miles' **Aaron's Door** (195) in which Aaron hides in his new room while his little sister quickly adapts to her new parents. On a more mature level, Pedersen's **At Sixes and Sevens** (397) relates the adjustment during the first year after the arrival of sisters, while Peipenbrink's **Forever Family** (399) and Mall's **P.S. I Love You** (387) describe their sibling adoptions.

Single-Parent Adoption

While children do not always arrive alone, some children arrive home to a single parent. On a young level, Van Workom's **Something to Crow About** (93) describes the caretaking of a bachelor rooster who takes on a brood of little chicks. **The Boy Who Wanted a Family** (50) by Gordon is adopted by a non-traditional single mother. For older readers, Koons' **Tony: Our Journey Together** (376) recounts a single mother's adoption of a young boy in Mexico and Margolies' **They Came to Stay** (389) tells about her struggles to adopt a little girl from Vietnam, then another from Korea.

Foster Parent Adoption

In addition to single parents, there are books which relate foster parent adoptions. In **Holly's New Year** (166) by Hamilton, Holly, who is very comfortable in her new foster home, has some interesting experiences which help her decide to be adopted by her new family. In Swetnam's **Yes, My Darling Daughter** (234), it is only after she finds she loves her foster mother's new baby that Josephine can understand love between people who are not related and agrees to her adoption.

Stepparent and Relative Adoption

Stepparent and other relative adoptions are the most common type of adoption in the U.S. and there are books that mirror that experience. Bates' **Bugs in Your Ears** (128), Platt's **Chloris and the Creeps** (213) and Colman's **Tell Me No Lies** (149) each have a resentful female main character who has a loving, patient stepfather who wants to adopt her and eventually gains her permission to do so. In both Cameron's **A Spell is Cast** (141) and Tripp's **Changes for Samantha** (240), an uncle adopts an orphaned niece. Books on stepparent or relative adoptions for older readers include Angelo's **Big Little Island** (270) and Shyer's **My Brother, The Thief** (318).

Transracial Adoption

Transracial adoptions of minority children by white parents is another common theme in these books. Bunin's **Is That Your Sister?** (2) has become the standard book for young children to explain how a biracial child became part of a white family. Other books include Warren's **Walk In My Moccasins** (244) in which a white family adopts a Native American sibling group, and Newfeld's **Edgar Allen** (311) which describes the eventual disruption of a black child's adoption by a white family due to community prejudice. Fitzgerald's **Chocolate Charlie** (460), for older readers, recounts the difficulties of a single white man trying to adopt a preschool black child and Rigert's **All Together: An Unusual American Family** (407) gives a father's perspective on his interracial family.

Intercountry Adoption

In addition to transracial adoption, intercountry adoption is also a popular theme in these books. Since most foreign-born adoptees are from South Korea it is no surprise there are more books about Korean children than children from any other single country. Fisher's **Katie Bo: An Adoption Story** (44) and Girard's **We Adopted You, Benjamin Koo** (49) relate the arrival and adjustments of two Korean-born children. Slightly older fiction featuring Korean-born children include McDonald's **Mail-Order Kid** (189), and McHugh's **Raising Mother Isn't Easy** (190), while Sass' **I Am Adopted** (79) relates the arrival and adjustment for a child from India. For older readers, Chinnock's **Kim: A Gift From Vietnam** (356) and Sheehy's **Spirit of Survival** (419) provide personal narratives, while Register's **"Are Those Kids Yours?": American Families With Children Adopted From Other Countries** (406) presents a more objective view.

Amerasian Children

A specific category of intercountry adoption is that of Amerasian children, or children who are part Asian and part American. After the Korean War, Pearl Buck took particular interest in these children in that country. In addition to establishing a foundation to help meet their unique needs, she also wrote books describing their situation. Her photographic story, **Welcome Child** (1), relates the first year in the United States of a kindergarten-age caucasian-Korean girl and **Matthew, Mark, Luke and John** (137) describes the Korean street life of four Amerasian boys who are found by American soldiers and adopted to the States. For older readers, Eitz writes a compassionate volume concerning the adoption of her black-Vietnamese son, **Dark Rice** (365) and Rogers' **Dearest Debbie** (408) focuses on the short life of an adopted Korean/Puerto Rican teen. While it does not deal specifically with adoption, Moen's **Written in the Stars** (479) portrays a two-generation story of life in Korea for Amerasians as Suki tries to locate her American birthfather.

Racial Identity

Problems regarding the racial identity of adopted children show up in several books. Irwin's **Kim/Kimi** (296) features a young teen coming to terms with her Japanese heritage. Terris' **Whirling Rainbows** (325) and Cheatham's **Life on a Cool Plastic Ice Floe** (283) both deal with the personal identity of Native Americans, while Becker's **All Blood is Red--All Shadows Are Dark** (342) concerns itself with an interracial couple and their family members' racial identity.

Minority Family

Adoptions by minority families, primarily black families as those described here, are portrayed in a few books. Caines' **Abby** (35) is a gregarious adopted little girl whose brother teases her, but also proudly brings her to school for show and tell. Sesame Street viewers will recognize the characters in Freudberg's **Susan and Gordon Adopt a Baby** (45) which reiterates the adoption of baby Miles which happened on national television. Myers' **Won't Know Till I Get There** (309) shares a fictionalized account of a family adopting a thirteen-year-old street-smart boy. For older readers, **Mixed Blessing** (385) by McMillon relates the story of a mixed-race child born in Germany.

Special Needs

Aside from older child, sibling and minority child adoptions, special needs adoptions are covered on a limited basis. Taylor's **Tuck Triumphant** (238) is about a family adopting a deaf Korean boy. For older readers there are insightful works such as **Adopting Children With Special Needs** (332) which describes the daily life of several families who have adopted special needs children, and Dorris' **The Broken Cord** (361) is one father's journey with his son who is afflicted by fetal alcohol syndrome (FAS). Steven's **Kim: "I Will Make Darkness Light"** (423) concerns itself with the life of a blind Korean girl who becomes a famous singer and Wheeler's **Tanya: The Building of a Family Through Adoption** (434) is a mother's recollections of living with and adjusting to the adoption of a school-age physically disabled child.

Large Families

Another type of family addressed in these books is large families, those having five or more children. Probably the most well-known large adoptive family is the DeBolt family depicted in Blank's **Nineteen Steps Up the Mountain** (347) with their brood of U.S.-born and foreign-born children with a variety of physical disabilities. Other large families are described in Lund's **Patchwork Clan** (384), Nason's **Celebration Family** (393), Doss' **The Family Nobody Wanted** (362) and Sandness' **Brimming Over** (416). Books about large families for younger readers include Weyn's **Make Room for Patty** (98), Doss' **A Brother the Size of Me** (155) and L'Engle's **Meet the Austins** (303).

Birthparents

In addition to the child and the adoptive parents, the birthparents make up the final section of the adoption triad. Becker's **To Keera with Love** (249) provides an insight to a young pregnant teen's thoughts and activities as she continues her adoption plans for her baby. In Eyerly's **He's My Baby Now** (292), the teen birthfather attempts to raise the baby himself only to realize how difficult it is, and decides adoption will give the baby the best opportunities. Musser's **I Would Have Searched Forever** (392) and Dusky's **Birthmark** (364) relate two birthmothers searching for the children they relinquished years ago.

Search and Reunion

Adoptees searching for birthparents and their subsequent meetings are dealt with in many books. Primarily written for older readers, there are, in fact, probably more books on this one aspect of adoption than all others. Fictionalized accounts include Lifton's **I'm Still Me** (304), Klass' **To See My Mother Dance** (299), Lowry's **Find a Stranger, Say Goodbye** (305) and Okimoto's **Molly By Any Other Name** (312). Informative books on search and reunion include Lifton's **Lost and Found** (379) and Gediman's **Birthbond**(368), while personal narratives relating searches and reunions include Begley's **Missing Links** (434), Savage's **I Heard My Sister Speak My Name** (489) and the story which started all the others, Fisher's **The Search for Anna Fisher** (366).

Surrogacy and Open Adoption

Two relatively new aspects of adoption, surrogacy and open adoption, are also represented in this bibliography. Landau's **Surrogate Mothers** (260) provides an objective view of the situation, while Bunting's **Surrogate Sister** (281) presents a fictionalized account of the effects on other family members. There are a greater number of books dealing with open adoption in which the birthmother is included in the decision-making process regarding the placement of her child as well as the opportunity to maintain contact. For the very young reader there is Sly's **Becky's Special Family** (85) in which a little girl talks about her relationship with her adoptive family and her birthfamily. For older readers, Anderson's **And With the Gift Came Laughter** (335) describes how the author's two children joined the family through open adoptions, while **Open Adoption: A Caring Option** (382) by Lindsay presents an overview of the process with insights from all members of the adoption triad.

Other Significant Situations

Other aspects of adoption handled in books include the secrecy of adoption and the abuse and neglect of children. Several stories deal with children erroneously believing they are adopted. These include Lindbergh's **Nobody's Orphan** (184), Martin's **Claudia and the Great Search** (191) and Coleman's **The Different One** (285). Other stories, usually gothic novels and mystery stories, feature a tragic heroine who has just discovered she is adopted and how it dramatically effects her life. These include books such as Arthur's **Requiem for a Princess** (272), Dwyer-Jones' **Reach for the Shadows** (458) and Robins' **Wait for Tomorrow** (488).

Abusive or neglectful situations which involve moving to live with new families include, for younger readers, Joy's **Benjamin Bear Gets a New Family** (174), Levinson's **Silent Fear** (182) and Sach's **A December Tale** (221). For older readers, these same themes can be found in Crawford's **Mommie Dearest** (359) and Johnson's **What Lisa Knew: The Truth and Lies of the Steinberg Case** (375).

Adoption-Related Situations

In addition to books directly dealing with adoption, there are also several titles to which adopted children may readily identify. These borderline titles involve such situations as foster care and orphanage or other group living arrangements since so many adopted children have that experience. Likewise, there are books involving stepparents or living with other relatives which may never speak directly of adoption, but since the process of becoming a blended family is so similar, the reader may find some benefit.

MATERIALS EXCLUDED

At the same time, certain material has purposefully been excluded from this bibliography. For the most part, Bible stories, such as those of Moses, Esther, Joseph and Samuel, which include a biblical character being raised by someone other than birthparents have been omitted. Likewise, books which are primarily reports, studies or other scholarly works have not been included. In addition, books on genetics have been excluded as have books dealing with interracial themes or cultural heritage unless they, in some way, include direct adoption implications. While these kinds of books are often useful to adoptive families, they fall outside the scope of this bibliography. Furthermore, guide books, that are designed with detailed instructions how to adopt, or how to search for birthparents or how to handle an unwanted pregnancy are not included here.

COMPILATION TECHNIQUES

To compile the list of titles to examine for possible inclusion in this bibliography, I used a number of different techniques. Initially, I consulted many published standard bibliographies, selection aids, and book lists which might have contained references to books dealing with adoption. Several of the more pertinent of these lists are included within Appendix A. During the same time, I queried over fifty adoption support groups and agencies requesting bibliographies and book lists they might have produced. The return rate was quite successful and the titles suggested added greatly to the growing list. In addition, I checked card catalogs in libraries I visited, as well as those I could access via computer. I also performed several online database searches of the Online Computer Library Center (OCLC) which provides access to thousands of library collections. Meanwhile, to complement my more formal approach to title-gathering, once people knew I was working on this project, I received title suggestions through the mail, over the phone, on scraps of paper, and in passing. What resulted from these various gathering techniques was a list of nearly 750 possible adoption-related titles for evaluation.

Once the book list was produced, I determined which titles were available locally, sought others through interlibrary loan, and purchased those that were not otherwise available. Over the course of a year, I systematically evaluated, read and annotated those books which I felt to be appropriate for this work. The result is a bibliography of 503 titles all of which, except when noted, have been personally examined.

ORGANIZATION

Following this introduction is the bibliography itself which is divided into four major categories each representing a different age/grade grouping of the potential readers. Each of the four categories is then divided into nonfiction and fiction. As a general guideline the chapter entitled "Preschool and Primary Readers" includes books appropriate for preschool children through grade three. Grades four through six are included in "Intermediate Readers," while grades seven through nine are included in "Junior High School Readers" and grades ten through twelve and beyond are handled in "High School Readers."

The age/grade divisions used within the grade categories were made in hopes of coordinating materials written within similar reading and interest levels. The first three grade categories are self-explanatory. The high school category, however, includes many adult titles as these young readers often read fiction and nonfiction originally published for the adult market. Consequently, adults may also find this bibliography helpful for determining appropriate reading for their own needs as well.

Following the bibliography are two appendices which provide adult readers with supplementary information. Appendix A is a selected list of sources used to compile the bibliography, as well as other relevant secondary sources primarily concerning adoption, children's literature and reading. Appendix B is a selective directory of adoption-related organizations which may be helpful.

Concluding the book are three indices assuring access to the books within the bibliography by author, title and subject. Effort was made to give each title at least two subject headings in hopes of enhancing this volume's usefulness. It should be noted that authors and titles cited within annotations are also accessible through the appropriate indices.

AVAILABILITY OF TITLES INCLUDED

No effort has been made to determine whether the books described in the bibliography are available for purchase since such information is quickly out-dated.

Checking with a local bookstore or library will verify that information.   With interlibrary loan cooperation among libraries most all of these titles are available by borrowing.   Contact a local public library for assistance and details.   The OCLC number for each book has been provided, when available, and can be found at the end of each citation.   This item identification number should assist libraries using the OCLC network for interlibrary loan purposes.   Also, in the event a title is no longer available for purchase, most bookstores and libraries will provide the names of out-of-print book dealers who can attempt to locate a book for purchase.

USES OF BOOKS AND READING

Once access to the appropriate materials has been gained, reading can fulfill a variety of needs for readers.   At its best, reading is a means of obtaining information, is a relaxing leisure-time activity and serves some therapeutic needs as well.

Information Gathering

Most obviously, reading imparts information to the reader.   It allows the reader the opportunity to learn new facts or to refine knowledge already learned.   Readers can be exposed to other lifestyles and perspectives on living.   In this particular instance, reading is one way children and young adults can learn about the adoption experience.   They can discover what children are available for adoption and reasons for their availability, what motivates parents to adopt children, what is a homestudy, how relinquishing birthmothers have felt and how others have gone about searching for birthparents.   Readers can also learn what it is like to be involved in different kinds of adoption, such as a intercountry adoption or a transracial adoption, or how different people feel about being adopted or how a sibling might feel when a child is adopted into the family.

Leisure-Time Activity

In addition to gaining factual information, reading is also an enjoyable leisure-time activity suitable for all ages.   Although recreational reading is often taken for granted, its benefits are as often overlooked.   Spending hours lost in other worlds, involved with other peoples' lives, in other places, and in other times can be a rewarding as well as pleasurable experience.   Recreational reading provides an escape from one's life and affords the opportunity to peer into someone else's or to become someone else.   It allows the reader to leave his/her own life and experience another by vicariously partaking in new activities and feeling a full range of emotions.   Reading permits the reader not only to learn about, but also to "try on" new situations, attitudes and feelings.   The pleasure of finding delight in the antics of storybook animal characters, the sadness felt at the death of a heroine in a drama, the spine-tingling chill as a murderer stalks his prey in a mystery, the joy and rapture felt as the lovers embrace in a romance, the anger and sympathy experienced when the innocent man is wrongly convicted of a crime in a detective story, are all affective benefits of becoming engrossed in other characters' lives.

Therapeutic Benefits

Aside from imparting factual information and providing enjoyable recreational reading, books, whether silently read, read aloud or experienced through storytelling, also provide valuable therapeutic benefits in helping children and young adults cope with personal difficulties. Reading can enhance self-perception, encourage problem solving and provide psychological relief. Masha Rudman points out in **Children's Literature: An Issues Approach** (2nd ed. New York: Longman, 1984) "the practice of bibliotherapy--the use of books to help children solve their personal problems--has become accepted as an important part of teaching. Librarians, counselors, as well as parents, search for books that mirror a problem they wish to help a child overcome." (p. 3) In mirroring a child's specific experience, books can demonstrate ways to handle difficult situations and the reader can learn from another's experience in a vicarious way. Within a framework of adoption, perhaps by reading about how another child made a move from foster to adoptive care could help a child do the same.

Books can also encourage children to express their thoughts, in fact, often books can give words to a child's feelings thereby stimulating insight, perceptions and discussion. Sometimes if a child is unable to understand a particular situation, he will create his/her own explanations which may be inaccurate. Perhaps a book about another child's situation could facilitate a dialogue which could help clarify a child's misconception about his/her own availability for adoption, for example.

Perhaps the most important therapeutic function books can provide is to help readers discover they are not alone. To be able to read about another child who has to put up with the adoption of siblings, for example, may make a child not feel so all alone. As stated by Charles A. Smith in **From Wonder to Wisdom: Using Stories to Help Children Grow** (New York: New American Library, 1989), "Through stories, they [children] will discover that they are not alone. The great mystery and the most painful contradictions in their life's journey can be shared with others in the human community." (p. 139)

In the article "Children's Literature Can Affect Coping Behavior" (**Personnel and Guidance Journal** 43 (May 1965): 897-903) Patricia Cianciolo sights three stages of the therapeutic effect of bibliotherapy: identification, catharsis and insight. She describes identification as the act of affiliating one's self with a literary character; the next step, catharsis, occurs when the reader not only identifies with the character, but can empathize with the character as he/she works through a problem and releases the associated emotional tension providing an emotional purge for the reader; at this stage, the reader is now in a better emotional condition to approach his/her situation more intellectually thereby achieving insight. (p. 898)

Although even professionals within the fields of psychology and library science disagree over the methodology, science, and effectiveness of bibliotherapy, Myra and David Sadker sum up the benefits of a bibliotherapeutic approach in **Now Upon a Time: A Contemporary View of Children's Literature** (New York: Harper and Row, 1977) when they state, "Although there is no research that definitively proves that literature helps children understand themselves and others and provides them with a means for coping with the complexity and reality of contemporary life, there are nevertheless, many personal testimonials concerning the powerful impact of literature. For example, consider this statement by James Baldwin: 'You think your pain and your heartbreak are unprecedented in the history of the world, but then you read. It was books that taught me that the things that tormented me the most were the very things that connected me with all the people who were alive or who had ever been alive.'" (p. 90)

PUBLISHING NEEDS

Although books on adoption appear to cover a great many types of adoptive situations, there are still several areas which are greatly lacking. Indeed, there are many adoptive situations not adequately reflected in literature suitable for children and young adults. Five major areas of need include books concerning the different ways children become available for adoption; books dealing with some of the less-pleasant aspects of adoptions; books covering the intercountry adoption of children from a wider variety of countries representative of families' real experiences; books reflecting adoption in minority families; and books not necessarily about adoption, but featuring adopted characters.

Availability Reasons

In the first concern, children come into the child care system, and subsequently adoption in many instances, in a variety of ways. In addition to birth parents choosing adoption for infants, which most books assume, some children are voluntarily relinquished at older ages, while other children often become available as a result of legal termination of parental rights, often for abuse and neglect. Very few books, such as Joy's **Benjamin Bear Gets a New Family** (174), concern themselves with these situations, from any point of view, even though many children share these experiences.

Less-Pleasant Aspects

Second, while it is true the majority of adoptions are successful, there are no books dealing specifically with adoption disruptions, situations in which an adoptive placement fails and other arrangements, often adoptive, are made for the child. Likewise, while books reinforcing the joy involved in adoption are prevalent, stories that validate children's and other family members' pain as they deal with problem situations within an adoptive placement are rarely brought forth in the literature. Problems associated with unattached children, acting-out behavior, mental and physical disabilities, the need for residential care, school problems, drug-affected children, as well as HIV-infected or other terminally ill children, situations often found within adoptive placements, are not widely reflected in books. While there are some titles that touch on these aspects of adoption, they are in the minority.

Sommer's **And I'm Stuck With Joseph** (226), for younger readers, attempts to address the frustration of living with a newly-adopted preschooler brother with irritating behavior problems, Sandness' **Brimming Over** (416) comes the closest in presenting the reality of living with an emotionally disturbed adopted child as well as with physically disabled children and Blank's **Nineteen Steps Up the Mountain** (347), also for older readers, honestly relates an estranged, but healing, parent/child relationship as well as presents an insight into a large family with several physically disabled children. As a rule, however, it appears that authors and publishers shy away from presenting the not-so-pleasant realities of some adoptive situations. There is a greater tendency to be maudlin and to romanticize the experience, perhaps in fear of discouraging potential adoptive families by painting a negative picture of the adoption scene. Citing the previously mentioned titles, however, it is possible to present even the most painful, difficult or controversial situations, on every reading level as well, in a sensitive, thoughtfu, and truthful manner, refraining from bitterness and undue hostility.

Greater Country Representation

The third area which needs to be addressed in the literature for children and young adults is for books which feature children adopted from various countries representative of the actual experiences of families. Books, on all levels, which feature the arrival, adjustment and feelings of children, adopted as infants as well as older children speaking no English, from Colombia, India, Philippines, Chile, Brazil, Hong Kong and Romania, to name a few, are greatly needed. Although South Koreans make up the largest group of foreign-born adoptees, and consequently, enjoy the greatest availability of book titles, the needs of children adopted from other countries are equally great.

Minority Adoptions

Fourth, there needs to be an increase in the portrayal of families of color with adopted children. While minority children of all backgrounds are often portrayed as adoptees, usually they are involved in transracial adoptions. Historically families of color have engaged in a less-formal approach to adoption such as that described in Tate's **Just an Overnight Guest** (237), but as minority families are recruited by such organizations as Homes for Black Children (see Appendix B) and gain better access to and reponse from traditional agencies, stories such as Caine's **Abby** (35) and Myers' **Won't Know Till I Get There** (309), help to strengthen the image of minority families actively involved in traditional adoption.

Adopted Characters

Finally, there is a need for more books which casually feature adopted children as characters within a story having nothing to do with adoption. Adopted children should easily be able to locate a wide variety of literature, including mysteries, biographies, adventure stories, science fiction, romance stories, that has a protagonist or other character whose life has been touched by adoption. Books like Cross' **Mystery at Loon Lake** (150), Blume's **Just as Long as We're Together** (132), Kuklin's **When I See My Doctor** (10) and Milton's **Greg Louganis: Diving for Gold** (113) illustrate the possibilities. These books mirror and give validation that for the most part adopted children are just children engaged with school, friends and family and that while adoption may be important to them, it is not the focal point of their lives.

The growing numbers of non-traditional adoptions which include single parents, minorities, siblings, older children, special needs, intercountry, as well as the realities which accompany them, attest to the fact that the adoption picture is changing. Hopefully, authors and publishers will continue positively responding to the growing needs of young readers for material which encompasses and reflects the diversity of adoption experiences.

DISCLAIMER

Of course, as with any undertaking of this nature, the chances of omissions and oversights are great. While I endeavored to locate as many appropriate titles as possible dealing in some way with adoption, up until the final days of editing I was still discovering additional titles. Since there was no systematic way to insure total inclusion, I made the best effort to establish an initial volume of this kind. Accordingly, all errors of judgment and inclusion are mine alone. Should readers discover omissions or errors, correspondence relating to such would be greatly appreciated.

ADOPTION LITERATURE
FOR CHILDREN
AND YOUNG ADULTS

Preschool and Primary Readers

NONFICTION

001   Buck, Pearl S. **Welcome Child**. Photographs by Alan D. Haas. New York: John Day, 1963. 96pp. (OCLC 1621431)
This story follows Kim, a young adopted Amerasian Korean girl, from her arrival in the States, through her insecure first days at home and at kindergarten, to her naturalization. Black and white photographs on nearly every page document Kim's growing confidence as she adjusts to her new family and life. The book concludes with a three-page message from the director of Welcome House, an agency founded by the author, which handles intercountry adoption. Although the photos are dated, the story and message of the adjustment process remain fresh.

002   Bunin, Catherine, and Sherry Bunin. **Is That Your Sister? A True Story of Adoption**. New York: Pantheon Books, 1976. [35]pp. (OCLC 1994055)
Full of family photographs, at least one every other page, this book tells about adoption in the words of transracially adopted biracial six-year-old Catherine. The authors not only detail encounters with friends who are curious about her life, but also describe the adoption of Catherine's younger sister, Carla. Reasonable, age-appropriate explanations for several situations are provided including why her birthmother did not keep her, why she does not look like other family members and how her family is just like everyone else's. This is an honest, thoughtful story with engaging text and charming photographs which add to its sense of warmth. This story is reprinted with some of the photographs in **Stories for Free Children** (New York: McGraw-Hill, 1982, pp. 107-109), edited by Letty Cottin Pogrebin. A new edition with black and white illustrations in place of the photographs is also available. (Wayne, PA: Our Child Press, 1991). For Carla's version of her own story at age twelve, see Jill Krementz's **How It Feels to be Adopted** (258).

003   Christenson, Larry. **The Wonderful Way That Babies Are Made**. Illus. by Dwight Walles. Minneapolis: Bethany House, 1982. [55]pp. (OCLC 8629186)

While primarily a Christian sex instruction book for young children, this also incorporates adoption as another way people become parents. Each section of text includes large print rhyming verse written for younger readers and accompanying small print narrative designed for older readers. The book relates biologically, emotionally and religiously the nature of love and babies. Using Jesus' adoption by Joseph as the example, the book weaves adoption as a natural outgrowth of the love which creates children. The full-color illustrations on each spread depict families of different racial backgrounds. This book features a strong Christian perspective and includes the virgin birth and Christian values regarding premarital sex.

004   Doss, Helen Grigsby. **All the Children of the World**. Illus. by Audrie L. Knapp. New York: Abingdon Press, 1958. [21]pp. (OCLC 1392847) Describing how children from around the world are alike and yet different from one another, Doss describes how God has given specific attention to eyes, skin, hair and abilities. Doss continues by relating how parents create families, see their children as special and care for them. Near the end of the story Doss includes adoption as another way parents create families and love their children. Using a Christian perspective, Doss compares a parent's love to God's love. Cartoon-like color illustrations depict multi-racial situations in this reassuring book for very young children on human differences.

005   Drescher, Joan. E. **Your Family, My Family**. Illus. by the author. New York: Walker, 1980. 32pp. (OCLC 5892508) Illustrating different kinds of families, Drescher explains families can be composed of varying numbers and kinds of people and can originate in several ways as well. After some general introductory statements about families, Drescher spotlights individual children and describes their family situations identifying a traditional nuclear family, a family with a stay-at-home dad, a divorced family, a family with two mothers and no father, an extended family, a foster family, a single-parent family, a grandparent-as-parent family, as well as an adoptive family. The book concludes with several pages devoted to qualities and positive aspects of family life. The full-page black and white illustrations, accented by the use of orange/gold, are both humorous and realistic as they complement the minimal text. This is a positive presentation that adoptive families are but one kind of family.

006   Erichsen, Jean. **My Journey Home From Colombia**. [Minneapolis: OURS, 1976.] [45]pp. Published as an adaptation of Partridge's **My Journey Home** (015), this hand-printed, photo-filled, soft-bound book is designed for Colombian-born adoptees describing Colombia and the adoption process. There are blank spaces throughout the book for a child's own pictures and drawings. Several pages at the end of the book, written for adults, describe Colombian culture and the needs of Colombian orphanages. Like the Partridge title, despite its publishing quality, it provides reassuring text and the opportunity for a personalized story.

007   Forrai, Maria S. **A Look at Adoption**. Text by Margaret S. Pursell. Minneapolis: Lerner Publications, 1978. [36]pp. (OCLC 3293018)

Designed for young children, this small book alternates a page of text with a full-page photograph thereby providing a simple explanation of adoption. It explains who adopts and why, reasons children are available for adoption, the process involved and how adoptive families learn to love and care. Intercountry adoption is briefly mentioned. The photos are real, warm and touching; the text is usually kept short, simple and honest. This title is part of the **Lerner Awareness Series**.

008   Goudy, Rosemary. **My Journey Home From Vietnam**. [Minneapolis: OURS, n.d.] [28]pp.
An adaptation of Partridge's **My Journey Home** (015), this large-type, photo-filled, soft-bound book is designed for use by Vietnamese adoptees. It describes the birth country, the war and reasons why a child might have been given up, orphanages, as well as the process of coming to the States and becoming part of a family. The text is designed so that the child's story and pictures can be made part of the book. Despite the unprofessional publishing quality, this book offers the opportunity for a personalized story as well as reassuring text.

009   Koch, Janice. **Our Baby: A Birth and Adoption Story**. Designed by Pat Goldberg. Fort Wayne, IN: Perspectives Press, 1985. 28pp. (OCLC 11916097)
In this sex education book for young children, the facts of birth and adoption are combined to help explain the two means children become part of families. Describing first the biological process involved in the birth of a child, Koch goes to describe that grownups can also adopt a child who has already been born. Using biologically specific terminology, this book successfully incorporates birth and adoption into one story for adopted children. The black and white borders and illustrations also include places to personalize the story by offering a place to write the child's name, paste in a picture of child alone and with the family, as well as to note details of the adopted child's arrival. While this provides a positive perspective, the book fails to address why babies are available for adoption. Unable to locate for evaluation is a possible earlier version, **Our Adopted Baby: How You Came Into Our World** (Roslyn Heights, NY: Parkway Press, 1983) by same author and illustrator.

010   Kuklin, Susan. **When I See My Doctor**. Photographs by the author. New York: Bradbury Press, 1988. [30]pp. (OCLC 16682290)
Speaking in the first person, four-year-old Thomas describes his annual checkup with his pediatrician. He begins his story in the waiting room and continues into the examination room with his mother helping him undress. The doctor arrives and gently engages the little boy in the examination while Thomas simply explains the procedures and the equipment used. The proper names of the medical instruments are given, often with their phonetic pronunciation. The full-color photographs complement the text and reveal that Thomas is Asian, probably Korean, and his mother is white. Not only a informative and comforting book about seeing the doctor, this is a also good example of a children's book casually featuring an adopted child as a character even though the book itself is not about adoption.

011   McNamara, Joan. **Families: A Coloring Book for Families to Share**. Illus. by Joanne Opel. Ossining, NY: Family Resources, 1976. [15]pp.

Explaining that a family is a group of people joined together to share and care for each other, McNamara goes on to say that families can be small or large and look like each other or not. Families with children have an adult, like parents or grandparents, to help them grow up. People become part of a family when they are born, adopted, married or just loved very much. When families grow they change and sometimes experience sad goodbyes and new beginnings. McNamara reveals families give people a start in life, teaching them how to share good times and bad, and about working, living and loving together. This is a coloring book depicting different family arrangements and providing spaces for readers to draw pictures of their own families, houses and activities. Although difficult to locate, this can be obtained through the publisher at 1521 Foxhollow Rd., Greensboro, NC 27410.

012   May, Julian. **Man and Woman**. Chicago: Follett Publishing Co., 1969. 46pp. (OCLC 21297)

Basically a sex education book aimed at young children, this book briefly explains the sexuality of plants and animals, then the human female and male reproductive sytems, citing the need for mental and emotional readiness, as well as physical ability, before being a parent. After tastefully describing intercourse and conception, May points out that couples who are unable to conceive a child will often adopt a child so they can become parents. He moves on to illustrate how a family can meet children's needs and teach them to grow to be healthy, respectful individuals. Adolescence, learning about sex and the human cycle concludes the book. Full-color, somewhat dated photographs, featuring people from a variety of ethnic backgrounds, are peppered throughout the book. There is a definite bias towards traditional nuclear families. This is part of the **Follett Family Life Education Program**.

013   Meredith, Judith C. **And Now We Are a Family**. Graphics by Pamela Osborn. Boston: Beacon Press, 1971. [32]pp. (OCLC 673162)

Using blue and red Corita Kent-style graphics, this picture book is designed as a read-aloud to help children think about and accept their adoptive situations. With help from the splashes of color and hand-printed text, Meredith carefully explains the adoption process from the perspectives of both the adoptive and birthparents. The book focuses on the plans of both sets of parents which resulted in the child's adoption. Included at the end of the book is a two-page note to parents from the author. Designed to initiate a thoughtful dialog, the book has a warm conversational tone which is effective with children from typical infant adoptions. It does not accommodate the needs of children who have been neglected, abused or abandoned.

014   Owens, Carolyn. **Color Me Loved**. Illus. by Lisa Falstad. Minneapolis: Bethany House, 1982. [32]pp.

In this creative-thinking activity book about families, Owens presents a Christian approach to family building, including adoption. The book attempts to reinforce God's love by comparing it to a family's love while making the relationship between being adopted into a human family and into God's family. The book engages its young reader in such activities as drawing completion and coloring. Resembling a coloring book, this title is most easily obtainable directly from the publisher (Bethany House, 6820 Auto Club Rd., Minneapolis, MN 55438).

015   Partridge, Jackie. **My Journey Home.** [Minneapolis: OURS, n.d.] [26]pp.
            (OCLC 5757402)
Designed for use by Korean-born adoptees, this hand-printed, photo-filled, soft-bound book tells of being adopted from Korea. It relates information about the country, why a child might have been placed for adoption, living in a foster care home or an orphanage and the process of coming to the States to become part of a family. The book also includes blank spaces throughout for a child's drawings and pictures. While this is not a glossy, high-quality product from an established publisher, the text is quietly reassuring and involves the child by referring to the reader as "you" and by providing the opportunity to personalize the story.

016   Patterson, Eleanora. **Twice-Upon-A-Time: Born and Adopted.** Illus. by
            Barbara Ernst Prey. Brattleboro, VT: EP Press, 1987. [48]pp. (OCLC
            17353499)
Concentrating on the uniqueness of a school-age boy, Patterson describes how all children have a set of birthparents and that some children also have a different set of parents to care for them. Briefly and simply, Patterson explains conception and birth and that sometimes the birthparents are unable, for a variety of reasons, to care for the child. Because birthparents do not always realize immediately they cannot care for their child, children are various ages when another family needs to be found for them. The book explains how the adoptive family has been excitedly waiting and preparing for the arrival of their new child no matter the age of the child. Patterson describes the personal and physical growth of a child, as well as an adoptive child's possible curiosity regarding birthparents, indicating that it is equally acceptable to wonder and want more information about them as it not to be particularly interested. The book concludes by explaining that the child's own story continues as he grows up. The use of clear text and simple, humorous black and white illustrations make this an especially engaging book as does the fact that it accounts for adoptions at all ages.

Pursell, Margaret S. **A Look at Adoption.** see Forrai, Maria S. (007)

017   Rippey, Carol. **Do You Know What Adoption Means?** Illus. by Sara Nelson.
            King George, VA: American Foster Care Resources, 1989. [17]pp.
Looking somewhat like a coloring book, this story is for children in foster care prior to their transition to an adoptive family. Rippey describes adoption as having new parents and possibly siblings, living in a new house, attending a new school and having a family forever. Assuring the reader that the adoptive parents have been waiting for a child to love, Rippey explains several possible reasons the birthparents were unable to continue caring for a child. She continues by telling about meeting and visiting the new family and the mixed feelings and questions that accompany the pending move. Once the family and child learn more about each other, the social worker helps pack belongings, facilitates saying good-bye to the foster family and saying hello to

the new adoptive family. The child begins to understand the permanency of adoption when the new family is finally together and the child really belongs. The black and white cartoon-like illustrations reveal a young school-age boy, but the text is not sex specific.

018   Rondell, Florence, and Ruth Michaels. **The Family That Grew.** Rev. ed.
        Illus. by Judith Epstein and Tom O'Sullivan. New York: Crown
        Publishers, 1965. 20pp. (OCLC 263822)
        Rondell briefly explains how everything, including people, begins to grow. She indicates that everyone wants to take care of the babies they grow, but sometimes they are not able to, like the reader's birthparents. So the birthparents are helped to find parents who will care properly for the child. Rondell describes how happy and excited the adoptive parents are and how they prepare for the baby's arrival. When at last they bring the baby home, family and friends gather to see the baby and share the parents' joy. Rondell tells how the baby grows and learns how to do new things and how the parents love and play with the child as he grows. Admitting that some days the child and parents do things to get the other upset, Rondell reassures that even though angry, the family love is still there and that the parents are always glad to have a family and this child. The sketchy black and white drawings, highlighted in an orange-red, depict a happy baby and family. On a very young level, Rondell addresses some significant issues. This is the second book of the author's **The Adopted Family.** Book One is called **You and Your Child: A Guide for Adoptive Parents.**

019   Rosenberg, Maxine B. **Being Adopted.** Photographs by George Ancona. New
        York: Lothrop, Lee and Shepard, 1984. [48]pp. (OCLC 9829123)
        Describing the family situations of children who are adopted into families with different racial or cultural backgrounds from their own, this story introduces its readers to seven-year-old biracial Rebecca, ten-year-old Andrei from India and eight-year-old Karin from Korea. Rosenberg relates events, feelings and experiences these children have encountered due to their transracial or intercountry adoptions. The black and white photographs on every page provide revealing insights into the text.

020   Schaffer, Patricia. **Chag Sameach! Happy Holiday.** Berkeley, CA: Tabor
        Sarah Books, 1985. [27]pp. (OCLC 12552003)
        Presenting an introduction to Jewish holidays, this book names the holidays then briefly describes the historical significance and present celebration activities. Beginning with Rosh Hashanah, the Jewish New Year, the author describes blowing the shofar, a ram's horn and eating apples dipped in honey. It continues by explaining Yom Kippur, Sukkot, Chanukah and Purim to name a few. The subject of the book is not adoption, however, the full-page black and white photographs which accompany the text reveal several kinds of families including transracial adoptive families. With no more than five lines of text on any page, this presents an introduction to Jewish holidays illustrated by interracial families.

021   Schaffer, Patricia. **How Babies and Families are Made: (There is More Than One Way).** Illus. by Suzanne Corbett. Berkeley, CA: Tabor Sarah Books, 1988. 52pp. (OCLC 14520640)

Rachel and Michael are friends who are alike in some ways, but different in others. While they each belong to a family, their family compositions are different. Rachel belongs to an intact nuclear family and Michael lives with his father and stepmother. The book explains that while all babies are born, the act of conception can happen in several ways. First describing the reproduction system of a woman, then a man, Schaffer briefly describes sexual intercourse as the most common way to start a baby, then discusses the reasons for and the process involved in artificial or donor insemination and in vitro fertilization. Michael was the result of sexual intercourse, while Rachel was the result of artificial insemination. After describing the growth involved in a normal pregnancy, Schaffer touches on miscarriage, hospital versus home birth, labor, natural childbirth, Caesarean section, premature birth and disabilities. Schaffer explains the difference between a biological family and families made up of stepparents, half-siblings and adopted family members. The soft black and white illustrations portray a multi-ethnic setting, wheel-chair-bound individuals and a nursing mother. This contains much information, using correct terminology, in a simple, tasteful format.

022   Simon, Norma. **All Kinds of Families.** Illus. by Joe Lasker. Chicago: Albert Whitman, 1976. [40]pp. (OCLC 1975154)

Acknowledging that all families do not fit the stereotypical nuclear family, this book presents the notion that many different kinds of groupings of people can be considered families. Recognizing that a family is the people who live with, love and care for a child, the book goes on to describe different family sizes, various family living arrangements made up of a mixture of adults and children. Simon shows families living in different ways; she depicts families whose children have moved away, families who move to different places and indicating that when children grow up they may begin their own families which then become part of their old families. Adoption is casually mentioned a few times throughout the text as a means by which families are made. Emphasizing families are for loving and caring, in good times and in bad, there is a mixture of celebration and sadness both in the text and in the illustrations. Lasker's illustrations, some in color, are on every page and provide a warm rendering of the text and feature children of diverse ethnic backgrounds. Compare this title to Tax's **Families** (089).

023   Simon, Norma. **Why Am I Different?** Illus. by Dora Leder. Chicago: Albert Whitman, 1976. 31pp. (OCLC 2425344)

Using the voices of young children as a narrators, Simon cites physical differences between people such as hair and eye color, size and allergies. She then progresses through differences in abilities and preferences, as well as family experiences and circumstances. Being adopted along with a baby sister, just one way to make a family, is cited as a possible reason for feeling different. Presenting differences in cultural and religious backgrounds, Simon portrays both some of the positive, as well as negative aspects of being or feeling different. The charming illustrations, detailed black and white drawings, highlighted in orange, aptly illustrate the text depicting differences, including racial differences, to complement the text. This book highlights the pride that can be found in differences.

FICTION

024   Althea. **Jane is Adopted**. Illus. by Isabel Pearce. London: Souvenir, 1980. [24]pp. (OCLC 16559636)

When Jane asks once again what adoption means, her mother invites her to sit on her lap as she lovingly relates Jane's adoption story. Mummy explains that she and Daddy wanted a child very much and since one did not grow inside her they decided to adopt a child. She describes the homestudy process, the home preparations for the arrival of a child and the announcement of a placement. Providing background on Jane's birthparents, Mummy tells Jane how nice it is that she has dark hair and eyes like her birthmother. Mummy concludes by telling Jane that adopted means belonging to a family and how happy she and Daddy were to adopt her and Jane agrees. The full-color illustrations are stilted and cartoon-like. This title, which uses a few British phrases, may be difficult to locate.

025   Anderson, C.W. **Lonesome Little Colt**. Illus. by the author. New York: Macmillan, 1961. 46pp. (OCLC 1211611)

In the spring, when all the new little colts are with their mothers, there is one little colt whose mother has died. The colt is rejected when trying to attach to the other mother ponies, until the children on the farm intervene and their father finds a mother whose colt had just died. The two are joined so that the little colt belongs to someone, feeling safe and loved. Providing a keen sense of rejection and sadness, this story also gives young readers the vocabulary to describe the need for, and good feelings that accompany, belonging. The soft full-page pencil drawings add to the warmth of the story.

026   Anderson, Deborah. **Jason's Story: Going to a Foster Home**. Illus. by Jeanette Swofford. Minneapolis: Dillon Press, 1986. 45pp. (OCLC 12752377)

This is the story of seven-year-old Jason, who lives with his mother after several foster home experiences. Using age-appropriate language, the narrator describes the family situations that led to Jason's foster home placements as well as the process and feelings involved as he and his mother separate and reunite. The story ends happily with Jason's mother better able to care for him. The book concludes with an explanation of foster care and notes to adults. Other titles of particular interest in this series by the same author include **Margaret's Story: Sexual Abuse and Going to Court, Robin's Story: Physical Abuse and Seeing the Doctor, Michael's Story: Emotional Abuse and Working with a Counselor** and **Liza's Story: Neglect and the Police** (all Minneapolis: Dillon Press, 1986). The books feature colorful watercolor-like illustrations that complement the text. Although these books do not specify adoption, they deal with situations, on a very young level, that may be familiar to many adoptive children. The happy endings may be considered unrealistic.

027   Averill, Esther Holden. **Jenny's Adopted Brothers**. Illus. by the author. New
          York: Harper, 1952. 32pp. (OCLC 8990128)
Jenny is a little black cat, happy and grateful for her life with her master, the
Captain. When Jenny comes across two stray cats, Edward and Checkers, she
wants her master to adopt them as well. Once the adoption plan is successful
and Jenny's brothers begin to settle into their new home, Jenny becomes
jealous and wishes they were gone. Realizing she is upset, the boys leave, only
to be found by a contrite Jenny who is willing to work out a new life sharing
the Captain and their home. Little black, white and red drawings nicely
complement the details of the story which, using animals, openly relates the
reality of sibling rivalry among adoptees. The author's Jenny series includes
other titles as well.

028   Bawden, Nina. **Princess Alice**. Illus. by Phillida Gili. London: A. Deutsch,
          1985. [32]pp. (OCLC 14239741)
Tidy Alice, transracially adopted from Africa to England as the wish of her
dying mother, lives with her large untidy interracial family where she feels she
does not fit in well. After visiting with her birthfather, an African prince, who
is temporarily in London, she changes her mind. With him she learns what
her life would have been like had she remained in Africa. She decides that
for all its faults, she likes living with her family rather than as a lonely, doted-
upon princess with a father who has very little time. When she returns home,
her adoptive father assures her that as far as he is concerned, all of his
daughters are princesses. Full-color illustrations reveal a messy, happy family.
This is an unusual adoption story giving a child's view of two lifestyles.

029   Bloom, Suzanne. **A Family for Jamie: An Adoption Story**. Illus. by the
          author. New York: C.N. Potter, 1990. (OCLC 22209934)
Dan and Molly have a full life in their rural home where they make so many
of the things they need, but they are unable to make a baby. They contact an
adoption agency and while they wait for their baby to arrive they make the
necessary preparations. One day they receive a call and welcome Jamie to
share their life and love and teach him to make things as well. The bright,
vibrant illustrations spill over onto the pages and effectively engage the reader.

030   Blue, Rose. **A Quiet Place**. Illus. by Tom Feelings. New York: Franklin
          Watts, 1969. 63pp. (OCLC 4053)
Young Matthew loves to visit the library and curl up and read in the big, soft
yellow chair, but when the library closes during reconstruction work, Matthew
is left feeling he no longer has a special quiet place. After having lived in
several foster and children's homes, Matthew feels comfortable with this
Mama who says he will stay here forever and although he enjoys the activity
and noise of the house at times, he misses having a special quiet place to read.
Teased by older children, including his foster sister, for his love of reading,
Matthew is defended by her boyfriend and is supported by his parents. One
day, Matthew takes a walk and, finding a peaceful secluded place under a big
tree, decides it will be his warm weather quiet place and settles down with a
good book and plans to find a cold weather place soon. The text together with
the black and white shaded illustrations portray a warm, loving and supportive
black family and a quiet, studious little boy.

031   Brandon, Sandra. **We're A Family**. Illus. by Helen Endres. Cincinnati, OH:
          Standard Publishing Co., 1986. [23]pp. (OCLC 15247747)
Stephen, the narrator and oldest child in his family, describes how he and his
sister, Kelly, look like their parents because they were born to them. Their
younger sister, Sara, however, is adopted from another country and does not
look like any of them. Despite the differences in looks, Stephen is quick to
point out the many ways Sara is like the rest of the family. Stephen tells of
his playmates expressing disbelief that Sara is his sister because she looks
different from him. He explains Sara is his adopted sister and does not want
anyone to hurt her feelings. Stephen points out God planned it so we would
each be different and special and that just as Sara belongs to his family,
everyone belongs to God's family. This is a reassuring story of differences
within a family created by adoption, however, while the text describes Sara as
having dark skin and a different eye shape, the full-color illustrations do not
reveal any physical differences and depict Sara looking very much like the rest
of her family.

032   Brodzinsky, Anne Braff. **The Mulberry Bird: Story of an Adoption**. Illus. by
          Diana L. Stanley. Indianapolis, IN: Perspectives Press, 1986. 48pp.
          (OCLC 13183713)
When a mother bird's egg hatches, she does her best to provide for the baby
by keeping a safe nest, gathering bugs for food and protecting the baby. When
a severe storm damages her nest, the mother bird is faced with new dangers
as she tries to keep her baby safe and fed while living on the ground. She
contacts a wise owl for guidance and he suggests that she make an adoption
plan for her baby. The mother is outraged and refuses, wanting to keep and
care for her baby herself. When additional problems make the situation
overwhelming, the mother bird realizes she needs a plan to make sure her
baby is taken care of properly if she cannot herself. She returns to the owl
and he takes the baby bird to his new, anxiously awaiting parents with whom
he grows up knowing his adoption story. With charming full-page black and
white illustrations, this is a warm, caring story of a birthmother's love and
struggling efforts which emphasize her part in planning for her child's future.
The mother bird and baby are goldfinches while the adoptive parents are
sandpipers.

033   Bulla, Clyde Robert. **Open the Door and See All the People**. Illus. by Wendy
          Watson. New York: Crowell, 1972. 69pp. (OCLC 591866)
After their home is destroyed by fire, Mamma and her two young daughters,
JoAnn and Teeney, go to live in the city where Mamma finds work. While
their mother slowly replaces their lost possessions, the girls miss their dolls.
They learn about The Toy House where children can take out toys on loan,
much like a library lends books, and they each choose a doll. JoAnn and
Teeney learn they can adopt the dolls, but they need to demonstrate they are
taking good care of them. Before the adoption day party, Teeney's doll is
tattered by a neighbor dog and, ashamed of herself, Teeney secretly takes the
doll back to The Toy Shop. At the adoption party, Teeney is surprised to
learn that she, too, is receiving an adoption certificate, and a fully-repaired
doll, being told that when accidents happen, seeking immediate help is the
most responsible thing to do. In doing so, Teeney proved the quality of her

care. When the shop owner realizes their mother has never had her own doll, she allows Mamma to take the china doll she has admired. While some readers may object to the adoption of things, rather than children, the message of love and care of special dolls may shed some insight on adoption for very young children. The black and white line drawings are simple, but charming.

034   Bulla, Clyde Robert. **Poor Boy, Rich Boy**. Illus. by Marcia Sewall. New York: Harper and Row, 1982. 63pp. (OCLC 6791027)
Baby Coco, who is left an orphan by the war, is taken to live with Rosa, a poor woman who is afraid to love him too much for fear he will be claimed someday. One day Coco's rich, childless uncle comes to take him home where Coco has everything he wants, but feels unwanted himself. After an episode where Coco expresses that a captured wild colt needs his mother, the uncle realizes that Coco needs to be wanted and sets out to help him feel that way. This is an **I Can Read** book with large print and illustrations on almost every page. One ends the book with the impression that Coco and his uncle will work out a mutual caring relationship.

035   Caines, Jeannette Franklin. **Abby**. Illus. by Steven Kellogg. New York: Harper and Row, 1973. 32pp. (OCLC 776398)
Using minimal text, this is the story of an adopted preschooler, Abby, who spends the day looking through her baby book and being teased by her older brother Kevin. Proud of her, Kevin later asks if he can take Abby to school for show-and-tell. The story ends with Abby wanting the family to adopt another child. The text and the black and white drawings convey a loving, warm home atmosphere of a black family, although the facial depictions are not always flattering.

036   Chapman, Noralee. **The Story of Barbara**. Illus. by Helen Schuyler Hull. Richmond, VA: John Knox Press, 1963. 24pp. (OCLC 1871656)
This story relates the adoption of infant Barbara, describing her parents' life before her arrival and afterwards. When Barbara is five years old, she asks her mother where babies come from and is given a tasteful biological, with religious overtones, explanation. When Barbara further questions her own beginnings, her mother explains, again with religious overtones, the difference between birthparents and adoptive parents. The black and white sketches, highlighted in red, are rather sparse and are outweighed by the amount of small-print text. The beginning of the story disturbingly describes Barbara's adoptive parents as sad because they do not have a baby.

037   Dauer, Rosamond. **Bullfrog and Gertrude Go Camping**. Illus. by Byron Barton. New York: Greenwillow, 1980. 38pp. (OCLC 4193858)
When Bullfrog and Gertrude go camping in the woods they meet a snake whom they accidentally name Itsa. Itsa takes to Bullfrog and Gertrude and tries to ingratiate herself to them by being helpful. Gertrude wants to take Itsa home with them when they leave, but Bullfrog resists until Gertrude reminds him that he was adopted by the Mouse family. The three of them leave the camp discussing the things they will do as a family. A flaw in this cute story is Bullfrog's statement that he was adopted by the Mouse family

because he was a good-looking tadpole. The bold, cartoon-like illustration are a humorous addition to the tale. This is a **Greenwillow Read-alone** book.

038   Dellinger, Annetta E. **Adopted and Loved Forever**. Pictures by Patricia Mattozzi. St. Louis, MO: Concordia Publishing House, 1987. [20]pp. (OCLC 15015317)
With a young child as a narrator, this story describes adoption using a Christian perspective. Dellinger explains why and how children are adopted, why adoption is forever and why it is alright for children not to look like their parents. Scriptural references, as well as the biblical story of Esther's adoption by Mordecai, are included. The soft water-color illustrations portray a young Asian boy adopted by a white couple. There is too much text for a small child, but this is a nice selection for readers seeking a Christian view. There is one disturbing comment indicating that the parents were lonely before they adopted a child.

039   Dubkin, Lois. **Quiet Street**. Illus. by Juliette Palmer. London: Abelard-Schuman, 1963. [40]pp. (OCLC 1392320)
Preschool-aged Lisa is an only child living on a quiet street. Some neighbors have pets, but no one has a child with whom she can play. Lisa approaches her parents about getting a sister, but her mother explains while they wanted another baby, none came. Lisa spends much time watching construction workers build a new building near her home and when it is completed she discovers it is an orphanage full of children needing families. Her parents inquire and soon Lisa has a sister, Amy, who is slightly younger than herself. Now that the two girls have each other to play with, the neighborhood street is no longer quiet. The full-color sketchy illustrations on each page depict aspects of the text of this charming story.

040   Eber, Christine Engla. **Just Momma and Me**. Illus. by the author. Chapel Hill, NC: Lollipop Power, 1975. 36pp. (OCLC 2066766)
Giving the impression of a single-parent adoption, this is the story of a little girl who happily lives with just her mother until a male friend begins to take up some of Momma's time. The little girl feels jealous, but learns to make room for Karl. After Karl moves in and Momma becomes pregnant, the little girl feels very left out. When her mother is in the hospital having the baby brother, the little girl and Karl grow closer and she is ready to see the positive side of being part of this growing family. The black and white sketches in this soft-cover book show a loving family. Some readers may object to this live-in, rather than marriage, family situation. In addition, at the beginning of the story there is a reference to the mother as now being the "real" momma.

041   Eisenberg, Eleanor. **The Pretty House That Found Happiness**. Illus. by Betsy Warren. Austin, TX: Steck Co., 1964. 31pp. (OCLC 4011203)
Describing in detail a house a child would like to live in, this book tells the story of how lonely a couple and their house are until they adopt a little boy. The story relates how much happier the couple, the child and the house are since his arrival and that an addition of an adopted little girl would make everyone happier yet. While obviously good intentioned, this book is disturbing for several reasons. The notion that a house or a couple's

loneliness is a problem to be solved by an adopted child places an unrealistic burden on the child, as well as young readers. In addition, the language and illustrations are sexist using passive/active stereotypes when referring to little girls smelling flowers or watching birds, and boys kicking rocks or climbing hills. The illustrations are in soft black and white pencil highlighted in greens.

042   Fairbank, Anna. **Lucky Me!: An Adoption Story**. Illus. by Martha Weston. Millbrae, CA: Mariah Press, 1988. [32]pp. (OCLC 18848846)
Using very large print, but very little text, the preschooler main character introduces herself as Emily and proceeds to tell readers she was adopted by her parents when she was a baby. She continues by saying that her parents chose her to belong to their family and lists all the activities she enjoys with her family such as hugging, loving, laughing, sharing, reading, talking and learning. She closes by emphasizing her parents adopted her so she could be happy and she is. The black and white sketchy drawings, highlighted in red, reveal a happy little girl warmly engaged with family and friends. Some readers may negatively react to the emphasis placed on Emily being a "chosen" baby.

043   Fall, Thomas. **Eddie No-Name**. Illus. by Ray Prohaska. New York: Pantheon Books, 1963. 48pp. (OCLC 5034345)
Timid Eddie, who appears to be about seven years old, is often teased by the older boys in the children's home. He is surprised, but inwardly excited and apprehensive, when Mr. and Mrs. Whalen, a farm couple, want him to visit because he knows it may lead to adoption. When Eddie runs from a chasing goat and rooster, Mr. Whalen begins to doubt Eddie's nature indicating he does not have much faith in people who scare easily; Mrs. Whalen is understanding and supportive of Eddie's need to learn new ways. One day Eddie gathers his courage and kills a snake around the corn bin only to be angrily told he has killed Boris, the snake that protects the corn cribs from rats and mice. When Mr. Whalen learns why Eddie killed the snake, he realizes how much Eddie needs to learn and that he needs to be teaching Eddie instead of letting him learn on his own. Later, Mr. Whalen introduces Eddie as his son and Eddie realizes he will stay and finally have a last name. Pen and ink drawings, washed in water colors, add to the story of young boy needing to belong.

044   Fisher, Iris L. **Katie-Bo: An Adoption Story**. Illus. by Miriam Schaer. New York: Adama, 1987. [52]pp. (OCLC 16226494)
Told in the first person by the older of two brothers, this story tells about his family adopting a Korean baby girl. Using short sentences, the narrator relates the activities and feelings of the family before, during and after Katie-Bo's arrival. The full-page illustrations, which alternate with pages of text, are colorful, stylized multi-media collages. The pages of text are also bordered in a similar collage style. The family and its experiences sound real: preparing the baby's room, sibling jealousy, the social worker's involvement, the airport arrival, the court finalization, all make for an enjoyable reading experience.

045   Freudberg, Judy, and Tony Geiss. **Susan and Gordon Adopt a Baby**. Illustrated by Joe Mathieu. Featuring Jim Henson's Sesame Street

Muppets and the Sesame Street Cast. New York: Random House, 1986. [30]pp. (OCLC 13216321)

Based on the television scripts, this story follows Sesame Street characters, Susan and Gordon, as they prepare for the adoption and arrival of baby Miles. Big Bird tries to help, but feels in the way and unloved until Gordon and Susan show him the ways he can be helpful and explain there is always enough love to go around. Since the characters and setting will be familiar to most children, it is a positive gesture to have adoption presented in comfortable surroundings. The story reinforces the message of a child's place in the family and love for that child.

046   Gabel, Susan L. **Where the Sun Kisses the Sea**. Illus. by Joanne Bowring. Indianapolis, IN: Perspectives Press, 1989. [30]pp. (OCLC 20131913)

Giving the illusion of an oriental setting, this story features a small, almond-eyed, dark-haired boy who lives in what appears to be a children's home. The story relates the children's daily activities, likes, dislikes, fears and hopes. They sometimes engage in an activity in which they describe families they would like to belong to, while trying with difficulty to remember living with their original families. One day the small boy is told that he will get his wish of having his own family because someone wants to adopt him. He travels by airplane to a new country where his new parents lovingly greet him at the airport and they go home together. Beautiful pen and ink and watercolor full-page illustrations enhance the story.

047   Garling, Gloria. **A is for Adoption**. Illus. by Georgia Oistad. Seattle, WA: G. Garling, 1979. [23]pp. (OCLC 7893395)

Roughly measuring six inches square and printed on heavy stock paper, this book begins with a list of ABCs of adoption, then tells the story of preparing for the arrival of an adopted child, relating how the parents became mom and dad. The print is in large type with no more than four lines per page. The bold, graphic illustrations and page borders, as well as the print, are in bright primary colors of blue, red and yellow. This is a charming little book self-published by the author whose address is listed as 1103 East Hamlin, Seattle, WA 98102.

048   Girard, Linda Walvoord. **Adoption is for Always**. Illus. by Judith Friedman. Niles, IL: Albert Whitman, 1986. [32]pp. (OCLC 13859959)

Although she had always been told she was adopted as an infant, little Celia has just realized what it means. She is angry and confused to learn that these parents are not her only Daddy and Mommy. The book explores her feelings and her parents' and teacher's attempts to help her understand and accept her adoption. The situation is resolved when Celia realizes that she was not given up because she was bad, but rather because it was part of a plan of her loving birthparents. Soft, full-page black and white pencil drawings framed in a flowery cranberry-colored border illustrate the text. On a young level, this book covers the topic of a birthmother as a real person and the need to understand what adoption means.

049   Girard, Linda Walvoord. **We Adopted You, Benjamin Koo**. Illus. by Linda Shute. Niles, IL: Albert Whitman, 1989. [29]pp. (OCLC 18383061)

Nine-year-old Korean-born Benjamin relates his birth and adoption story while describing his experiences and feelings about growing up adopted from another country. The adoption of his sister from Brazil provides him additional perspective as he recounts specific situations, such as his surprise when he discovered that he did not look like his parents, his anger and confusion in reconciling the notion of having two mothers, his frustration at peer name-calling, comments from strangers and his comfort in accepting his place in his family. The color illustrations throughout reveal a typical middle-class home and activities. Many Korean children and their parents will relate to the little referral picture on the title page. This book gives an accurate and realistic portrayal of a Korean adoption. Due to the amount of text and the nature of the story line, this may also be appropriate for older children.

050   Gordon, Shirley. **The Boy Who Wanted a Family**. Illus. by Charles Robinson. New York: Harper and Row, 1980. 90pp. (OCLC 5499030)
This is the story of seven-year-old Michael, once almost adopted by a family, as he begins his new life with a single mother whom he thinks is a rather odd, but nice, character. The story follows them through the one-year probationary period up to the court finalization; through all the holidays, birthdays and the usual experiences which help create a family. Gordon captures the hope and fear of a young boy who learns some dreams do come true. Scattered pen and ink drawings break up the text and provide a visual extension for the young reader.

051   Green, Phyllis. **A New Mother for Martha**. Illus. by Peggy Luks. New York: Human Sciences Press, 1978. [32]pp. (OCLC 4004405)
First-grader Martha is distraught over the death of her mother. Not receptive to her father's plans for remarriage, she clings to the fantasy her mother will soon return. Believing she is helping out, Martha first plans to fix up the guest room, then when June and her father marry and June moves into her father's bedroom, Martha fixes the guest room for her mother. Each day she waits in the guest room for her mother to return. June, who had also lost her mother, is kind and understanding using subtle opportunities to provide the mothering Martha needs and wants. In a late night, lonely situation, Martha makes a hard choice and decides to join her father and new mother. The full-page black and white detailed illustrations, accented with shades of pink watercolor, heighten the emotional story of a small girl as she accepts her new mother.

052   Greenberg, Judith E., and Helen H. Carey. **Adopted**. Photographs by Barbara Kirk. New York: Franklin Watts, 1987. 32pp. (OCLC 15318067)
Sporting full-page black and white photographs on every other page, this book features the adoption of baby Ryan which causes sister Sarah, adopted seven years earlier, to question her own past and place in the family. She hears the explanation of her birth, how this family wanted her and cares for her and how she is special, not because she is adopted, but because she is herself. A quiet, reassuring story, this book also includes extended family and school situations. This book is part of the publisher's **My World** series.

053   Guy, Anne. **A Baby for Betsy**. Illus. by Priscilla Pointer. New York: Abingdon Press, 1957. 32pp. (OCLC 1648168)

Betsy Bright and her parents have a happy life, except they want a baby in their family. Betsy's next door neighbor and friend, Tommy has a baby sister and Betsy likes to go to his house to watch and play with their baby. At other times, Betsy treats her dog Cooky as a baby, dressing him up and taking him for buggy rides. One day Betsy learns that Tommy's family adopted their baby and she runs to ask her parents if they can too. Her parents tell her that they have been thinking about adopting a baby and have begun the process. A year later they receive a call to come get their baby, but when two babies are brought into the room at the agency, Betsy cannot decide between the two and is overjoyed to learn that the babies are twins, a boy and a girl, and the family is adopting both children. The black and white illustrations are realistic and the full-page illustrations are accented in pink and blue. The pink and blue theme is also carried out in the story. This, together with Harwood's **The Widdles** (054), is one of the few stories for young readers relating the adoption of twins.

054   Harwood, Pearl Augusta. **The Widdles.** Illus. by Henning Black Jensen. Minneapolis: Lerner Publications, 1966. [27]pp. (OCLC 4045582)
Mr. and Mrs. Widdle live in Hawaii in a large house and decide they need children to help fill it. They go to a local orphanage to adopt a two-year-old child and are met at the door by an eight-year-old Chinese boy who claims that he will be at the orphanage forever because adults always want to adopt smaller children. The Widdles are charmed by Lee Chan and he becomes their first child. The same events repeat themselves several times and the Widdles bring home an eight-year-old Japanese boy, then an eight-year-old Puerto Rican boy and later, one-year-old twin Hawaiian girls making the family complete. The soft, but primitive, full-page pencil drawings are enhanced by golds, greens and blues. An interesting story promoting older child and transracial adoptions, while providing the gentle reminder that families often find joy and happiness in a child other than the one they originally had in mind. There is a disturbing reference on the first page to suggest that the Widdles wanted to adopt because they were lonely.

055   Haywood, Carolyn. **Here's a Penny.** Illus. by the author. New York: Harcourt Brace and World, 1944. 158pp. (OCLC 300368)
Penny, named because his red hair is as shiny as a new penny, is his adoptive parents' first child. The story portrays Penny's young life in his family and neighborhood relating everyday activities. The story culminates with the family adopting Peter, a friend of Penny's who lives at the local orphanage. The antics of the two boys continue in the sequels **Penny and Peter** (New York: Harcourt, Brace and World, 1946) and **Penny Goes to Camp** (New York: Morrow, 1948). While the stories and illustrations are sometimes dated and there is not much substance to the adoption theme, children who are becoming independent readers still like Haywood titles.

056   Hess, Edith. **Peter and Susie Find a Family.** Illus. by Jacqueline Blass. Translation of **Peter und Susi Finden Eine Familie** by Miriam Moore. Nashville, TN: Abingdon Press, 1984. 33pp. (OCLC 11371006)
The Findleys have been married for some time and have a dog and many friends, but sadly, no children. Since no babies have been born to them, they

approach an adoption agency to locate a child. They wait for the agency to match them with a child, all the while preparing their home for a new baby. When the agency at last calls to offer Peter, they are overjoyed, anxiously awaiting the day they can bring Peter home. Peter is welcomed by an extended family and grows into a confident little boy who eventually wants a sister to play with. The Findleys once again approach the adoption agency, which acts much quicker this second time, and are soon the happy parents and sister of baby Susie. The colorful full-page watercolor illustrations are stiff, yet detailed. In a two-page afterword parents and educators are urged to promote adoption stories for both the benefit of adopted children, but also for the edification of their non-adopted friends. This is an interesting story in that it relates the life of active parents prior to the adoption of children, as well as briefly describes the adoption process the parents go through.

057   Hutchins, Pat. **Our Baby is Best**. New York: Greenwillow, 1991. (OCLC 21230645)
Although this book was unavailable for evaluation, the pre-publication information reveals it is about a child describing the messy, noisy and lovable qualities of a newly adopted baby sister.

058   Jeschke, Susan. **Firerose**. New York: Holt, Rinehart and Winston, 1974. [32]pp. (OCLC 677620)
When Zora, the fortune teller, finds a baby on her doorstep, she is surprised to learn the baby breathes fire and has a dragon's tail. Zora calls upon Lucia, another fortune teller, who advises her to help the child, now called Firerose, to like her tail. Instead, Zora concentrates on ways to make the tail disappear. When she realizes the tail is going to stay, Zora follows Lucia's advice and works on helping Firerose like and accept herself. Lucia's crystal ball informs them a dragon was born without a tail the same time Firerose was born with one. Zora and Firerose find the little dragon and the dragon doctor switches the tail. Although she misses her tail, Firerose understands she does not need one since she is a person. The soft pencil drawings add a humorous element to this fantasy adoption story.

059   Johnson, Doris. **Su An**. Illus. by Leonard Weisgard. Chicago: Follett, 1968. 30pp. (OCLC 438026)
A solemn withdrawn Korean orphan, Su An, still clinging to the bittersweet memories of her Korean mother, is reluctant to partake of her new life in America and harbors false hopes that her birthmother will soon be with her. Not wanting to acknowledge the end of her past life, Su An stubbornly resists the caretaker's efforts to take her to her new family. In heartrending sparse poetic prose, Johnson reveals the needs of the small girl as she reluctantly reaches out to her new mother who hugs her and gives her a new doll and a sense of security she has not felt for some time. Su An surprises herself by feeling taken in and shares a small smile with her new parents. The black and white line drawings, by a Caldecott award-winning artist, are as quiet and frail as Su An herself. Johnson provides a touching story of acceptance.

060   Keller, Holly. **Horace**. Illus. by the author. New York: Greenwillow, 1991. [28]pp. (OCLC 21339156)

Little Horace, who looks like a leopard, has spots while his adoptive parents, tigers, have stripes. Every night at bedtime his mother tells him his adoption story, but Horace falls asleep before she finishes. Even though he loves his parents, Horace feels that he belongs with a family who looks like him. He runs away and finds such a family, joining them for a day in the park, and has a wonderful time. But, as night comes, he realizes how much he misses his parents and considers they miss him too. So, instead of going home with the new family, he runs to his waiting parents. That night at bedtime, Horace listens to the whole story his mother tells and learns they wanted him to be their son. After the day's events, he, too, chooses them for his family. The brightly colored illustrations enhance the text with the message that belonging has more to do with feelings than appearances.

061   Koehler, Phoebe. **The Day We Met You**. Illus. by the author. New York: Bradbury Press, 1990. [36]pp. (OCLC 20016483)
This book, with its large type printed right over the illustrations, tells the simple story of how a newly adopted infant's parents prepared for the baby's arrival. It simply and lovingly describes preparing the nursery, getting baby supplies and receiving a teddy bear from Grandpa. With illustrations rendered in pastel crayon, the book beautifully describes the parents' joy as they welcome their new child. At the conclusion of the story is a two-page afterword to parents.

062   Kornitzer, Margaret. **The Hollywell Family**. Illus. by Shirley Hughes. London: Bodley Head, 1973. 31pp. (OCLC 7049683)
Robert and Freda Hollywell are happy with their first child, Mary, and decide a baby brother would be a wonderful addition to the family. A doctor tells the Hollywells that they are not able to have another baby, so the family seeks out an adoption agency. They are told that the wait will be long and the Hollywells spend the time preparing for the new baby's arrival. When they receive the awaited call to go see their new baby, George, they bring him home. Later, the Hollywells go to court and the adoption is finalized. There is a decided British flavor to this book, both in vocabulary and dialog. The colorful detailed, yet sketchy drawings which accompany the story give the only clue the story involves an transracial adoption. It is a refreshing story that concentrates on the adoptive family without mentioning that George is black and the Hollywells are not.

063   Kornitzer, Margaret. **Mr. Fairweather and His Family**. Illus. by Margery Gill. London: Bodley Head, 1960. [32]pp. (OCLC 18509529)
After the Fairweathers marry, they realize something is missing from their lives and they acquire a dog and then a cat, but discover they really would like a baby. Set in Great Britain, the couple inquire at Sunshine House about adoption, since a baby has not been born to them, and once the director is satisfied they will be good parents, they are shown a baby boy sleeping in a crib, but the couple turn him down because he is not the right child for them. The director contacts them sometime later to come see another child. This time the baby boy they are shown is the right one and they take Andrew home. The family settles down to living with their new baby and at the proper time, the Fairweathers go to court to finalize Andrew's adoption. Later, the

family goes back to Sunshine House to adopt a baby girl and Sarah goes home to live with her new family. The color and tinted illustrations, sketchy, muted and blurry, reveal a somber home and family; there are very few recognizable smiles. Not only is there not much feeling in the story, it is also a stilted and abbreviated version of an adoption.

064   Korschunow, Irina. **The Foundling Fox: How the Little Fox got a Mother**.
            Illus. by Reinhard Michl. Trans. of **Finderfuchs** by James Skofield. New
            York: Harper and Row, 1984. 48pp. (OCLC 10559270)
A baby fox is left alone, abandoned by his mother when she is killed by a hunter. Unable to fend for himself, the baby fox is soon found by another mother fox who is on her way home to her babies. The vixen, while initially reluctant, feeds the little fox and takes him home with her. On their journey they confront danger, but the mother fox protects her new charge and they arrive safely home and join the other three babies. The vixen is ridiculed by her neighbors, but remains fiercely protective of the foundling fox. When there is the opportunity to show off her new little one, she is unable to recognize him from her other little foxes. She feeds, protects and teaches all the little foxes until it is time for them to be on their own. The natural color illustrations, as well as the black and white drawings, add a warmth and charm to this blending of families.

065   Lapsley, Susan. **I Am Adopted**. Illus. by Michael Charlton. Scarsdale, NY:
            Bradbury Press, 1974. [26]pp. (OCLC 1449401)
A preschool-age child named Charles narrates this story in which he reveals that he and his younger sister, Sophie, are adopted. The bulk of the story relates, in sparse text, routine family activities such as getting a small tractor as a birthday gift, playing with a friend, playing piano, making things, cooking with Mommy, working with Daddy on the car and Daddy helping with their bath. Within the story Charles also explains his understanding of adoption when he tells that he and Sophie were given to their parents when they were small and their parents brought them home to make a family. In the end, Charles' summation is that adoption means belonging. The brightly colored illustrations portray a warm, happy family, albeit sexist, atmosphere for this straightforward story.

066   Long, Carol. **It's Fun to Be Me!** Illus. by Jan Smulcer. Washington, D.C.:
            National Committee for Adoption, 1983. 24pp.
Lee, the narrator, tells about family life and celebrations while discussing how adoption agencies and parents work together to create families. Lee tells about being born to another mother who was not able to provide care, but that his/her parents prepared a nursery, anxiously waited and received a call that made them parents. Picking up baby Lee was an exciting and happy day and many friends came to welcome him/her. Lee's parents continue to reassure him/her of their love because he/she is special to them. Approximately the size of a coloring book, this paperback, illustrated in yellow, orange, white and black, is arranged with the text centered on the left side of the page with a border appropriate to the text, eg., hearts, suns, smiley faces, telephones. The right side is made up of activity pages to help parents talk to their small children about adoption, while actively including them in the discussion. Since

the sex of the narrator is not given, this is equally appropriate for use with boys and girls. While this book is difficult to locate in libraries, it is available directly from National Committee for Adoption (see Appendix B). Activity books for older children include Gabel's **Filling in the Blanks** (107) and Kalil's **Adoption: Let's Talk** (257).

067   Lowe, Darla. **Story of Adoption: Why Do I Look Different?** Illus. by Christina S. Carney. Minneapolis: East West Press, 1987. [16]pp. (OCLC 17797703)
Just after her third birthday, an Asian girl realizes she looks different from the rest of her family. She has darker hair and skin and her eyes look different as well. Mom takes advantage of the opportunity to share her daughter's adoption story with her telling the little girl about Korea, where everyone looks like her. Continuing the story, Mom tells how their family wanted to adopt a little girl and how another woman gave birth to a baby girl she could not care for. Mom tells how the little girl's new big sister first held her and how special her arrival was. Mom reminds her that God created all children everywhere so, no matter the differences, we can all be proud. The book ends with the arrival of a new baby brother who looks just like the little girl. This paperback has rather primitive black and white illustrations on every page; the story addresses physical differences.

068   MacKay, Jed. **The Big Secret**. Illus. by Heather Collins. [Toronto]: Annick Press, 1984. [22]pp. (OCLC 11618809)
Mario, a six-year-old who was adopted by his family last year, is suspicious about the activities of his family when they tell him a special day is coming on Saturday and he does not have a clue. To further complicate matters, Mario's friends and neighbors seem to know more than he does. In an attempt to discover the secret, Mario rummages through the basement, but does not find anything. On Saturday, his mother sends him off to the library as usual even though his friend, Doug, cannot go and none of his friends are even there. Feeling lonely, Mario walks home and is greeted by a big surprise party as he goes through his door. His family and friends have gathered to celebrate his one year anniversary of joining the family. A full-color, full-page illustrations, featuring a multi-ethnic neighborhood, faces each page of text. Celebrating his arrival day, this story reveals a temporarily confused, but eventually contented little boy.

069   MacLachlan, Patricia. **Mama One, Mama Two**. Pictures by Ruth L. Bornstein. New York: Harper and Row, 1982. [32]pp. (OCLC 7738200)
Maudie lives in a foster home with Mama Two while her birthmother, Mama One, is hospitalized for depression. Getting up to feed the crying baby in the middle of the night, Mama Two and Maudie retell the story of how Maudie came to have two mothers. While not actually an adoption story, children who have lived in foster care will recognize the fears and concerns expressed by Maudie. In addition to the pictures, which appear on almost every page using soft and muted colors, the story also provides a calm positive image of the foster mother and the male social worker.

070   Martin, Ann M. **Karen's Little Sister.** Illus. by Susan Tang. New York: Scholastic, 1989. 101pp. (OCLC 20740004)
Six-year-old Karen and her four-year-old brother Andrew live part-time with their father, his wife Elizabeth and her four children. Daddy and Elizabeth have also adopted Emily, a two-year-old Vietnamese child. Karen feels ignored, left out and jealous of the attention Emily gets. Feeling angry, yet despondent, Karen tells her mother about this problem and asks for a pet to care for and love her. Karen finds a homeless baby bird and with her family's help carefully nurses it back to health. Karen plays with Emily while she in the hospital and helps take care of her when she comes home. Presenting a blended family, this story provides insight into the feelings of a birthchild after the arrival of a newly adopted younger sibling. The occasional soft black and white illustrations enhance the text. This book is #6 of the **Baby-Sitters Little Sister** series, which features the younger sisters of the main characters of the **Baby-Sitters Club** series. Emily is a permanent character in both series. For related titles featuring the Baby-Sitters Club members and their families see Martin's **Claudia and the Great Search** (191) and **Kristy and the Mother's Day Surprise** (192).

071   Milgram, Mary. **Brothers Are All the Same.** Illus. by Rosemarie Hausherr. New York: Dutton, 1978. [32]pp. (OCLC 3517127)
Rodney, the second-grader next door, cannot believe that Joshie is Nina and Kim's little brother because he is black and they are white and he did not come from the hospital. Nina and her other second-grade friends try to explain to Rodney that brothers and sisters can arrive in different ways. When his own older brother is mean to Rodney, the other children use the opportunity to claim that all brothers, no matter their age or how they joined the family, can be pests. When Rodney and the girls make paper airplanes, he learns that like airplanes, there are different kinds of siblings. The large black and white photographs make the children in the story seem like real people. In the text and photographs, Rodney is initially characterized as a know-it-all who becomes more humble as the story continues, while Joshie is portrayed with a mischievous sparkle in his eyes. This is a warm, matter-of-fact story about adopted siblings.

072   Miquelle, Jean B. **It's Neat to Be Adopted.** Illus. by Peggy Fenner. [Darien, CT: FANA], 1979. 30pp. (OCLC 8024021)
Eight-year-old Katie, adopted from Korea as an infant, is asked so many questions about adoption she includes the answers in this book to satisfy readers' curiosity. Using her own experience, Katie explains the two older birthchildren in her family, as well as her own adoption and that of her brother, Chris, adopted from Colombia when he was two years old. She explains what an adoption agency is and the process parents must go through to adopt a child as well as the situation of waiting children. In addition, Katie thinks about her birthmother and wonders about her life and why she might have given her up. Katie also discusses school problems, her parents' love for their children, the awkward times when strangers make comments about their looks and that her parents believe that although a child's heritage is important, there is not much heritage in an orphanage. Katie is glad that she and her brother did not grow up in an orphanage and hopes other children get adopted

too. The calligraphic text and primitive drawings in brown ink printed on yellow paper, are not particularly aesthetically attractive, however, this book realistically approaches issues such as sibling jealousy, prejudice, maintaining heritage and children's past life.

073   Munsch, Robert N. **David's Father**. Illus. by Michael Martchenko. Toronto: Annick Press, 1983. [30]pp. (OCLC 11070482)

One day as little Julie is skipping home from school, she notices someone moving into a house in her neighborhood. Seeing the life-size eating utensils the movers are carrying in scares her so that she runs home and hides, but the next day as she comes home from school she meets David who has just moved into the house and he invites her to play. When Julie accepts David's dinner invitation, she meets his father, who is a kindly giant. When Julie mentions to David that he does not look like his father, David explains he is adopted. After dinner the three of them go for a walk together and David's father uses his size to stop traffic so they can walk across the street, get the kids waited on in a store and scare away six big bully kids from eighth grade. When Julie gets a scraped elbow in the brawl, David's father gently bandages her arm. Julie admits to David his father is really nice, even though she still finds him rather scary. To which David replies that if Julie thinks his dad is scary she should meet his grandmother. The delightful colorful illustrations, on every other page opposite the text, provide a humorous complement to the story. This is a charming and fun fantasy featuring an interracial friendship; Julie is black and David and his father are white.

074   Munsch, Robert N. **Murmel, Murmel, Murmel**. Illus. by Michael Martchenko. Toronto: Annick Press, 1982. [25]pp. (OCLC 20489271)

While five-year-old Robin is playing in her sandbox, she discovers a baby down a deep hole. Realizing she is unable to care for the child, Robin tries to find a grown-up to take the baby, but nearly everyone refuses. She asks a woman who tells her she already has a baby and is being chased by seventeen diaper salesmen; she asks a old woman who does not like how a baby behaves and prefers her seventeen cats; she approaches a business woman who has many jobs, much money and little time and is followed by seventeen secretaries. Likewise, a selfish man refuses when he cannot find a benefit for having a baby. Dejected, Robin is then approached by a man who drives a large truck. He is delighted with the baby and they happily walk off together. Robin asks him about his truck which he is forgetting. He replies he has lots of trucks, but he needs a baby and Robin can keep the truck. The full-color, busy illustrations humorously enhance the text of this fantasy story which finds a parent for a baby. The title refers to the extent of the baby's vocabulary.

075   Parrish-Benson, Barbara. **Families Grow in Different Ways**. Illus. by Karen Fletcher. [available through Before We are Six, 12 Bridgeport Road East, Waterloo, Ontario], 1973. [27]pp. (OCLC 1530950)

Sara and Jamie are best friends who live near each other and play together almost every day. One day Jamie's mother tells him she is going to have a baby. He is so happy he runs to tell Sara who tells her parents about the news and asks if they, too, can have a baby. Her mother tells her they are hoping to adopt a baby soon instead of growing one. Jamie's baby sister is born and soon thereafter, Sara's parents receive the call to pick up their baby girl. Jamie and Sara dance around happy to have their new babies, loving them the same even though they came from different places. The dark blue ink of the calligraphy and the sketches are set on a creamy colored paper. This provides a simple joyful story of two special friends and the different ways babies are added to their families.

076   Piepgras, Ruth. **My Name is Mike Trumsky**. Illus. by Peg Roth Haag. Elgin,
        IL: Child's World, 1979. 32pp. (OCLC 4858067)
        Appearing to be early elementary school age, Mike Trumsky is the Westons' foster child since his mother needed to be hospitalized. It has been three months and, unlike his last foster home experience, his mother has not called or written. Mike is worried about her and that he might forget her. He likes this foster family, but he is teased by other children about whether his last name is Trumsky or Weston. When Miss Hunt, his caseworker, takes him to visit his mother, he is shy when he first sees her, but is happy that he recognizes her. His mother talks of the unexpected length of her hospital stay, her plans for a new job and her desire to bring him home so they can be a family again. He confesses that he calls his foster mother "Mom," but his mother is understanding because Mike knows who his real mother is. Mike returns to the Westons' with a renewed sense of himself. Miss Hunt is a black caseworker and Mike's friend Jim tells Mike about his adopted cousin. Following the text of the story is a short section discussing the story and foster care in general indicating that sometimes the children involved return to their parents, get adopted or stay in permanent foster care. Some adopted children may relate to Mike's confusing feelings while in foster care.

077   Rhoda [Bontrager, Rhoda]. **God Gives Me a Family**. Illus. by Sara Beachy.
        Goshen, IN: God Gives Me a Family, [1990]. [18]pp.
        Using an unnamed child as the narrator, this book describes the love two happy parents have because they love God. The parents want a child to hug, love and play with. The narrator exclaims his parents want him and that they knew God had a special child in mind for them telling how his parents prayed and God lead them to him. Explaining adoption means belonging to a family God made just for him, he continues to say he was a special gift from his birthparents when his birthmother was unable to care for him. Now at home with his new family he has a loving extended family, as well as his parents, and is hoping for brothers and sisters. Grateful for a special place in the hearts of his parents, the narrator thanks God for his Christian parents who teach him to love and obey God. The soft shaded blue illustrations, as well as the text, reveal a Mennonite lifestyle, but would be appropriate for others seeking a Christian approach to adoption.

078   Sanford, Doris. **Brian Was Adopted**. Illus. by Graci Evans. Portland, OR:
        Multnomah, 1989. [27]pp. (OCLC 19388640)
        Eight-year-old Brian, who was adopted from Korea when he was a baby, describes his adoption and his life in America. Interspersed throughout the text are Brian's brief letters to God in which he shares his thoughts. Revealing a loving family, Brian tells about his relationship with his parents and his brother and how he feels about looking different from his other family

members. When Brian asks, his parents tell all they know about his earlier life. They remind Brian of the day he arrived in the U.S. and of his Korean baby clothes which he takes to show and tell. Brian tells about going to court for finalization and admits to fantasies about his birthmother; he also admits he does not like kimchi. Having mixed feelings at times, Brian says his father is not his real father when he is punished, but at the same time wants to have been born from inside his adoptive mother. Ending with an illustration of Brian and his mother in front of a Christmas tree, there is also a letter to God from Brian's mom thanking Him for Brian. The detailed colorful crayon-like illustrations are lifelike and reveal realistic details about a Korean-born child, such as a referral picture, kimchi and traditional Korean dress. This book attempts to show parents who give their foreign-born child a sense of deep love as well as his own heritage. This is part of the publisher's **In Our Neighborhood** Series.

079   Sass, Norma Jean. **I Am Adopted**. [Novi, MI: Norma Jean Sass], 1987. [24]pp.
Kara, the narrator, relating that children can be adopted from many countries, tells of her own adoption from India when she was two years old. She relates living in an orphanage with other children, of her siblings, both of whom are adopted, and reveals she does not look like her parents because her skin, eyes and her hair are different. Reassuring readers that parents love their children for themselves, not how they look, Kara tells of her initial fear of strange people, food, smells, clothes and weather, while slowly warming to her new family whom she grew to trust and love. In a final word, Kara describes adoption as adults and children coming together as a family and loving each other. Although not widely circulated, this is one of the few books at this level on the adoption of a child from India. The cartoon-like full-color watercolor illustrations depict varying racial backgrounds and complement the text. This book is available directly from the author at 28680 Summit Court, Novi, MI 48337.

080   Saunders, Lowell. **The Kitten Who Was Different**. Illus. by June Talarczyk. Minneapolis: T.S. Denison, 1966. [28]pp. (OCLC 953013)
When the master's cat has a litter of five kittens, one of them, Feelee, is born with eight toes on each front paw instead of the usual four. The master's grandchildren will soon visit to each pick a kittens to take home as their own pet. While the others are convinced they will be chosen first, Feelee, feeling different and inferior, runs away. Deep in the woods, Feelee encounters a wise owl who questions him until Feelee realizes it is best for him to return home. When the grandchildren arrive, one of the little girls, Betsy, has leg braces and uses crutches and moves more slowly than the other children. Their grandfather allows her to choose her kitten first. Although Feelee tries to hide his front paws Betsy notices and chooses him because just as she is different from the other children, Feelee is different from the other kittens. Knowing he was Betsy's first choice, Feelee happily and proudly goes home with her. The illustrations, some in color and others in black and white, support the idea of being wanted despite differences.

081   Schindel, Ronnie Levine. **I Am Jungle Soup**. Illus. by Tom Hall. Syracuse, NY: Singer, 1967. 32pp. (OCLC 3130072)
Jung Sook is a little girl who describes living in a Korean orphanage. One day Jung Sook is told to put on a pretty traditional Korean dress, a hambok, to have her picture taken in hopes a real mother and father will see it and want her for their daughter. Sometime later, Jung Sook is taken away from the orphanage wearing a dress and a bracelet with her name on it to travel to live with her new family and is met by her new father in the United States, but Jung Sook is afraid. After a long car ride home, Jung Sook meets her new mother and smiles. She is given toys, dresses and a doll she straps to her back as Korean mothers do. Jung Sook is still afraid of Daddy until he shares with her the picture of her wearing the hambok and she knows this is her daddy. He tells her she is not Jung Sook, she is his very own "Jungle Soup." The black and white drawings, highlighted and sometimes washed in red, reveal, along with the text, many features of Korean orphanage life, as well as the fear of the small girl as she joins her new family. The story also uses some Korean words and spells Jung Sook's name in Hangul.

082   Schnitter, Jane T. **William is My Brother**. Illus. by Gerald Kruck. Indianapolis, IN: Perspectives Press, 1991. (OCLC 22707670)
According to the pre-publication information, the two young brothers in this book, which was unavailable for evaluation, are the same in many ways except that one was born into the family and the other was adopted. Together the boys anxiously await the arrival of a new sister.

083   Seuling, Barbara. **What Kind of Family is This?: A Book About Stepfamilies**. Illus. by Ellen Dolce. New York: Golden Book, 1985. [25]pp. (OCLC 12069366)
After his parents' divorce, Jeff's mother remarries and the two of them move in with Henry and his two children. Jeff feels resentful and he rebuffs Henry's friendly overtures. Scott, Henry's son who is the same age as Jeff, shares a bedroom with Jeff and the two behave angrily toward each other. When the boys have an argument over a lost hamster, they discover each other has some good play ideas. Slowly, the boys find ways to play together, usually getting along and learning to be brothers. They talk of how they each feel about having a new parent and discover their similar reactions. Although his life with his new family is not perfect, Jeff now agrees with his mother that in time he will get used to it. While not dealing directly with adoption, the experience of a child blending with a stepfamily has many similarities to becoming part of an adoptive family.

084   Silverman, Helen. **Special You: A Story of Adoption**. Illus. by Laurie. Lincoln, NE: Linc Publications, 1955. [23]p. (OCLC 11448320)
Told in rhyme with one line per page, this book relates the adoptive parents' search for a baby. It starts with their idea of wanting a baby, going to a children's home where the staff promises to find the best baby for them and tells them to wait. They wait patiently for months until the home calls to tell them it is time to pick up their baby. Rushing to the home, the parents are taken to a little room where a nurse comes to them with a small bundle that is their baby. The very last page has a cut-out space in which to place a baby's

picture to personalize the story. The pastel illustrations are cartoonish, but sweet, however the story is too simplified.

085   Sly, Kathleen O'Connor. **Becky's Special Family**. Illus. by Leland D. Sly and
            Robert F. Urfer. Corona, CA: Alternative Parenting Publications, 1985.
            [56]pp. (OCLC 15062255)
        Centering on the mutual love of both the adoptive parents and the birth-
        parents, Sly presents Becky's open adoption in a picture book format.
        Preschool Becky introduces herself in words and photographs and tells the
        reader she was born to her birthmother and adopted by her parents when she
        was a baby. She relates the story of family and friends coming to welcome her
        and love her. She continues by saying that although her birthparents live far
        away, they, too, love her and care about her. They keep in touch with her by
        phone and letters and she has a special blanket from her birthgrandmother.
        Becky loves her adoptive family, but thinks both of her families are special.
        The remainder of the volume provides space for the reader to make a picture
        book of his/her own special family and adoption with room for photographs
        of birthparents and adoptive parents. This book is significant as it is the only
        picture book examined that deals with an open adoption. While the black and
        white photographs enhance the book's warmth, the photographic quality is not
        consistent.

086   Stanek, Muriel. **My Little Foster Sister**. Illus. by Judith Cheng. Chicago:
            Albert Whitman, 1981. [32]pp. (OCLC 7672639)
        When preschooler Penny goes to live with a foster family after the death of
        her parents, she is rejected by the only child of the foster family. The only
        child, who is the narrator of the story, gives her perspective on having a foster
        sister. Her experiences are quite negative until an older child bullies Penny
        and the narrator comes to her rescue. By the time Penny leaves to be adopted
        by an aunt and uncle in California, the narrator has grown to care about her
        and is sad to see her go. The black and white sketches are enhanced by the
        addition of gold strokes of color. This is an unusual picture book describing
        a foster situation from the point of view of one of the siblings, rather than the
        foster child, and describes how such relationships can grow. Some readers
        may be offended by the initial selfish and rude attitude of the birthchild.

087   Stein, Sara Bonnett. **The Adopted One: An Open Family Book for Parents
            and Children Together**. New York: Walker, 1979. 47pp. (OCLC
            4515146)
        With dual texts on the same page, the story uses large print for a child and a
        small print narrative for an adult. This book attempts to facilitate growth and
        discussion with and about the adopted child and his feelings and perceptions.
        While the adult text discusses the needs of adoptive children, the child's story
        tells of a Thanksgiving gathering where four-year-old Joshua is feeling left out
        because he is adopted and needs to hear his adoption story once again. When
        fantasizing a better life with birthparents, Joshua angrily accuses his adoptive
        parents of not being his real parents. Some readers may object that instead
        of disputing the use of the word "real," Joshua's father snaps back that he is
        not their real child either. Even though the father saves the situation, the
        story ends with an unsettled feeling.

088   Taber, Barbara Gilchrist. **Adopting Baby Brother**. Illus. by Margaret K.
Anderson. Rochester, NY: self-published, 1974. [15]pp. (OCLC
1950780)
The Kemp family is excited because they are adopting a baby brother. Daddy
and Mommy have already explained to the two daughters, little Jenny and
Lisa, how some families have babies born into them while others adopt babies
who have been born to others. Happily, the two girls help their parents
prepare the room for baby Peter William's arrival and shop for new baby
things. They are so excited when the baby arrives home Daddy suggests a
backyard party the following week to celebrate Peter's adoption. While the
girls grow bored with the baby and wish their mother had more time with
them, Jenny and Lisa also like helping with the baby. At the party a child asks
why Peter is brown and Jenny responds it is because his birthmother was
brown and reminds him that Lisa is brown too. She continues by telling him
it is the same as having different color hair or eyes. This self-published spiral-
bound book has lovely sketchy illustrations, outlined in brown, that are
sparsely and selectively colored in various shades. They reveal a loving warm
family created by transracial adoption. The author's address is listed as P.O.
Box 5061, River Station, Rochester, NY 14627.

089   Tax, Meredith. **Families**. Illus. by Marylin Hafner. Boston: Little, Brown,
1981. 32pp. (OCLC 6666792)
Six-year-old Angie tells about many of her friends to describe several kinds of
family groupings, human and animal, defining family as the people you live
with and love you. Angie describes her own situation living with her mother
in a large apartment in New York and her father who lives in Boston with his
new wife and baby. Angie's friend George lives with his brothers and their
father while Marisel lives with her large Hispanic extended family. Angie's
cousin, Louie, is adopted and her friend Frederick Douglas lives alternately
with his mother and grandmother while his mother works. Susie lives with her
mother and godmother and claims not to have a father. Angie also tells about
lions, ants, dogs and their families. She concludes by restating that there are
many different kinds of families, but they are held together by the same
common bond of love. The black and white detailed drawings reveal the
warmth the text delivers while depicting Angie and her friends who represent
several ethnic backgrounds. Similar in scope and approach to Simon's **All
Kinds of Families** (022).

090   Thompson, Jean. **I'm Going to Run Away**. Illus. by Bill Myers. Nashville,
TN: Abingdon Press, 1975. [31]pp. (OCLC 922773)
Little Jimmy wakes up to a bad day when his favorite shirts are dirty, he has
trouble tying his shoelaces, there are no corn flakes for breakfast, his sandbox
fort is destroyed by the next door dog and his friend Steve is not home. Since
the day is so bad Jimmy decides to run away. Packing some things, Jimmy
tells his mother he is running away to find a place where people are nicer to
him. His mother tells him that most people already have their own families,
but to be careful and not go off the street. As he travels from house to house,
Jimmy receives a variety of responses to his request for a new home. Some
neighbors are kind and offer cookies, while others are mean or busy and some
already have enough kids. After going to many houses, and as the evening

gets darker, Jimmy happens upon a nice house with a nice smiling woman who says they always wanted a little boy just like him. Feeling warm and wanted, Jimmy washes his face and hands for dinner and sits down to join his very own mother and father for dinner. Bold black and white sketches, highlighted in muted blue and olive, are a nice addition to this cute switch story in which the child looks for a new family.

091   Turner, Ann Warren. **Through Moon and Stars and Night Skies**. Illus. by James Graham Hale. [New York]: Harper and Row, 1990. [31]pp. (OCLC 17443502)

An unnamed preschool boy begs his mother to let him tell the story of how he came to America carrying the pictures of his new parents and house. He tells about living in an unnamed southeast-Asian country and needing a bed and parents of his own. Fearful of flying and encountering new experiences, he describes his long flight clutching the pictures of his new family. Although he is frightened when they land at the airport, he soon sees the man and woman who are in his picture. They are holding a picture of him and waiting with outstretched arms. Still fearful, he travels home with his new parents and when they arrive, he recognizes his house from his pictures and is happily welcomed by the dog, whom he also recognizes. Still afraid, he soon comes to know his mother's smile and his father's face. Momma and Poppa put him to bed with the teddy bear quilt that he had seen in the pictures. They tuck him in and, knowing they will watch over him, he falls asleep to dream of their comfort and protection. The watercolor illustrations are evocative and include subtle, appropriate details. While initial adjustments are not quite so quick, relating a child's emotions from fear to fond acceptance is captured beautifully.

092   Udry, Janice May. **Theodore's Parents**. Illus. by Adrienne Adams. New York: Lothrop, Lee and Shepard, 1958. [28]pp. (OCLC 5011519)

Theodore is a competent little boy who takes care of himself, his house, his garden and his pets. He is intrigued when the other children at school talk about their parents and he questions them about how old they are, what they do and if they are much trouble. Deciding that parents sound pretty good, Theodore places an ad in the newspaper for a set of parents. He is very surprised when so many couples arrive at his house on the interview day. Discouraged by unsuitable applicants, Theodore sadly turns them all away and sits in his now-lonely house. When the doorbell rings, Theodore greets another couple, with their small daughter, who arrive late because of traffic problems. The family seems to fit right into Theodore's house. The family likes pets, the mother helps fix dinner and knits sweaters and mittens, the father has always wanted a boy to take to the zoo. Although he did not advertise for one, the parents thought Theodore would like a sister as well. Happily, Theodore invites them to move in tomorrow and they plan to go to the zoo. Delightful full-color illustrations complement the text. Despite the parental sexist overtones, this is a cute story that humorously turns around the traditional adoption process so the child chooses his parents.

093   Van Woerkom, Dorothy. **Something to Crow About**. Illus. by Paul Harvey. Niles, IL: Albert Whitman, 1982. [32]pp. (OCLC 8131926)

One morning when Ralph, a bachelor rooster, performs his daily job of crowing to wake up the neighborhood, he discovers a basket of three warm abandoned eggs on his doorstep. He nervously calls his friend Harriet for advice and she suggests Ralph sit on the eggs to keep them warm so they can hatch or to take them over to the hatchery and they will find someone else to adopt them. Ralph decides against the hatchery and gently sits on the eggs. The next morning the eggs began to crack open and Ralph calls Harriet to find out how to care for the baby chicks. Unfortunately, when Ralph crows his morning alarm, the chicks awaken. Harriet helps Ralph get the chicks under control so they can all rest peacefully. When they are old enough, the chicks go to school and Arabelle learns to dance, Sarabelle learns to sing and Paul learns to draw. When the chicks contract chicken pox and Ralph cares for them, he gets so tired himself that he accidentally crows at the light from the new supermarket instead of the sun. Ralph and the little chicks organize a special birthday party for Aunt Harriet. The cartoon-like black and white illustrations, highlighted in orange, which appear on every page, are a humorous addition to this story of an adoptive single father and his support system.

094   Waber, Bernard. **Lyle Finds His Mother**. Boston: Houghton Mifflin, 1974. [47]pp. (OCLC 866582)
Lyle, the famed crocodile featured in a series of books highlighting his antics, is happy living with the Primm family in their house on East 88th Street. His former stage manager, Hector P. Valenti, star of stage and screen, is out of work and hungry. After Hector sees Lyle with his family, he misleadingly lures Lyle back to work as a stage star with the promise to take him to his birthmother, then puts off Lyle's repeated requests. Hector finally relents and the two travel to a tropical area where Lyle notices a crocodile surface in the water and soon he is in the water playing with his mother. Lyle's mother returns with Lyle to the Primms' where she is warmly received. Since she is as theatrically inclined as Lyle, Hector offers to help her if she wants to seek a stage career. The delightful illustrations add humor to the text of this story, however, Lyle's status in the Primm household is unclear and the search and reunion theme may appear too pat for young readers.

095   Wagstaff, Sue. **Wayne is Adopted**. Photographs by Chris Fairclough. London: A. & C. Black, [1981]. 25pp. (OCLC 16563433)
Wayne, a biracial child who was adopted by the King family when is was eight years old, is now eleven. This book relates the activities of the King family, a white British family with four other children, including Emma, a biracial child adopted as an infant. Explaining adoption, the story relates the circumstances of Wayne's birth and his years in foster care; Mrs. King tells why they wanted to adopt Wayne; siblings, Emma and Paul, reveal their feelings about the adoption; and Mr. King describes the brief finalization court ceremony. The Kings' lifestyle is portrayed with the children having chores and typical sibling spats, family vacations, school sports and birthday treats. The family encourages Wayne and Emma to learn about their mixed heritage. The book concludes with a brief bibliography and a list of primarily British adoption resources. The photographs are interesting and help present an appealing story of a transracial adoption abroad.

096   Wasson, Valentina Pavlovna. **The Chosen Baby**. Illus. by Glo Coalson. rev.
 ed. Philadelphia: Lippincott, 1977. [46]p. (OCLC 2777173)
 Originally published in 1939, then revised in 1950 and again in 1977, this is the
 classic children's adoption book. The story follows James and Martha Brown
 as they go through the adoption process, first adopting Peter, then, a few years
 later, Mary. The story is drawn from the author's personal experience and as
 the foreword points out, the story gives an accurate account of infant adoption
 while genuinely relating the joy of the adoptive parents to the young reader.
 The soft watercolor-like illustrations, updated for the 1977 edition, capture a
 warm loving family atmosphere. Some readers may object to the chosen child
 theme.

097   Waybill, Marjorie Ann. **Chinese Eyes**. Illus. by Pauline Cutrell. Scottdale,
 PA: Herald Press, 1974. [34]pp. (OCLC 867964)
 Korean-born Becky is teased at school for having "Chinese eyes". She spends
 a long school day feeling very confused, angry and sad. When she gets home
 her mother comforts her and then helps her discover that their eyes are
 different in shape as well as color. Becky's mother explains that Becky's eyes
 look similar to those of children in China and that is why they have Chinese
 eyes. Her mother continues by reassuring her that her eyes are beautiful and
 Becky chimes in that one way their eyes are the same is that they both can
 see. The author attempts to explain a common taunt in order to help the
 child understand. While the colorful chalk drawings and story are charming,
 some readers may have preferred some discussion on name-calling and ways
 to help a child respond.

098   Weyn, Suzanne. **Make Room for Patty**. New York: Scholastic, 1991.
 The Bakers, with their eleven adopted children, welcome a new sibling, Patty,
 to their multi-racial family. With twelve children from a variety of ethnic
 backgrounds and personal circumstances, the family is always lively. To make
 matters more interesting, five of the Baker children are eight years old. This
 first in a series called **Bakers' Dozen** was unavailable for review.

099   **Who Wants to Adopt Willy the Wandering Kitten**. New York: Derrydale
 Books, 1988. [24]pp. (OCLC 19329245)
 Willy is a curious little tiger kitten who grows tired of watching his brother
 play with a butterfly and sets off to explore the area surrounding the garden
 in which he lives. Although warned against going into the house, Willy takes
 advantage of an open door and scampers inside where he encounters several
 dangers. Outside again, Willy discovers several animals before returning to his
 mother. This is a misleading title since there is no mention that Willy is
 actually in need of a new family. Realistic full-color illustrations reveal a
 lovely little kitten and other animals. Originally published in Great Britain,
 other titles in this series in which the baby animals always find their way back
 home include **Who Wants to Adopt Paddy the Playful Puppy, Who Wants to
 Adopt Georgie the Bold Baby Goose** and **Who Wants to Adopt Billy the Brave
 Bunny** (all New York: Derrydale Books, 1988).

100   Wickstrom, Lois. **Oliver**. Illus. by Priscilla Marden Johnson. Wayne, PA:
 Our Child Press, 1990. 32pp. (OCLC 22002568)

Although unable to obtain for evaluation, pre-publication information indicates this is a story of an adopted alligator who, when punished, wonders who his "real" parents are and how his life would be different with them. An earlier edition, which is difficult to locate, was also published (Denver: Sproing, 1979).

101   Williams, Vera B. **"More More More" Said the Baby: Three Love Stories**. Illus. by the author. New York: Greenwillow, 1990. [32]pp. (OCLC 19354500)
      In three short stories, three babies are given loving attention by a significant adult in their lives. Little Guy is a blond whose father gives him raspberry kisses on his stomach; Little Pumpkin, a black child, has a doting white grandmother who kisses his toes; and Little Bird is a small Asian child whose mother cuddles and lovingly puts to bed. The bold illustrations, characteristic of Williams, add to the delightful text. The transracial presentation of a grandparent and grandchild is a welcome addition to picture books as transracial adoption stories featuring grandparents are rare.

102   Wright, Betty Ren. **My New Mom and Me**. Illus. by Betsy Day. Milwaukee: Raintree Children's Books, 1981. 30pp. (OCLC 6890226)
      A little girl with her pet cat sadly remembers the death and funeral of her mother. In describing the cat's changed, stand-offish behavior, the girl is actually describing her own. The little girl's father is supportive, but when he remarries, she is unable to get past her anger and grief to accept the woman. She remains distant from Elena, her new stepmother, as does her cat. One evening when her father is not home, the little girl discovers her cat is in trouble and can only call on Elena for help. Together they discover the cat has lodged himself behind a wall in a closet and Elena breaks through the wall to rescue the frightened cat. Much to the little girl's surprise, the cat then jumps into Elena's waiting arms. They sit together and the cat allows Elena to comfort him. Elena explains that the girl's mother taught the cat how to love and, although he will never forget her, he must be tired of keeping all the love locked inside. The cat begins to purr and Elena puts her arm around the little girl and it feels good. The realistic lifelike full-color illustrations reveal a sad, angry little girl in this somewhat contrived story of attaching to a new parent.

103   Young, Miriam. **Miss Suzy's Birthday**. Illus. by Arnold Lobel. New York: Parents' Magazine Press, 1974. [40]pp. (OCLC 797842)
      While Miss Suzy is busy inside her oak tree house sewing for her four adopted little squirrels, Mrs. Chipmunk, gathers some friends to plan a birthday party for her. All the animals, including the little squirrels, have a meeting and argue how the present should be wrapped and whether the gift should be practical or fancy. Stevie, Miss Suzy's youngest, has the best idea and the party is planned for the next day. Despite Stevie's unintentional hints, Miss Suzy is delightfully surprised at the party. Crow gives her a big basket with a single acorn and the others all give acorns wrapped to their own liking. Soon the basket is full of acorns, enough for Miss Suzy to use for baking for months. The warm illustrations by award-winning Lobel enhance the story of family

and friends. Miss Suzy found the orphaned squirrels during a storm in **Miss Suzy's Easter Surprise** (New York: Parents' Magazine Press, 1972).

Intermediate Readers

NONFICTION

104   Berman, Claire. **"What Am I Doing in a Stepfamily?"** Illus. by Dick Wilson.
        Designed by Paul Walter. Secaucus, NJ: Lyle Stuart, 1982. [48]pp.
        (OCLC 8765133)
        This is a helpful work for exploring and coming to terms with having more
        than one set of parents, although adoption is not specifically mentioned.
        Focusing on situations which result in stepfamilies and on specific experiences
        stepfamilies have, Berman offers insight and advice to readers on stepfamily
        adjustments. This would be of particular use to those involved in stepparent
        adoptions. Designed and published by the same group as **Why Was I Adopted**
        (111), it offers a light-hearted, positive treatment to a serious topic.

105   Doss, Helen Grigsby. **The Really Real Family**. Illus. with photographs
        furnished by the author. Boston: Little, Brown, 1959. 75pp. (OCLC
        1668834)
        Elaine and Diane, sisters who appear to be about four and five years old, live
        in a foster home in Honolulu, Hawaii with their foster mother and four foster
        babies. The girls are delighted when their caseworker tells them a family
        wants to adopt them. They have a good-bye celebration and fly to California
        to join their new family, that includes seven other adopted children. As the
        new family settles in, one of the new sisters, Laura, who is the same age as
        Elaine, has a jealous time adjusting to the new arrivals and behaves very
        uncooperatively. The two clash until Elaine recalls her foster mother's advice
        to put herself in another's shoes to see how they feel. Doing so, Elaine is able
        to understand how threatened Laura must feel and tries to be more coopera-
        tive herself; Laura responds positively. Even though the children appear too
        altruistic, this is a delightful story enhanced by dated, though appealing black
        and white photographs providing an inside look at a large adoptive family in
        the 1950s. Other versions of the Doss family story can be found in the
        author's **The Family Nobody Wanted** (362) and **A Brother the Size of Me**
        (155).

106   Fredkove, Ann. **Advice for Adopted Kids**. Illus. by the author. Edina, MN:
Ann Young Ran Fredkove, 1989. 44pp.

Adopted to the U.S. at age seven, Korean-born Fredkove relates the story of
her own adoption and adjustment offering other adopted children advice from
her experience. Under the guidance of her family counselor, Ann covers such
topics as why birthparents do not keep children, orphanages, abuse, foster
parents, adoption adjustment, feeling different, getting along with a new family,
special days and feelings of adopted children. Two epilogues follow, one
written five months after the book, and the other two years later. In addition,
the book begins with selections written by Ann's parents and her counselor.
Fredkove includes several of her own black and white drawings to illustrate
her text. This is a readable, helpful, realistic book and Fredkove's text is
written in the language and from the point of view of a child. Although
difficult to locate in libraries, this paperback spiral-bound book is available
through Adoptive Families of America (see Appendix B). The book indicates
that readers may write to Ann Fredkove or her parents at 5712 Wooddale
Ave., Edina, MN 55424.

107   Gabel, Susan L. **Filling in the Blanks: A Guided Look at Growing Up
Adopted**. Illus. by Julie Seregny. Fort Wayne, IN: Perspectives Press,
1988. 158pp. (OCLC 21139820)

Using a workbook approach, this consumable book is designed for the middle-
school-age child to complete with an adult. Divided into four major sections,
"My Birth Family," "My Adoption Process," "My Adoptive Family" and "My
Self," each section has a general introduction. Each chapter within a section
has narrative introductory material, sometimes offering vocabulary, or
background information, followed by open-ended questions which are
appropriate for that chapter. The book is proceeded by an eight-page
introduction to the adult that explains the structure of the book, preferred
method for use and a plan for using the book. A glossary of terms introduced
is also included. This is potentially a beneficial source for helping adults who
assist adopted children focus on meaningful adoption issues. An activity book
useful for an older child is Kalil's **Adoption: Let's Talk** (257), while for a
younger child use Long's **It's Fun to Be Me** (066).

108   Holz, Loretta. **Foster Child**. Illus. by the author. New York: Julian
Messner, 1984. 63pp. (OCLC 10277676)

Appearing to be a junior-high-school-age child, Peter relates his life in a foster
home while his birthmother works on her alcoholism-related problems. Peter
tells of his concern and anxiety when joining the foster family and proceeds to
describe the differences between this temporary family and his own. He
relates differences concerning punishment, school work, chores, cooperation,
family rules, responsibility and trust. Peter, learning new positive values and
habits in his new home, questions his birthmother's ability to convince a judge
she will be able to care for him properly. Adoption is mentioned once when
an adopted friend compares himself to Peter and although adoption is never
specifically referred to as a possibility for Peter, this book realistically portrays
and parallels the foster life of many children who were adopted at an older
age. The black and white photographs make the story more realistic.

109   **It's Only FAIR: A Child's View of Adoption.** Palo Alto, CA: Families
        Adopting in Response (FAIR), 1989. [110]pp.
        This spiral-bound book is a collection of writings and drawings on adoption by
        children whose families belong to the adoption support group that published
        the book.   Divided into sections on family life, birth families, disabilities,
        feelings, teens, brothers and sisters, culture and getting together, the offerings
        provide children's perspectives on the adoption experience.   Sometimes in
        original handwriting and other times in various size of typeface, the authors
        and illustrators, all between the ages of two and eighteen, honestly reveal bits
        of their own backgrounds, memories, feelings and hopes.   This would also be
        an appropriate title for older readers, including adults.   There may well be
        additional volumes to come as the preface indicates this is the first volume of
        the title.   Although it may be difficult to locate in libraries, this title can be
        ordered from Families Adopting in Response (FAIR), P.O. Box 51436, Palo
        Alto, CA   94303.

110   Jenness, Aylette. **Families: A Celebration of Diversity, Commitment, and
        Love.** Illus. by the author. Boston: Houghton Mifflin, 1989. 47pp.
        (OCLC 19554496)
        Derived from material originally part of a traveling exhibition started at the
        Children's Museum in Boston, this book devotes two pages of text and
        photographs to each of seventeen children and their families. While there are
        a few traditional nuclear families containing only birthchildren, most of the
        families highlighted reveal a variety of living arrangements. Family circles
        formed by step relationships, adoption, gay parents, foster siblings, are
        examined as are large families, small families, extended families and families
        living in religious communities. Several minority, as well as interracial families
        are also represented. A two-page introduction defines the word family and
        includes children's actual written responses to questions about families. A
        one-page bibliography of children's books on families completes the book.
        The combination of the black and white photographs, as well as the families'
        own words, make each of these family systems seem alive and real.

111   Livingston, Carole. **Why Was I Adopted? The Facts of Adoption with Love
        and Illustrations.** Illus. by Arthur Robins. Designed by Paul Walter.
        Seacaucus, NJ: Lyle Stuart, 1978. [47]pp. (OCLC 3770728)
        This oversized book with cartoon-like illustrations sets forth the facts about
        adoption in a humorous yet straight-forward manner. By using a questioning
        approach, Livingston handles such concerns as identity, why birthparents do
        not keep a child, can new parents send a child back and an explanation of why
        and how people adopt. The drawings and texts are designed to be light and
        humorous, just as the artistic collaborators' previous book, **Where Did I Come
        From?** by Peter Mayle (New York: Lyle Stuart, 1975), and offers just a
        serious enough touch to approach some very sensitive issues. Unfortunately,
        only famine and war are cited as reasons that would result in intercountry
        adoption. The accompanying illustration features a stereotypical portrayal of
        an Asian child sitting in a battlefield wearing a military helmet. Some readers
        may find the text and illustrations too blunt. A Spanish language version, **Por
        Que Me Adoptaron?** (Barcelona: Ediciones Grijalbo, 1987) is also available.

112 McNamara, Bernard and Joan. **Ordinary Miracle**. Ossining, NY: Family
Resources, 1977. [19]pp.
Explaining that love is an ordinary miracle, the authors explain how adoption
is one kind of ordinary miracle. Describing a pregnant woman who, for
perhaps one of the several reasons given, is not able to care for her child by
providing all the important things a child needs to grow up, the McNamaras
indicate other grown-ups help. Judges, social services workers, foster care
workers and adoption workers try to find the child a home in which to be
important and lovable. When the adoption agency finds the right family, even
though good-byes can be frightening, the child has a new beginning to grow
and work hard in a new family. Sharing good times and bad, the child learns
about belonging and love slowly grows. Black and white photographs illustrate
this paperbound book that could be used with younger children, as well as
older children. Although this title can be difficult to locate, the publisher's
current address is Family Resources, 1521 Foxhollow Rd., Greensboro, NC
27410.

113 Milton, Joyce. **Greg Louganis: Diving For Gold**. Illus. by Stephen Marchesi.
New York: Random House, 1989. 87pp. (OCLC 18986188)
A biography of the Olympic medal winner, this relates the story of Louganis
who was adopted shortly after birth. He and his older adoptive sister took
dance lessons and he continued with gymnastics which provided his background for diving. Louganis, a mixed-race child (he is part Samoan and part
northern European) also experienced an early reading disability and asthma.
Unable to obtain title for evaluation.

114 Quinn, Barbara. **Were You Adopted?** New York: Vantage Press, 1970. 31pp.
(OCLC 1998113)
The narrator in this book tells the story of her own two children's adoptions
in the hopes it answers questions about the reader's adoption. Quinn proceeds
by relating the arrival of their second child, a son, and the questions asked by
their then three-year-old daughter. Indicating children are curious about their
adoptions, Quinn encourages children to ask their parents for answers. By
providing an anecdote regarding a schoolmate whose mother is going to have
a baby, Quinn tells about the difference between being born to one mother
and being cared for by another. She covers the idea of families being created
by fate, the idea of "real" parents, the uniqueness of each person, anger and
reaching out and touching each other's lives. Rough black and white drawings
accompany the text. Some readers may object to the drawing which shows a
father spanking a little girl over his knee. The purpose, execution and
usefulness of this vanity press publication is questionable. The text rambles,
uses an inconsistent vocabulary and is primarily concerned about the feelings
and beliefs of the adoptive parents.

115 Rosenberg, Maxine B. **Growing Up Adopted**. New York: Bradbury Press,
1989. 107pp. (OCLC 19777115)
After interviewing many children and adults concerning their adoptions,
Rosenberg presents fourteen fascinating life stories. With each chapter
focusing on an individual, Rosenberg delves into each adoptee's background,
as well as current thoughts on explaining adoption, feeling different from other

family members, relationships with other members of the family and searching for birthparents. The responses of the eight children and six adults, some of whom were adopted as infants, some as older children and some of whom were foreign-born while others were from the U.S., provide interesting insights into the thoughts and feelings of adoptees. While similar to Krementz's **How It Feels to be Adopted** (258), which contains photographs, and uses only children and teens as subjects, Rosenberg's book is significant for the inclusion of adult perspectives. The book concludes with a bibliography, sources of help and an index.

116   Scott, Elaine. **Adoption**. New York: Franklin Watts, 1980. 58pp. (OCLC 6251842)
Aimed primarily at children not familiar with the topic, this provides an introduction to adoption briefly covering some of the major issues. Beginning with a historical overview and citing the biblical story of Moses and the Code of Hammurabi, Scott discusses the difference between an adopted child's birthparents and adoptive parents. She refers to the adoptive parents as the child's "real" parents since they are the ones who serve in the caretaking role. Scott analyzes the role of both heredity, as well as environment, on the development of an adopted child. In addition, she looks at the issues of identity and searching for birthparents. The black and white photographs depict various adoptive situations including infant adoption, a Korean toddler with a single mother and Yul Brenner with his two adopted Vietnamese daughters. The book concludes with a short bibliography and an index. Focusing on infant adoptions by couples unable to bear children and on the importance of physically and intellectually "matching" adoptive parents and children date this book.

117   Sobol, Harriet Langsam. **We Don't Look Like Our Mom and Dad**. Photographs by Patricia Agre. New York: Coward-McCann, 1984. 32pp. (OCLC 10185353)
Korean-born Eric and Joshua Levin, at ages ten and eleven, are the subjects of this photo essay explaining what it is like to grow up in family where the children do not resemble the parents. The boys, adopted separately and before the age of three, discuss their Korean heritage, their curiosity about their birthparents, as well as their hobbies, likes and dislikes. The book shows, through the text and photographs, that despite differences, this is loving, sharing, caring family because they choose to be.

118   Stanford, James. **So, You're Adopted**. Illus. by Sylvia Woodcock-Clarke. Edinburgh: Macdonald, 1981. 48pp. (OCLC 16024328)
Using vignettes of adopted children, Stanford covers such topics as why and how children become available for adoption, why parents want to adopt and how adoptive parents are prepared. A chapter on the positive and negative aspects of a children's home is also included. Stanford continues by describing the first meetings of parents and their prospective adoptive child and then uses a few chapters to discuss the early adjustment period where everyone is on best behavior, as well as later on when they all settle down and find the new family routine. He advocates accepting one's past and determining the parts for which one can reasonably be responsible. The role of, status of and

emotions involved when talking about birthparents, called natural parents here, and the possibility of searching for them when the adopted child is older is also discussed. One page is devoted to minorities and includes transracial adoption. Stanford explains the adoption experience well enough to introduce the topic to the uninitiated as well as to validate the feelings of readers who are adopted. A revised edition (Edinburgh: Chambers, 1986), not examined, is also available.

119   Stewart, Gail. **Adoption**. New York: Crestwood House, 1989. 48pp. (OCLC 19516601)
Looking at issues from both adoptive children's viewpoint and that of the adoptive parents', Stewart covers a brief history of adoption, the motivation to adopt, the process of adoption, as well as sources of adoptive children and what it feels like to be adopted. Stewart includes a discussion of the child's birthfamily, but firmly defines "real" as the parents who raise, love and care for a child. By examining topics such as name-calling, transracial adoption, gray and black market adoptions, wondering about one's past and searching for birthparents, Stewart provides a thoughtful work. The book concludes with an address for more information on adoption and a combined glossary/index. While the pages seem crowded, the use of several specific examples of adoptive children and families along with many full-color photographs make this an interesting inside look at adoption for those directly involved or just curious.

FICTION

120   Adler, C.S. **The Cat That Was Left Behind**. New York: Houghton Mifflin/ Clarion Books, 1981. 146pp. (OCLC 7172295)
Thirteen-year-old Chad, recently relinquished for adoption by his birthmother, resentfully spends the summer with yet another foster family. He befriends a skittish stray cat while walking alone instead of joining in family activities. As the story progresses, the cat's trust in Chad slowly grows as does Chad's trust in the foster family who wants to adopt him. While not overjoyed at the prospect, Chad exhibits a willingness to try this new life and accept his birthmother's decision. This is a poignant story which realistically portrays a foster child's unwillingness to form significant relationships for fear of being rejected. The foster family is also realistically presented with its own foibles. Use of an animal to bridge bonding is similar to Hall's **Mrs. Portree's Pony** (165).

121   Alcock, Gudrun. **Duffy**. Illus. by Robert Clayton. New York: Lothrop, Lee and Shepard, 1972. 192pp. (OCLC 379234)
Following an accident which killed her father, eleven-year-old Duffy discovers her injured mother is actually her stepmother. Duffy is made a ward of the state and put in several homes until it is determined whether she will return to her stepmother or be sent to live with her long-lost birthmother and new husband. Sometimes humorous, other times serious, this story recounts Duffy's experiences as she goes from a caring temporary foster home as an only child, to a large foster family with a manipulative disturbed and rebellious foster

daughter, to a children's home. Duffy eventually meets her immature birthmother and helps decide she will remain with her stepmother. The story provides an insight to the confusion of a foster child who feels like a victim.

122   Ames, Mildred. **Without Hats, Who Can Tell the Good Guys?** New York: E.P. Dutton, 1976. 133pp. (OCLC 1735529)
Although it has been years since he has lived with his widowed father, eleven-year-old Anthony remains convinced his father will come for him as soon as he is settled down with a job. Consequently, he sees no reason to invest himself in the Diamonds, his foster family. Eleven-year-old Hildy, the Diamonds' birthchild, is resentful of Anthony's presence, Mr. Diamond is moody and volatile and Mrs. Diamond tends to fade into the woodwork. On his first day with the family, Mr. Diamond tell him they will call him Tony and expresses his joy at finally having a boy in the house. Mr. Diamond forces Tony, who is not fond of baseball, into Little League, but later, when angered, he pulls Tony from the team. Tony and Hildy slowly find a friendlier relationship when Hildy brings home a stray cat and they find a good home for him. When Anthony's father visits, Anthony mistakenly thinks his father has come for him. As Tony describes his present life to his dad, he grudgingly realizes he has found a good family. Setting his delusions aside, Tony decides to stay with the foster family. All the characters have rough edges on their personalities, but find ways to form relationships. A good example of a young boy with one foot in yesterday and one in today.

123   Angel, Ann. **Real for Sure Sister**. Illus. by Joanne Bowring. Ft. Wayne, IN: Perspectives Press, 1988. 72pp. (OCLC 16950861)
Nine-year-old Amanda, adopted as an infant, and her family prepare for the addition of a new child, a biracial baby girl. The family remembers the adoptions of their other children, baby Joey from Mexico and seven-year-old Nicky from the U.S. Involving their social worker and friends, the family eagerly greets the new child, Stevi, and Amanda spends the next several months of the probationary period adjusting to the changes in the family. This is a delightful story featuring a realistic racially-mixed family that does not pretend to be perfect. Amanda's best friend is an adopted Korean girl. The black and white pencil sketches are warm and humorous.

124   Angell, Judie. **Tina Gogo**. Scarsdale, NY: Bradbury Press, 1978. 196pp. (OCLC 3396919)
During the summer, eleven-year-old Sarajane becomes friends with a strange new girl, Tina, who turns out to be a foster child vacationing in the resort town. Tina is brash, uncaring and untruthful, but seems to need and want a friend. She begins to help out at Sarajane's parents' restaurant and slowly begins sharing her real life. Supplemented by information from the foster mother, Sarajane and her family discover that Tina is a tough little girl only on the exterior. Just as Tina starts trusting her new surroundings and hopes to stay with this family, her birthmother reclaims her. Knowing which life she prefers, she chooses, out of obligation, to live with her birthmother. While the adoption angle of this story is weak, this is a realistic portrayal of the behavior of an angry and confused young foster child who learns to trust herself and others.

125   Auch, Mary Jane. **Pick of the Litter**. New York: Holiday House, 1988.
         152pp. (OCLC 16683735)
         Only-child eleven-year-old Catherine, known as Cat, was adopted as an infant.
         Her mother, who has been taking fertility drugs, is now pregnant and will
         probably experience multiple births. While excited, Cat feels she and her
         ballet are being pushed aside for the babies and fears that her parents will
         love them better because they are birthchildren. Cat's mother is hospitalized
         right before the annual ballet recital and Cat's father leaves in the middle of
         the performance when he learns his wife is having the babies. Cat spends the
         night at a friend's and is greeted with a morning newspaper story exclaiming
         her mother had quadruplets. A few weeks after Cat's mother comes home
         from the hospital, so do three of the babies, but Max, in critical condition,
         remains in the hospital. Cat feels displaced by the babies, runs away, but
         returns when she learns Max is in danger. Max dies and at Max's funeral, Cat
         meets and forms relationships with distant relatives and feels her place in the
         family. This is a thoughtful story portraying the inadequate feelings of an
         adopted child with the addition of a birthchild.

126   Auch, Mary Jane. **A Sudden Change of Family**. New York: Holiday House,
         1990. 112pp. (OCLC 21409705)
         While on their annual visit to her grandmother's to join the large, warm
         extended family at the beach, eleven-year-old Katy and her mother discover
         her mother had been privately adopted as an infant. Feeling betrayed, Katy's
         mother angrily takes Katy and the two set off to find Katy's birthgrandmother
         whose name and residence was provided. When they arrive at her home, a
         dilapidated, trashy house, they are greeted by two eccentric birthparents who
         are delighted to see them. Katy's birthcousin, Elijah, who is close to her own
         age, lives with them since his mother, who intermittently is involved with his
         life, is not able to make a commitment to him. Katy wants to return to the
         beach so badly that she and Elijah secretly catch a bus to take them there, but
         they take the wrong bus and are picked up by the police and spend a night in
         a juvenile center until Katy's mother picks them up. Katy and her mother stay
         for two more days, learn about their new family, about their adoptive family,
         as well as about themselves, then return to the rest of the family at the beach.
         Juxtaposing two very different lifestyles, the author presents a setting for Katy's
         mother to realize the meaning of family.

127   Baker, Margaret Joyce. **The Family That Grew and Grew**. Illus. by Nora S.
         Unwin. New York: Whittlesey House, 1952. 121pp. (OCLC 1600393)
         Miss Basingstoke, who has always been fond of toys, is a single older woman
         who lives in a British hotel. When she acquires a dog, she looks for another
         place to live and answers an ad for a toy shop with living quarters. The
         Currant family next door help her set up the shop and she and her dog are
         quite happy. One day when she discovers a small boy trying to steal from her
         shop, she learns he is an orphan living in squalid conditions and decides to
         adopt him. When the toy shop begins to have economic problems, Miss
         Basingstoke is forced to sell it. Happily, she sells it to a former friend from
         the hotel who also marries her. Although the title is somewhat deceiving, this
         is a cute story in which a child arrives first, then the father. The black and

white drawings are rather detailed. There is one dated reference to Prince Charles and Princess Anne as little children.

128   Bates, Betty. **Bugs in Your Ears**. New York: Holiday House, 1977. 128pp. (OCLC 2966203)
Eighth-grader Carrie is not happy that her mother is marrying Dominic, a widower with three children. After the wedding, they live in Dominic's house where Carrie shares a room with one of her new, standoffish stepsiblings. Very unhappy with her current living arrangements and feeling she has lost her mother, Carrie is very negative when she learns that Dominic wants to adopt her. Although she pleads with the judge not to allow Dominic to adopt her because she wants to find her birthfather, when the judge questions her regarding her birthfather's actual care for her compared to Dominic's, the judge proceeds with the adoption telling Carrie someday she will understand how lucky she is. One day, Dominic shyly gives her back her favorite treasure box he has secretly repaired and refinished. This serves as a bridge between the two and a symbol of their new cautious, but caring relationship. Feeling more confident of her place in the new family, Carrie suggests and coordinates with the other children a special two-month anniversary dinner for their parents. This is a gentle story of the difficulties, as well as the joys, of the adjustment of a blended family as told by one of the young children involved.

129   Bates, Betty. **It Must've Been the Fish Sticks**. New York: Holiday House, 1982. 136pp. (OCLC 7999607)
Having just learned his birthmother is still alive, eighth-grader Brian is unhappy with his life and his parents' control. Against their better wishes, Brian's parents allow him to spend a few weeks with his birthmother, Imogene. Brian is taken aback by Imogene's bohemian lifestyle and live-in boyfriend. At first Brian feels he is in the way, but eventually he takes on the role of protecting his birthmother from her boyfriend's abuse. Brian feels pulled between his two homes, wanting to stay because his mother needs him, but wanting to go back to the safety of his father's. After the boyfriend causes a house fire by smoking marijuana and falling asleep, Brian tells him to leave his mother. Brian then returns to his father's with a new perspective. This provides an interesting look at the differing lifestyles which often accompany adoptions. It also provides an inside look at a dysfunctional family unit.

130   Bawden, Nina. **The Outside Child**. New York: Lothrop, Lee and Shepard, 1989. 232pp. (OCLC 18834995)
Thirteen-year-old Jane, adopted by her eccentric aunts when she was seven, happily maintains contact with her widowed father, a marine engineer. While visiting him she discovers her father remarried ten years ago and has two children, ten-year-old Annabel and eight-year-old George. Feeling she has been cheated, Jane does not heed her father's wish to keep his families separate and slowly, deceptively enters their lives in hopes of learning more about them. A gift Jane brings to the children betrays her real identity to their mother, Amy, who angrily sends Jane away. Amy later visits Jane and tries to explain her behavior by telling her she originally wanted to be a good mother to Jane, who at one time lived with them, but when Annabel was born with a deformed hand, the headstrong Jane was too much for Amy and it was

then Jane moved to live with the aunts. Although plans are made to remain in contact, Jane cannot trust Amy, but realizes her place with her aunts. A deft storyteller, Bawden presents a child whose family foundation is shaken and how she comes to terms with her families.

131   Blue, Rose. **Seven Years From Home**. Illus. by Barbara Ericksen. Milwau-
        kee: Raintree Editions, 1976. 58pp. (OCLC 1974020)
        Mark, adopted as an infant, is an angry eleven-year-old who wants to know his "real" parents. He acts out his anger, disrupting family life as his parents and younger brother, a birthchild, bear the brunt. Mark is portrayed as brooding, confused and manipulative. It is only when both boys are punished the same for a shared infraction that Mark once again feels the safety and equality of his family. The sketchy black and white drawings add to the sense of Mark's feelings of incompleteness. Even though there are less than sixty pages of text, the print size is very small.

132   Blume, Judy. **Just As Long As We're Together**. New York: Orchard Books,
        1987. 296pp. (OCLC 15548961)
        Stephanie's relationship with her seventh-grade classmate, Rachel, changes with the arrival of Allison, a new girl from California. Allison, the adopted French-born Vietnamese daughter of a TV personality, becomes part of the new threesome which is endangered when the girls' personal problems get in the way of their friendship. Rachel is insecure in spite of her advanced academics, Stephanie is distraught over her parents' separation and Allison become morose when her mother becomes pregnant. The girls learn and find solace that their friendship will help them through their troubles. A typical Blume story which so well portrays the attitudes, moods and behaviors of young teens.

133   Bonzon, Paul Jacques. **The Orphans of Simitra**. Translation of **Les Orphelins
        de Simitra** by Thelma Niklaus. Illus. by Simon Jeruchim. New York:
        Criterion Books, 1962. 160pp. (OCLC 2115585)
        Twelve-year-old Porphyras' family lives in Greece and are setting up a garage and gas service station as a means of livelihood when an earthquake occurs and all his family, except his sister, ten-year-old Mina, are killed. The children are taken to a shelter from which they are sent to Holland as child refugees. Mina is so unhappy there that she runs away and Porphyras leaves as well to try to find her. He goes to France thinking she will be there and he lives with a kind French family. Eight months go by until the authorities discover Mina in Norway and reunite the two children in France where they will continue to live with the Barbidoux family. Accompanied by occasional black and white illustrations, this is an exciting story of two young children fighting to survive.

134   Braenne, Berit. **Trina Finds a Brother**. Translation of **Historien om Tamar
        og Trine** by Evelyn Ramsden. Illus. by Borghild Rud. New York:
        Harcourt, Brace and World, 1962. 155pp. (OCLC 1873996)
        Little Trina's father is a captain on an ocean-going freighter based in Norway, their home, and often Trina and her mother accompany him on his trips. On one such trip they travel to North Africa and while there they discover five-year-old Tamar, a very sick Arab orphan boy. Trina's parents seek medical

attention and eventually decide to adopt the boy and take him home when they return to Norway. The sequel to this story is **Little Sister Tai Mi** (New York: Harcourt, Brace and World, 1964) in which the family travels to Korea where they discover Tai Mi and she returns with them as their daughter and sister. The occasional pen and ink sketches accompany the unusual international adoption stories which also impart cultural information about the countries.

135   Bragdon, Elspeth. **That Jud!** New York: Viking Press, 1957. 126pp. (OCLC 466963)
Twelve-year-old orphaned Jud, who lives with Captain Ben in a small coastal town in Maine, has a reputation for getting into trouble. Jud, lonely and neglected, secretly fixes himself a hideaway on a small island. When a fire starts in a shed, Jud is there to put it out. Instead of treating him as a hero, however, the townspeople are divided whether Jud started the fire. When his name is cleared, Jud gains new respect from the town. Although the story never describes the nature of Jud's living arrangements with Captain Ben as adoptive, it clearly relates the child's loneliness and feelings of not belonging.

136   Branscum, Robbie. **Toby, Granny, and George.**   Garden City, NY: Doubleday, 1976. 104pp. (OCLC 1945308)
Abandoned as an infant, resourceful thirteen-year-old Toby lives with Granny and her dog, George, in the Arkansas mountains where there is a series of bizarre murders implicating the preacher.   During the summer, Toby negotiates to build up the collection of livestock on their farm, helps the preacher discover the murderer, learns she is the daughter of Granny's youngest child and befriends a boy who has not spoken in years. Black and white sketches begin each new chapter of this story in which Toby grows up to see life with a new perspective.

137   Buck, Pearl S. **Matthew, Mark, Luke, and John.** Illus. by Mamoru Funai. New York: John Day, 1966. 80pp. (OCLC 299554)
Matthew is an eleven-year-old Amerasian Korean child who is abandoned by his mother in Pusan, South Korea. He makes a home under a bridge and cares for himself until he finds little Mark, who is also a mixed-race Korean child. They live together and are eventually joined by Luke and John. When they are very hungry they approach a U.S. military base to discover many children hurrying into what turns out to be a Christmas party. One GI, Sam, takes a liking to Matthew who is tired of being responsible for the boys and needs someone himself. Sam adopts Matthew and takes him back to the States to live with him and his wife. The next Christmas, Matthew and his new family help find families for Mark, Luke and John. Although this is dated publication, it describes for young readers the plight of mixed-race children in Korea. The illustrations are shady sketches.

138   Budbill, David. **Bones on Black Spruce Mountain.** New York: Dial Press, 1978. 126pp. (OCLC 3396627)
Thirteen-year-old Daniel, adopted five years ago, and his friend, Seth, get permission from their families to go on a multi-day camping trip up Black Spruce Mountain. Somewhat fearful of the legend that a lonely, mistreated

foster boy hid and died in the mountain and that his bones are still there, the boys continue their adventure. They discover not only a cave with some of the legendary artifacts, they also find another cave with the skeletal remains of a boy. The mountain journey and discoveries force Daniel into confronting the events and fears of his past and to make a decision whether to choose a life of isolation like the mountain boy or to take the chance on this family and trust their love. In addition to the moving comparison of the boys' journey up the mountain and Daniel's journey of self-discovery, this is also an interesting survival adventure story.

139   Burch, Robert. **Skinny**. Illus. by Don Sibley. New York: Viking Press, 1964. 127pp. (OCLC 170936)
Eleven-year-old Skinny, an orphan who is waiting for space to open at a local orphanage, is living at Miss Bessie's hotel where he helps out. He would much rather just stay living at the hotel and Miss Bessie would like to adopt him, but she thinks it is important that he have a man around to help him grow up. When Frank "Daddy" Rabbit, a hotel guest, starts dating Miss Bessie, Skinny's hopes rise and, when Daddy proposes, Miss Bessie tells Skinny they will adopt him. Unfortunately, Daddy's sense of wanderlust does not allow him to make the commitment after all and he leaves them. Skinny goes to the orphanage where he begins his education and makes friends with the assurance that he can go back to Miss Bessie's for holidays and summer. Set in a small town in Georgia in the 1930s this story uses non-standard grammar and may be difficult to read. Black and white sketches open each chapter.

140   Byars, Betsy. **The Pinballs**. New York: Harper and Row, 1977. 136pp. (OCLC 2645673)
Three very different children, eight-year-old Thomas J., and teenagers Harvey and Carlie, arrive at the same foster home from very different situations. In each their own way, they begin to develop care, trust and age-appropriate behavior. Early in the story, the always distrustful and sarcastic Carlie compares herself and the two boys to pinballs in a pinball machine, always bouncing around, out of control. Later in the story, she has gained perspective to realize that they do have control and can help determine their own lives. This powerful story by a popular children's writer, may provide insight for adoptees who have had a foster home experience. Two of the characters come from abusive backgrounds.

141   Cameron, Eleanor. **A Spell is Cast**. Illus. by Beth and Joe Krush. Boston: Little, Brown, 1964. 271pp. (OCLC 3912648)
Pre-teen adopted Cory is sent, over a school break, to stay with her Uncle Dirk and Grandmother whom she has never met while her actress-mother is on tour in Europe. While there she learns although her ever-busy mother is her legal guardian, she has never taken the time to adopt her legally. Distressed by the news Cory sets out to find out why and in doing so changes the lives of her relatives. She rekindles her Uncle Dirk's romance with Laurel and the two plan to marry and adopt Cory. Told by a master storyteller, this is an intriguing, suspenseful tale of a girl wanting to belong. Occasional black and white illustrations complement the text.

142   Carlson, Natalie Savage. **Ann Aurelia and Dorothy**. Illus. by Dale Payson.
          New York: Harper and Row, 1968. 130pp. (OCLC 299220)
        This is the story of Ann Aurelia, who is finally living with a foster mother she
        likes, and Dorothy, a local girl who befriends her. The girls share several
        adventures and Dorothy provides support for Ann Aurelia when her
        birthmother shows up after an absence of several years and Ann Aurelia must
        decide with whom to live. After much soul-searching and acting-out behavior,
        Ann Aurelia decides to try a new relationship with her birthmother. The
        confusing and conflicting feelings regarding this decision are appropriate for
        children who have been in situations where they help decide their future.
        Portraying a warm close interracial friendship, this story is enhanced by
        occasional black and white illustrations. Some readers will object to the dated
        term "negro" when referring to Dorothy.

143   Carlson, Natalie Savage. **The Happy Orpheline**. Illus. by Garth Williams.
          New York: Harper, 1957. 96pp. (OCLC 299216)
        With Brigitte as their leader, the twenty little girls in this French orphanage
        plot so they will not be adopted. When the girls visit a dog cemetery, Brigitte
        is accidentally left behind and is found by a woman who claims to be the
        Queen of France and who wants to adopt her to use as a housemaid. Brigitte
        successfully shows the woman she is too mean a child to be adopted so she can
        stay in the orphanage with her friends. Sequels include **A Brother for the
        Orphelines** (New York: Harper, 1959), **A Pet for the Orphelines** (New York:
        Harper, 1962), **The Orphelines in the Enchanted Castle** (New York: Harper
        and Row, 1964) and **A Grandmother for the Orphelines** (New York: Harper
        and Row, 1980). These are humorous stories providing a light, albeit not real,
        look at orphanage life. The familiar detailed black and white sketches are by
        the same artist who illustrated **Charlotte's Web**, **Stuart Little** and the Laura
        Ingalls Wilder **Little House** books.

144   Cassedy, Sylvia. **Behind the Attic Wall**. New York: Thomas Y. Crowell,
          1983. 315pp. (OCLC 9555577)
        Now adopted by a family, this story recounts the nine months twelve-year-old
        neglected, orphaned Maggie lived with her two great aunts. Maggie, having
        been expelled from several boarding schools, is sent to live with her spinster
        health-conscientious aunts in their gothic mansion that used to be a girls'
        school. While there, isolated Maggie, who has never learned proper manners
        and frequently acts out her anger and confusion, begins to hear voices behind
        the attic wall. Through her interactions with these "people" Maggie comes to
        care for others and slowly finds herself loveable too, although not to the aunts,
        who, finding Maggie unwholesome, eventually send her away. Humorous
        conversations with Uncle Morris weave the fantasy and realism aspects of the
        story together. An exciting and memorable story which aptly portrays the need
        to love and be loved.

145   Caudill, Rebecca. **Somebody Go and Bang a Drum**. Illus. by Jack Herne.
          New York: Dutton, 1974. 132pp. (OCLC 698825)
        When Edie and Julian get married they decide they will have two birth
        children and then adopt two Mexican American children. Instead, they go on
        to have one birth child, Eric, who is then followed by seven adopted children,

only one of whom is Mexican American. The story relates, one by one, the adoption stories of the children as they join the family, arriving from abroad, as well as from the States. The author tells, in good humor, the fun and the problems of a large interracial family of closely spaced children. With two full-page illustrations per chapter, this is a delightful story of becoming family. Although for older readers, a somewhat similar story is Doss' **The Family Nobody Wanted** (362).

146   Christopher, Matt. **Touchdown for Tommy**. Illus. by Foster Caddell. Boston: Little, Brown, 1959. 145pp.   (OCLC 299356)
Orphaned four months ago when his parents were killed in an accident, young Tommy is now living with foster parents, the Powells, and their daughter, Betty. Tommy wants to be able to stay with the Powells and worries that his less-than-perfect performance on the midget football team will be a determining factor. Explaining to Tommy that foster families are not usually permitted to adopt their foster children, the Powells promise to petition the court so that perhaps they can keep him. Thinking he will be leaving, Tommy earns some money and gives gifts to each family member the same time they tell him their petition to adopt him has been approved. Using a large typeface and one full-page black and white illustration per chapter, this is a good young readers' football story, as well as a story of a young boy's fears about his future, although his behavior and attitude do not reveal much grief for the death of his parents.

147   Clark, Margaret Goff. **Barney and the UFO**. Illus. by Ted Lewin. New York: Dodd, Mead, 1979. 159pp.   (OCLC 5100890)
Barney and his four-year-old brother, Scott, have recently been placed with the Crandall family to be adopted and are now in the six-month probationary period waiting for the adoption to be finalized. Because Barney fears jeopardizing their adoption, he is afraid to tell his new parents he has seen a UFO because they might think he is crazy. His eventual trust in his new parents saves him from going off in the spaceship with his new friend, Tibbo, when Barney has to choose which life he really wants. This is an interesting story combining the intrigue of science fiction with the realistic situation of a young boy's decision about his adoption. The book is enhanced by occasional black and white water color illustrations. Sequels to this story include **Barney in Space** (New York: Dodd, Mead, 1981) and **Barney on Mars** (New York: Dodd, Mead, 1983).

148   Cleaver, Vera. **I Would Rather Be a Turnip**. Philadelphia: Lippincott, 1971. 159pp.   (OCLC 195445)
Imaginative and dramatic twelve-year-old Annie Jelks is devastated when her eight-year-old nephew Calvin, the son of her unmarried sister, comes to live with her and her father. The bigotry expressed toward the Jelks family due to Calvin causes Annie to resent the little bookwormish boy. During the long hot summer Annie's friends are forbidden to associate with her and she devises several pranks and diversions to entertain herself. Annie spends much time with Calvin and slowly finds herself appreciating him, although it is difficult for her to express. On their summer vacation, Annie saves Calvin's life and, while still a fantasy-prone young girl, this event marks a subtle change in her

maturity. While a sad, painful story of prejudice and learning to live together, there are several humorous episodes as Annie, sometimes with Calvin, enjoys childish pranks.

149   Colman, Hila. **Tell Me No Lies**. New York: Crown Publishers, 1978. 74pp.
         (OCLC 3627054)
       Twelve-year-old Angie's mother is about to be married and Larry, her fiance, wants to adopt Angie after the wedding. Angie defiantly opposes the adoption because it would negate any ties to her birthfather whom she has never seen. After the wedding, Larry convinces her mother to tell Angie the truth about her birth. It seems that the story her mother has told her over the years about her birthfather has been a lie to protect her. Actually, her birthfather is a Portuguese fisherman, Jose, who never knew she was born. Angry and determined to meet her birthfather, Angie convinces her reluctant mother to allow her to travel, stay with a family friend and meet Jose. Angie meets Jose's children first and later, she meets Jose. When she and Jose's son are detained by a storm during their fishing trip with him, a friend of Jose's comments on how much his daughter, meaning Angie, looks like him. Angie later talks with Jose, and while it remains unspoken, he realizes who she is. Angie returns home, with renewed love and respect for the two people who want to be her parents and willingly consents to the adoption. An interesting story in which a young girl's unrealistic expectations of an absent birthparent forces her to reexamine her life.

150   Cross, Gilbert. **Mystery at Loon Lake**. New York: Atheneum, 1986. 127pp.
         (OCLC 13268759)
       One summer, Jeff Glover, his recently adopted Vietnamese brother and another friend discover and explore an old abandoned tunnel in a cliff and disturb someone who attempts to murder them. In the sequel **Terror Train!** (New York: Atheneum, 1987), the two brothers meet a mystery writer and together they investigate another passenger's sudden death. Although unable to obtain for evaluation, reviews indicate this has much excitement and adventure.

151   Cunningham, Julia. **Dorp Dead**. Illus. by James Spanfeller. New York:
         Pantheon Books, 1965. 88pp. (OCLC 301881)
       When ten-year-old Gilly Ground's grandmother dies he is sent to live in an orphanage where he lives unhappily, not cooperating or applying himself in school, until he goes a year later to live with Mr. Kobalt, the local ladder maker. There, Gilly finds comfort in the silent, highly ordered and regimented life. While there is no emotional warmth from Mr. Kobalt, Gilly befriends his listless dog, Mash, and the two form a close relationship. One day, Gilly discovers that Mr. Kobalt has beaten Mash because he is getting old and needs to learn to die. Gilly feels his own safety threatened and snoops around and finds a cage just the size for himself. Although injured while snooping, Gilly makes his escape through the chimney, only to be followed by an ax-wielding Mr. Kobalt. While defending himself, Gilly is aided by an angry, growling Mash who attacks Mr. Kobalt and wounds him. The boy and dog escape to find the kindly man who befriended Gilly while he was in the orphanage and

to become his family. The pencil drawings reveal the sad, lonely boy who learns to trust himself in this eerie, chilling story.

152   Dalgliesh, Alice. **The Blue Teapot: Sandy Cove Stories**. Illus. by Hildegard Woodward. New York: Macmillan, 1931. 73pp. (OCLC 171822)
This is a collection of five stories all set in Sandy Cove, a village by the Bay of Fundy. The title story introduces Miss Letty, who, happily living alone with her cat, realizes she is really rather lonely. She approaches the orphans' home to adopt a fourteen-year-old girl, but instead chooses seven-year-old twin girls with straight braids who claim they have not been adopted because most people want one girl with curly hair. To Miss Letty's delight, Abigail takes to cooking and Sara takes to gardening so she always has help and companionship. When the three deplete their savings by frequently using a mail-order catalog, they cooperate by using their talents to raise money to replenish their savings so that they can have the house roof reshingled. The eight bold color illustrations, as well as the several in black and white, are quaint additions to the text. While a charming story, the adoption portion of the book is unrealistic. Another story about Sandy Cove is **Relief's Rocker** (New York: Macmillan, 1932).

153   Daringer, Helen F. **Adopted Jane**. Illus. by Kate Seredy. New York: Harcourt Brace Jovanovich, 1947. 225pp. (OCLC 1118468)
Jane Douglas, plain and practical, now the oldest girl in the orphanage, is delightfully surprised when Matron invites her to visit two different families during the summer. In the first visit, she lives happily with widowed Mrs. Thurman who lives simply in an old house and whom Jane thinks must be poor and lonely. Her next visit is with the Scott family on their bustling farm and Jane is overjoyed with the activity associated with farm life. When there is an emergency at the orphanage, Jane, although disappointed, returns dutifully. Mistakenly thinking her days of fun are behind her, Jane is pleased, but confused when Matron asks her to decide when both families ask to adopt her. Because she feels more needed by the widow, Jane chooses Mrs. Thurman realizing, due to Mrs. Thurman's financial status, she may be giving up a chance for college. Jane is surprised when she learns that Mrs. Thurman is wealthy and has donated enough money for the orphanage to replace its infirmary. Set at the turn of the century and accompanied by charming black and white illustrations, Jane consistently recites and uses good judgement and exhibits unrealistic altruistic behavior.

154   Doane, Pelagie. **Understanding Kim**. Illus. by the author. Philadelphia: Lippincott, 1962. 126pp. (OCLC 1861701)
Ten-year-old Penny Crandall is best friends with Judy, when the Crandall family decides to adopt Kim, a ten-year-old Korean girl. Both Judy and Penny are initially excited about the prospect of adding Kim into their secret friendship, but after Kim arrives, Judy is aloof and teases about Kim's accent and behavior and pits Penny between herself and Kim. Penny feels torn between her loyalty to her new sister and her best friend and tries to find a way to reconcile the two so they can all be friends. When the family's house catches fire, and Kim risks herself to save the family pets, Penny and Kim discover their true feelings for each other and Judy recognizes Kim's positive

qualities. Sprinkled with bits of Korean heritage, this book is disappointing as it presents Kim as a small Asian philosopher with an unrealistically good grasp of English rather than a child who has just arrived from Korea. The book, with one black and white illustration per chapter, also perpetuates the myth that an adopted child must perform in heroic ways to be accepted.

155   Doss, Helen Grigsby. **A Brother the Size of Me**. Illus. by Robert Patterson. Boston: Little, Brown, 1957. 88pp. (OCLC 1666202)
Donny's interracial adoptive family keeps growing with the addition of more adoptive children, but always children who are much younger than he is. Donny keeps asking for a brother is own age and although his parents request such a child, agencies keep referring infants and toddlers to the family. When his father says they cannot afford another child, Donny tries a few ill-fated money-making projects. When a brother his age is finally referred to the family, he is part of a placement which includes another sister and a baby brother which brings the total to twelve children for the family. Donny goes with his mother to meet the new children and provides the sibling link with the rest of the children. Black and white shaded illustrations complement the text of this caring story of a loving family and the ernest little boy who wanted a brother. A nonfiction version of this family's story for older readers can be found in Doss' **The Family Nobody Wanted** (362) while a nonfiction version for younger readers is told in her **The Really Real Family** (105).

156   Downes, Mary. **Son of Fortune**. London: Harrap, 1958. 80pp.
Part of Harrap's **African Library**, this book features Sani, the youngest son of an African village chief, who is despised by his two lazy older half-brothers. When he is still small, his father calls his three sons to find a lost lamb, but only Sani honors his father and seeks the lost animal. Sani saves the lamb's life and later, after his father's death, when his jealous brothers try to kill him in the desert, the lamb helps save his life. The lamb leads a desert traveler to Sani's aid and they travel to the Emir's palace to report the brothers' injustice. Because Sani is still young, he remains in the city as the son of the Emir's scribe. Sani's brothers are not found until much later, after Sani saves the life of the Emir's only son, Ibrahim, and becomes a second son to the Emir. Sani goes to the aid of his robbed village and becomes a captive of his brothers, the robbers. Ibrahim sets out without his father's knowledge wanting to help his brother. The Emir soon follows and his guards save Sani and they return to the city where Sani and Ibrahim grow up as twins and justly rule together when the Emir dies. An African adoption story with a right-makes-might twist.

157   Dunlop, Eileen. **Fox Farm**. Oxford: Oxford University Press, 1978. 149pp. (OCLC 4135034)
Ten-year-old Adam, a foster child, finds a baby fox and although he has not cared much for his foster family during the two years he has lived there, he shares his find with Richard, the family's youngest child, because he needs his help and money to hide and take care of Foxy. Now that his savings are depleted, Adam writes to his father in Australia in hopes he wants him, but his letter is answered by his stepmother who tells him of his three new sisters and admonishes him to behave so maybe the foster family will adopt him

because he is not coming to Australia. Finally understanding his father does not want him, Adam pours more energy, time and affection into Foxy and, in so doing, finds himself more drawn into the family. An impending flood endangers Foxy's hiding place and the boys reluctantly approach the foster father for advice. Upon hearing the story and seeing the animal, they learn Foxy is actually a mongrel dog and Adam may keep him. Over time, Adam learns this family can be trusted and, when his dreams of going to Australia are dashed, this family is waiting to become his. A subplot dealing with a local legend provides additional excitement to this story, set in Scotland, of letting go and trusting.

158   Enright, Elizabeth. **Then There Were Five**. Illus. by the author. New York: Farrar and Rinehard, 1944. 241pp. (OCLC 299613)

Set in a summer during World War II, this is the story of the four Melendy children, Mona, age fifteen, Rush, age fourteen, Randy, age twelve and Oliver, age seven. While on a metal scrap drive in the area, Rush and Randy meet several neighbors including Mark, an young unhappy, overworked boy who lives with an abusive, negligent relative. The Melendy children, self-sufficient and reliable, are left on their own for two weeks when their widowed father is on a Washington D.C. business trip and their housekeeper is inadvertently called to aid a sick relative. When Mark's relative is killed during a fire, Mark moves in with the Melendys. The five children enjoy the summer as Mark learns how to relax and play. When the children's father returns he makes arrangements for the family to adopt Mark with Mark's consent. Mark fits in well and happily in his new home. Unfortunately, while this is a fun, interesting story of the summertime activities of five siblings during war time, there are a few racial slurs against the Japanese.

159   Evernden, Margery. **Lyncoya**. New York: H.Z. Walck, 1973. 212pp. (OCLC 667064)

In this piece of historical fiction the author relates the story of Andrew Jackson's adopted sons. Narrated by Andrew Jackson, Jr., both as an older man and with flashbacks to his childhood, the story revolves around the life of Lyncoya who, at age four, is the only survivor of a massacre of the Red Stick Indians. Jackson finds him and carries him home to the Hermitage to be raised as his son along with Andrew Jackson, Jr., an adopted nephew, who is also four. The boys grow up as brothers, but Lyncoya remains distant and aloof. The boys share episodes of fun and danger and young Andrew continues to be loyal to this brother he does not fully understand. As an older child, Lyncoya forfeits a silver gorget, the only tangible link to his past, to help free a runaway slave. When the boys are older, young Andrew is sent to college and Lyncoya, who prefers not to go, becomes apprenticed to a saddlemaker who had earlier helped free the slave. When Lyncoya takes ill, it is young Andrew who discovers him and makes arrangements to take him home where he is welcomed and receives a gift of a horse he loved long ago. Claiming to be historically accurate, the author presents a heartbreaking story of a child who never gains a sense of belonging, who always feels separate from the family. Jackson, Sr. is presented as an magnanimous, yet insensitive autocrat.

160   First, Julia. **I, Rebekah, Take You, the Lawrences**. New York: Franklin,
          Watts, 1981. 123pp. (OCLC 6862215)
          After having spent most of her life in foster homes and orphanages, spunky
          twelve-year-old Becky is surprised and cautious when a family actually wants
          to adopt her. The Lawrences, her new family, lovingly help her adjust to her
          new upper middle-class life and as Becky lets her guard down, she begins to
          enjoy being part of a family. Her confused feelings surface at her combination
          birthday and adoption party when her new fashionable friends contrast with
          her shabby best friend from the orphanage. Becky feels guilty about her new
          life and the conflicting feelings are further challenged when the Lawrences
          decide to adopt a pre-teen boy into the family. Angry that she is not good
          enough to be an only child, Becky runs away returning to the orphanage to
          discover things are not as she remembered and the experience helps her to put
          her new life into perspective. She returns home with a new attitude. This is
          an interesting, fast-paced book dealing with the need for an older adopted
          child to reconcile the present with the past in order to live fully the future.

161   Fisher, Dorothy Canfield. **Understood Betsy**. Illus. by Ada C. Williamson.
          New York: Henry Holt, 1917. 217pp. (OCLC 8175066)
          Nine-year-old Elizabeth Ann has been overprotected by her citified elderly
          aunts since the death of her parents. When they are unable to care for her
          any longer she is sent to live in Vermont with the dreaded Putney cousins.
          Instead of overprotecting her, the Putneys comfortably assume she will be a
          contributing member of the family and do things for herself. Elizabeth Ann,
          now Betsy, happily learns she can rely on herself. When her little friend,
          Molly, needs a place to stay while her mother is ill, Betsy convinces the
          Putneys to let her live with them and the two have many adventures together.
          When the girls miss their ride home from the fair, Betsy takes charge and
          earns some money at the fair to pay for their bus ride home. The Putneys,
          who had been so worried, are so happy to see the girls, and Betsy knows she
          has become self-reliant and well-loved. When it appears her aunts want her
          back, Betsy has mixed feelings about whom to live with until her wish to stay
          with the loving Putneys is the best arrangement for everyone. Available in
          many editions, some recent, this is an ageless story of a young girl's awakening
          to the possibilities within herself and how she develops relationships with the
          very different adult figures in her life. The author uses an interesting device
          of occasionally speaking directly to the reader.

162   Fitzgerald, John Dennis. **Me and My Little Brain**. Illus. by Mercer Mayer.
          New York: Dial Press, 1971. 137pp. (OCLC 212896)
          When the hero of Fitzgerald's **Great Brain** series goes off to school, his
          younger brother, John, known as J.D., tries to follow in his footsteps as a
          wheeler-dealer conniver, but usually ends up unsuccessful. One time J.D.
          entices some poor neighbor children to do his chores for half of his allowance
          and then convinces his parents he is helping them earn money to buy candy.
          His plan, however, backfires when his parents, realizing he has so much extra
          time, give him additional household work to do. Four-year-old Frankie
          Pennyworth temporarily comes to live with J.D.'s family when his own family
          is killed in a landslide. When no living relatives are found, J.D.'s aunt and
          uncle want to adopt Frankie, but Frankie wants to stay with J.D.'s family and

they adopt the boy. Frankie's initial behavior is so mean and spiteful that J.D. dons a catcher's mask and a football uniform to play with him. J.D. resents the child and his behavior, but when an escaped convict kidnaps Frankie, it is J.D. who finds a way to save him and learn that his own little brain works well. He and Frankie find they can have a brotherly relationship. This humorous story, charmingly illustrated in black and white drawings by the well-known Mayer, portrays the feelings of a sibling when an acting-out child enters the family.

163   Gates, Doris. **Sensible Kate**. Illus. by Marjorie Torrey. New York: Viking Press, 1943. 189pp. (OCLC 203824)
Known for being sensible rather than pretty, ten-year-old Kate, orphaned at an early age and then shuffled among relatives, is left a ward of the county when her irresponsible, but demanding cousin does not want her anymore. When Kate goes to live with the elderly Tuttles as their family helper she discovers a clean, organized household in which she has relatively few responsibilities. While there, she befriends the Clines, a young artist couple, who are somewhat eccentric, but who value Kate as a bright addition to their lives. Kate settles into her new home and school and learns more about herself and how others live. Having always been fearful of adoption, she is afraid the Tuttles may want to adopt her, but is delightfully surprised when it is the Clines who ask her to be their daughter following the birth of their son. A sweet story with occasional black and white full-page illustrations depicting a young girl who, although wise beyond her years, learns that there are more important things than outward beauty.

164   Green, Phyllis. **Grandmother Orphan**. Nashville, TN: Thomas Nelson, 1977. 76pp. (OCLC 3121143)
Following a shoplifting incident, eleven-year-old Christy is punished by being sent to spend a week with her grandmother, who is a truck driver. The first few days she is dragged to plumbing shops, helps install a new water heater, and sits in a hospital waiting room, observing life and death, while her grandmother undergoes tests. At first complaining, Christy begins to learn about her grandmother, about herself and her family. She learns her mother was also adopted as a child and that her grandmother spent her childhood in a orphanage wanting to be adopted and that grandmother's rough exterior is a defense she learned long ago. She also learns being adopted is not the worst fate in the world and, putting that in perspective, goes back home to her parents. Using strong characterization, Green presents an eye-opening look at a multi-generation uncommunicative family touched by adoption. This book was reissued under the title of **It's Me, Christy** (New York: Scholastic, 1977).

165   Hall, Lynn. **Mrs. Portree's Pony**. New York: Charles Scribner's Sons, 1986. 89pp. (OCLC 12974282)
At age thirteen Addie, a foster child with the Everett family for seven years, feels unloved and unwanted. One day while wishing for a guardian angel to watch over her, she discovers a pony in whom she seeks comfort. She slowly forms a caring relationship with the pony's owner, Mrs. Portree, a hardened woman who has alienated her own daughter. The relationship changes both of them into feeling wanted and needed and Addie, with permission from her

birthmother, moves in with Mrs. Portree. A touching story of blending families using an animal as the bridge. A similar device is used in Adler's **The Cat That Was Left Behind** (120).

166   Hamilton, Dorothy. **Holly's New Year**. Illus. by Esther Rose Graber. Scottdale, PA: Herald Press, 1981. 127pp. (OCLC 7464789)
Now that thirteen-year-old Holly is with her foster family after the children's home closed, she realizes how much happier she is. She is fond of Cleo and Barney and their two young sons, Scott and Douglas Mark, but is unsure of her feelings about their offer to adopt her. Holly is happy that Trina, one of her best friends from the home is living in a foster home in the same town so they can remain close. Another friend from the home, Sally, comes to visit, but is so bitter and uncooperative about her living arrangements, the other girls realize how settled they really are. Holly deals with jealousy, guilt and a mystery regarding a silent grouchy neighbor. She slowly adapts to her new family and quietly comes to her decision to allow the adoption. The warm communicative family envelopes Holly with love, responsibilities and privileges as she finds her place within the group. This is a sequel to **Christmas for Holly** (Scottdale, PA: Herald Press, 1971).

167   Hansen, Joyce. **The Gift-Giver**. Illus. by Ed Towles. Chicago: Follett, 1979. 118pp. (OCLC 5007510)
Set in a Bronx neighborhood where fifth-grader Doris feels her parents are too protective, this is the story of a group of friends as they end the school year and spend the summer. Although shocking to friends, one of the children, Sherman, is separated from his family and is sent away to live with a foster family, as are his seven brothers and sisters. A new friend, Amir, who seems quieter and wiser than his peers, lends support and advice to his friends. Amir has spent years in foster homes and has learned how to cope following the death of his parents. Doris' father is laid off and while he takes part-time jobs, her mother also goes to work leaving Doris to stay home to take care of the baby. When Amir's current foster family decide to move to California he is moved to an upstate group home. Amir's special friendship teaches Doris to value herself and her ideas rather than to bow to peer pressure. This is a bittersweet story of a young girl growing up.

168   Hark, Mildred, and Noel McQueen. **A Home for Penny**. Illus. by Arnold Spilka. New York: Franklin Watts, 1959. 202pp. (OCLC 1418159)
School-aged Penny lives in a children's home with many other children who are waiting to be adopted. Although Penny dearly loves the staff at the home, especially Mrs. Brown, she continues hoping and waiting for her own family. Penny is upset and confused by her conflicting feelings when her best friend, Lottie May, who is often forgetful, is adopted by a farm family. Later, Joe, a friend who has been at the home less time than she has, is adopted by a family Penny mistakenly thought was interested in her. Always trying to make the best of bad situations, Penny and Mrs. Brown discuss the kind of family Penny needs and wants and Mrs. Brown assures her that the home will do its best to fill her needs as she grows up. Penny begins to look upon Mrs. Brown in motherly terms and, in short, begins to accept the children's home may end up

being her home. This is a somewhat Pollyanna-ish story with a unexpected ending, as well as a romantic view of orphanage life.

169   Hermes, Patricia. **A Place for Jeremy**. San Diego: Harcourt Brace Jovanovich, 1987. 150pp. (OCLC 15019014)
Eleven-year-old Jeremy happily stays with her grandparents and attends school there while her parents travel to Colombia to adopt a baby. Not at all pleased with the idea of a sibling, Jeremy refers to the new child as S.B., or Stupid Baby. While staying with her grandparents, Jeremy learns new construction in the area calls for the demolition of her grandparents' store and home. Jeremy feels sad, angry and helpless over these two major changes facing her. Not willing to change her feelings about the baby, through a social studies project Jeremy contacts the historical society and learns her grandparents' building may be saved, although she finds out her grandfather does not want to stay. Her parents call to tell her about Nichole, the half-Colombian, half-American sickly baby girl they will be bringing home soon. Grandfather helps Jeremy become willing to accept Nichole, although she may not be able to love her right away; Jeremy is surprised how attracted she is to Nichole when her parents arrive with the baby. Jeremy was first introduced in **What If They Knew?** (New York: Harcourt Brace Jovanovich, 1980) when Jeremy was diagnosed with epilepsy. Parallel subplots of loss present the strong resentful feelings of a birthchild awaiting the arrival of an adopted child.

170   Howard, Ellen. **Her Own Song**. New York: Atheneum, 1988. 160pp. (OCLC 17547293)
Ten-year-old Mellie, whose mother has died and whose caretaker aunt is on holiday, is left alone when her father is hospitalized after a factory accident. Set in Portland in the early 1900s during which time children taunted the Asian workers, Mellie is embarrassed, yet relieved to be befriended by Geem-Wah, a Chinese laundryman, who helps her locate her father and takes her to his home to care for her. Mellie locates her adoption papers which identify her as Mei-Li and Geem-Wah reluctantly reveals she was once part of their family when Mellie's birthmother sold her as an infant to them for thirty-five dollars. At age three, Mellie was forcibly removed from the family by the authorities who then placed her legally with an adoptive family. Mellie returns home to discover her father is out of the hospital and her aunt home early from her holiday. The family is initially distraught to learn that Mellie has been with the Chinese family, but now aware of her past, both families become friends. The flashbacks, both in the storyline as well as in Mellie's memory, are printed in italics. This is a fascinating adoption story which also touches on racial prejudice.

171   Jenkins, Jerry B. **Daniel's Big Surprise**. Illus. by Richard Wahl. Cincinnati, OH: Standard Publishers, 1984. 128pp. (OCLC 10274065)
Daniel Bradford, the youngest of three children, has just finished fifth grade. Dan's parents arrange for him to spend two hours a day at the local children's home to make friends and do something useful. He explores the home and meets a ten-year-old Hispanic girl, Yolanda, who is kind, helpful and beautiful. She becomes Dan's host and stands up to Tony, a bully, who threatens them. Although Dan's parents urge him to pray for Tony and to act good towards

him, Tony continues to bully. When they learn the home is planning to close in six weeks, Dan and Yolanda are saddened as it will end their friendship, but Yolanda tells him she has good feelings that she may soon be adopted. Dan has mixed feelings about her pending adoption having harbored a fantasy she could become his sister. Dejected, but wanting to be happy for Yolanda, he returns home and stays in his room until he is called for dinner where he meets his new sister, Yolanda. This is #1 of the Bradford Family Adventures. Told with a Christian perspective, this story accurately relates a young boy's feelings, but unrealistically portrays the adoption process and its purpose as a quick fix.

172   Jones, Adrienne. **So, Nothing is Forever**. Illus. by Richard Cuffari. Boston: Houghton Mifflin, 1974. 252pp. (OCLC 940605)
When the children of an east coast interracial couple are left orphaned, they run away to their grandmother's on the west coast to wait until their uncle comes home from the service next year and adopts them. Talene, age fifteen, Joey, age thirteen, and two-year-old Adam had never seen their grandmother until their parents' funeral because she estranged herself when her daughter married a black man. Although their reception is chilly, the widowed bitter old woman eventually allows them to stay. The older children try to make themselves useful and slowly they forge a rocky relationship with their grandmother. The old woman's feelings begin to change after she saves the baby who gets lost in a dangerous storm. The children gain a new perspective on her unhappy life and are receptive to her slow warming. When she is injured, the children take care of her and they learn to depend on each other. At the year's end, the uncle comes home to adopt them and the children go back to the east coast to live with him, promising to visit their grandmother next summer. A beautiful, complex story enhanced by the shaded black and white drawings of a renowned illustrator, that tells of the struggle of staying and becoming a family.

173   Jones, Rebecca C. **The Believers**. New York: Arcade Publishing, 1989. 176pp. (OCLC 19921330)
Sixth-grader Tibby was adopted at age eight by Veronica, a workaholic single woman television reporter after doing a story on foster care. Because her mother's job keeps her away from home so much of the time, Tibby's need for love and security remain unmet and Veronica's aunt is Tibby's most recent in a series of caretakers. Tibby befriends Verl and Esther, children in a local fundamentalist religion sect that does not believe in seeking medical attention. When she sees Esther pray so earnestly for a Barbie doll, Tibby thinks by secretly joining the sect and praying, perhaps her mother will come home. Tibby's mother researches the sect and comes home to do an expose on the religious group. When little Esther becomes very ill, Verl takes advantage of his parents' absence and takes her to Tibby's aunt so Esther can get proper medical help. Tibby's aunt takes her to the hospital which gains a court order to keep the girl there. Veronica rushes off to another story and Tibby and her aunt come to a better realization of their relationship and the security it entails. Tibby suggests they both move to the aunt's house and make the best of the situation. Tibby's need for closeness and love are expressed very well in both the text and in her acting-out behavior.

174   Joy, Deborah Berry. **Benjamin Bear Gets a New Family**. Illus. by J.B. Bauer.
       Chicago: Adams Press, 1988. 41pp.
       Sharing the story of Benjamin Bear and his older sister, Betty, this tells how
       the Bear parents became increasingly unable to care for their children. When
       Children's Services discover the poor condition of their home, the two children
       are sent to different foster homes and the parents begin receiving training.
       When his parents cannot learn, Children's Services finds Benjamin a new
       adoptive home so he can grow up happy and safe. Benjamin has mixed
       feelings, but remembers his worker telling him that his part in adoption is to
       tell his new parents about his feelings so they can help him. Benjamin feels
       even better when Betty gets a new family and the two can maintain contact.
       Each chapter is divided into two sections, the first relates the story of
       Benjamin and the second presents questions for the reader to answer and
       compare and contrast his or her experiences and feelings with those of
       Benjamin. There are black and white cartoon-like drawings at the beginning
       of each chapter. Although not a particularly attractive book and difficult to
       locate, it is one of the very few children's book dealing with abuse and neglect,
       termination of parental rights and subsequent adoption. Could also be used
       with older or younger children with proper assistance.

175   Kiser, Martha Gwinn. **Sunshine for Merrily**. Illus. by Eloise Wilkin. New
       York: Random House, 1949. 130pp. (OCLC 5850948)
       Sisters Meady, Merrily and their baby brother Bucky are among a small
       number of children who live in the county poor house because there is no
       room in the orphanage. Merrily, the middle child and narrator, is a spunky
       livewire who looks on the bright side. They are delighted when Miss Allie, the
       town spinster, requests they come live with her for the November and
       December holidays. The children thrive in the warmth of their new surround-
       ings along with Uncle Richey who has been betrothed to Miss Allie for twenty
       years. Miss Allie and Uncle Richey begin to realize what they are missing by
       not making a sincere commitment to one another and the children realize this
       is the kind of home they always dreamed of. Wealthy, elderly Miss Posey,
       Miss Allie's landlord, befriends the new family, enjoys their company and helps
       them out practically and financially, finding a way to keep the family together.
       Occasional black and white intricate drawings accompany this warm, but dated
       story of a small girl who gets her wish of a home and family.

176   Klein, Norma. **What It's All About**. New York: Dial Press, 1975. 146pp.
       (OCLC 1324343)
       Eleven-year-old Bernie, an only child of a Jewish woman and a Japanese
       American man who divorced when she was four, is excited when her remarried
       mother and stepfather, Gabe, adopt a Vietnamese child. The arrival of three-
       year-old Suzu, who adores Bernie, marks the beginning of changing relation-
       ships within the family. Gabe looses his teaching job, does not attempt to
       form a relationship with his new daughter and becomes verbally abusive and
       threatening to everyone. Bernie is invited to Boston by her father and his
       fiance, Peggy, who is seven months pregnant, to act as a bridesmaid at their
       wedding. Returning home, Bernie finds Gabe gone and her mother anxious
       and distraught because she does not know where he is. Bernie, Suzu and their
       mother settle in to a new family routine and divorced Grandma continues her

visits telling them about the new man in her life, Sol. Bernie's dad and Peggy have a baby boy, Jacob, and they send tickets so Bernie, Suzu and their mother can visit them for a restful much-needed vacation. They return home to find Gabe at the house, but having decided how she wants to live her life, Mom tells Gabe to leave. While Suzu's adoption adjustment is chronicled, this is really a story about Bernie's perceptions and confusion regarding relationships.

177   Lampman, Evelyn Sibley. **The Bounces of Cynthiann'**. Illus. by Grace Paull. Garden City, NY: Doubleday, 1950. 260pp. (OCLC 1687053)
Set in the 1860s, the four orphaned Bounce children, Matthew, age 14, Markia, age 12, Luke, age 10 and baby Johanna, sell their family home in the east to join an uncle in Oregon. They send a message announcing their arrival, but arrive in Cynthianna to learn their uncle has recently died. Four close families generously each take a child as the local judge attempts to locate the children's distant relative in Maine to make arrangements for the children's return. Meanwhile, the children and their new families are adjusting and learning to care for one another. Although each family would like to adopt each child, Matt is not happy with the idea because he promised their mother he would keep the family together. A solution is found when the children are willed a house and property and an Asian housekeeper agrees to stay with the children. The town agrees to adopt them all together and take care of them. While unrealistic, this is an exciting, Disney-like story, with occasional black and white illustrations, of an enterprising sibling group. The Asian houseboy and an old Native American are stereotypically portrayed.

178   Lampman, Evelyn Sibley. **Elder Brother**. Illus. by Richard Bennett. Garden City, NY: Doubleday, 1951. 217pp. (OCLC 3028706)
Set in Portland, Oregon at the turn of the century, Lampman portrays a Chinese enclave and highlights one family, the Chans. Because they have six daughters and no sons, the Chans follow Chinese custom and adopt a son from China so they will have a son necessary for ancestral worship. They adopt Jeong who, at twelve years old, is the same age as Mr. Chan's oldest daughter, Molly. Jeong soon learns that the traditional role of women in China does not hold in America. While Molly tries to be a good Chinese daughter at home, she is a feisty American girl everywhere else. Political troubles in China cause problems in the town and Molly is chosen to organize a band of children to keep watch and sound warnings. She is successful and although she lost her place as first in the family, her work in determining the local cause of trouble brings pride to her family. In the meantime, she and Jeong begin to see the good in each other and find mutual admiration and a good sibling relationship. Illustrated by infrequent black and white drawings, this story presents the difficulty of a young boy in adapting to a new way of life as well as that of a young girl as she learns to accept her new brother. Another title involving the Chinese in the U.S. northwest is Howard's **Her Own Song** (107).

179   Lattimore, Eleanor Frances. **The Chinese Daughter**. Illus. by the author. New York: William Morrow, 1960. 125pp. (OCLC 470601)
Little Alice, or Ai-li as she is called, is a Chinese preschooler who lives in North China with her American medical missionary parents. She is the darling

of the missionary compound except with a houseboy who is jealous of her elevated social standing now that she is adopted. His family knows Ai-li's birthfamily and makes an attempt for them to reclaim her. When Ai-li's adoptive mother has a baby, Martha, or Mei-mei, Ai-li is pleased because she has a sister and they both have American and Chinese names, however, other people make comments that cause Ai-li to want to be more Chinese. One day, when Ai-li is visiting a friend, arrangements are made to take her to see her birthfamily. She meets her birthparents and siblings and is intrigued by them, but does not want to leave the parents she has grown to love. Caught between two families, Ai-li happily returns to her adoptive family and they soon return to the States with Ai-li claiming she wants to be a missionary when she grows up and return to China. Having lived in China for the first sixteen years of her life, Lattimore weaves a story of cultural and physical differences and a heroine who wants to include all aspects in her self-definition.

180   Lawrence, Mildred. **Peachtree Island**. Illus. by Mary Stevens. New York: Harcourt, Brace, 1948. 224pp. (OCLC 736064)
Orphaned nine-year-old Cissie has been shunted from one relative to another and is now sent to Uncle Eben, an apparently antisocial single man who has a peach orchard on an island. Delighted in the island, as well as Uncle Eben and his housekeeper, imaginative Cissie is happy as can be. Wanting to live somewhere forever, Cissie has her hopes dashed when she hears Uncle Eben say he would keep her if she were a boy. That combined with next-door Jody, a boy in her class who thinks girls cannot do anything, causes Cissie to prove her worth to both of them by working on the farm. In the summer when Cissie and a friend sell peaches at a roadside stand, Jody shows off and overturns all the peaches on his truck. The girls help the embarrassed boy right his load and the next day, Jody sends a peace offering with a note acknowledging girls do know something. After Labor Day, the busy selling season is over, Cissie's aunt calls to take her back, but to Cissie's surprise and delight Uncle Eben says he wants to keep her forever; he wants and needs her to stay until she grows up and gets married. While somewhat dated, this book, with its occasional black and white full-page illustrations, is a warm story of a young girl finding her place in an unlikely family.

181   Lawrence, Mildred. **Tallie**. Illus. by Paul Galdone. New York: Harcourt, Brace, 1951. 213pp. (OCLC 1632180)
Eleven-year-old Tallie is sent from the children's home to live with the Jarrett family and when Mr. Jarrett is forced to leave his newspaper editor job in Florida, the family, Tallie included, moves to Pennsylvania to take over the abandoned Jarrett family chicken farm. Instead, they work long and hard and change the large chicken coops into a tourist motel while hearing stories about hidden Jarrett family silver and getting to know their new neighbors. When Mr. Jarrett is hospitalized, the children are left to manage the tourist motel and Tallie tells uncooperative little Celia the only way she can eat is to help with the work. Angry, Celia works, drops her grudge and actually enjoys being helpful. The director of the home contacts Tallie and the Jarretts to let them know a family wants to adopt Tallie and she is to write back with her decision. Disappearing during a Jarrett family meeting, Tallie gets stranded in a tree and finds the hiding place of the Jarrett family silver. The family rescues her,

rejoices in the find and tell her they want to adopt her and Sara consents. Although Tallie is almost too sensible, living by axioms she remembers from her birthfather, this is a good story of growing self-confidence.

182   Levinson, Nancy Smiler. **Silent Fear**. Illus. by Paul Furan. Mankato, MN: Crestwood House, 1981. 63pp. (OCLC 7459651)
Thirteen-year-old Sara, whose mother died and whose father abandoned her, is sent to live in a foster home. She is apprehensive about the prospect and although her social worker assures her it is the best foster home she could find, Sara quickly realizes she is in an abusive situation. Dixie, the foster mother whose trucker husband is usually on the road, is oppressive, neglectful and abusive to Sara and the two young boys also in her care. Sara tries to confide in a favorite new teacher, but only leaves Ms. Light with the impression that something is not right. Taking a risk, Sara reveals her situation to a new friend, Dave, whose father tries to help. When Dixie's house catches fire, Sara makes sure the two boys are out safely then runs away. Dave finds her and she changes foster homes and enjoys her new school, friends and freedom. The cartoon-like drawings are effective as they illustrate this story to which some adopted children who have been in abusive foster homes may relate. This title is part of the publisher's **Roundup Series**. Another title which utilizes an abusive foster home, Sach's **A December Tale** (221), features a less aggressive foster child.

183   Lewis, Mark. **Kaliban's Christmas: A Special Tale of Magic**. New York: Tom Doherty Associates, 1987. 55pp. (OCLC 18768629)
Seven-year-old orphan, Calafia, sneaks away from the rest of the orphanage children and hides in the museum until it closes and rejoins Kaliban, a statue, who comes to life for her. When they hear a noise, Kaliban resumes his stone stance, but Calafia's sweater is caught under his hoof so she cannot hide and is discovered by Mark, the friendly guard, whose gentleness allows Kaliban to come to life. Bitter Calafia downplays the Christmas holidays since it is the time of year her parents died, but Mark and Kaliban take her to the creche exhibit and tell her the Christmas story. Calafia relates to the baby left in the cold and the magic in the air helps Kaliban to know, and Calafia to feel, they have the power of love within themselves so they will never be really alone. Mark and Calafia make a wish on a falling star that they become father and daughter and Mark calls his wife and tells her of this great news. Kaliban reverts to his original position knowing he is loved and will be visited often. The story ends with Mark, now a grandpa, telling this story to his family and Calafia, surrounded by her husband and children, placing a small Kaliban on the top of their creche. A light fantasy, which speaks to the healing nature of love and care, has occasional black and white illustrations depicting scenes from the text.

184   Lindbergh, Anne. **Nobody's Orphan**. San Diego, CA: Harcourt Brace Jovanovich, 1983. 147pp. (OCLC 9489104)
As the only green-eyed member of an otherwise brown-eyed family, and due to the limited number of baby pictures available, eleven-year-old Martha erroneously believes she was adopted by her family. Her vivid fantasy of life with exotic birthparents fares better than her traveling government-employed

family that does not even let her have a dog. Martha finds a black Labrador, which she names Ronald Reagan and, through many delay tactics, is able to keep him for quite a while. In the meantime, Martha meets an elderly couple, the Ables, whose daughter has left them.   Martha fantasizes she is their birthgranddaughter and spends all her money to place ads to locate the Ables' missing daughter. The family goes to the Ables' for Christmas dinner and they meet the Ables' daughter who is not at all how Martha expected her. Parker, Martha's now-reconciled friend, reveals to Martha that she is adopted and that the orphan life Martha dreams of is not actually appealing. Martha, always scheming, changes her fantasy to that of finding Parker's glamourous birthmother.   A cute story with a lively effervescent conniving pre-teen heroine. For another story of a girl who mistakenly thought she was adopted see Martin's **Claudia's Search** (191).

185   Lindgren, Astrid. **Rasmus and the Vagabond**. Translation of **Rasmus pa Luffen** by Gerry Bothmer. Illus. by Eric Palmquist. New York: Viking, 1960. 192pp. (OCLC 471389)
Disliking the orphanage and having waited long for a family, nine-year-old Rasmus runs away to look for parents who might want a straight-haired boy rather than a curly-haired girl.   When he hungrily awakens in a barn one morning he is befriended by Oscar, a tramp, who share his breakfast and agrees Rasmus can travel with him until he finds his new parents. The two have many adventures as they wander the countryside. A friendly farm couple wants to adopt Rasmus and he happily agrees only to change his mind in the morning.   He realizes how fond he is of Oscar and chooses to continue wandering with him. Shortly thereafter, they arrive at what must be Oscar's real home and Rasmus meets Oscar's wife, Martina. Martina and Oscar agree that Rasmus would make a wonderful son and they plan to adopt him. Occasional sketchy black and white drawings supplement this story written by the author of the **Pippi Longstocking** stories. This delightful adventure story won the international Hans Christian Andersen Medal.

186   Little, Jean. **Home From Far**. Illus. by Jerry Lazare. Boston: Little, Brown, 1965. 145pp. (OCLC 301982)
After the death of her twin brother, Michael, eleven-year-old Jenny's parents, also parents of nine-year-old Alec and six-year-old Mac, foster eleven-year-old Mike and his sister, six-year-old Hilda.   Hilda fits right into the family and enjoys her new surroundings, but Mike wants so much to live with his birthfather, who is unable to care for them, he resists investing emotionally in this temporary family. Mike and Jenny remain at odds until they are drawn together by jointly building a playhouse for the younger children after Jenny accidentally starts a fire in Mike's secret hideout.   The children vacillate between enjoying the living arrangements and resenting each other. Jenny and her mother acknowledge each other's grief over the loss of twin Michael and help each other carry on. When Mike's father gives him the option of moving with him and leaving Hilda with Jenny's family, he admits he would rather stay where he is and reconciles himself to "home".   Occasional black and white drawings illustrate this lovely story that describes the children's fun activities, as well as the hard times and negative behaviors, which are part of adjustment.

While the parents have different personalities, they are presented as complementary and united.

187   Lively, Penelope. **Boy Without a Name**. Illus. by Ann Dalton. London: Heinemann, 1975. 45pp. (OCLC 1694518)
Set in England in the 1600s when Charles Stuart was king, this is the story of a orphan pauper boy. When the miller to whom he was apprenticed dies, the boy travels to his mother's town of birth. The priest there gives him a first name, Thomas, and he takes his last name from the stone mason who apprentices him and takes him into his family. Adoption is not specifically mentioned in this historical fiction, but Thomas, after early years of hardship, is treated as the mason's other children. The detailed drawings, most of which are black and white, are one-dimensional and primitive.

188   Lowe, Patricia Tracy. **The Different Ones**. Indianapolis, IN: Bobbs-Merrill, 1964. 153pp. (OCLC 1815179)
After his parents are killed in a plane crash, thirteen-year-old Mark is taken in by the Wilsons to remain with the family until the school year is finished, when he will go to his grandparents' in Wisconsin and decide where he would like to live. The Wilsons, who have offered to adopt him, welcome Mark warmly, but their only child, eleven-year-old Chris, who suffers from a heart condition, has mixed feelings. Because of his medical condition, Chris is kept from regular physical activities and is teased by other boys because he is perceived as weak; is sometimes belittled by his father who expects more of him; and is overprotected by his mother. Buff, a school bully from a nonsupportive family terrorizes Chris daring Chris to shoplift to prove himself. Wanting to be accepted, Chris shoplifts only to be confronted by Mark. Mark, Chris and Mr. Cook, a teacher, organize a boys track team in which Mark is team captain and Chris is team manager. In the end, Chris is invited to Mark's grandparents' farm as well and Mark decides to become a Wilson. As Mark and Chris develop their relationship, Mark helps Chris become more confident, which improves his relationship with his parents, and Chris helps Mark once again feels as if he belongs. Illustrating self-sufficiency in dealing with one's problems, this is also an interesting sports story.

189   McDonald, Joyce. **Mail-Order Kid**. New York: Putnam, 1988. 125pp. (OCLC 16982462)
Because he was first seen in a newsletter and then arrived on an airplane, fifth-grader Flip thinks his first-grade Korean-born brother, Todd, was ordered through the mail. Believing it is a similar situation, Flip mail-orders a red fox as a pet for himself. The fox's fear and apprehension of his new living environment help a somewhat resentful Flip understand Todd's adjustment difficulties during his first months in his new home. There is an initial disparaging remark by Flip that Todd is not his real brother, but it is made before the reader quite realizes Flip's resentment of Todd. Todd's English is uncharacteristically good for a school-age child who has been in the States for only three months. While some readers may object to the comparison of a child to an animal, this humorous story holds up well.

190   McHugh, Elisabet. **Raising a Mother Isn't Easy**. New York: Greenwillow, 1983. 156pp. (OCLC 8554059)
Fifth-grader Karen, adopted from Korea at age four by a single parent, is worried about her mother's future and sets out to find her a husband. Although her mother is a successful veterinarian, she is somewhat absent-minded and Karen feels her mother cannot possibly get along without her. Her mother starts dating Brian and they tell her they have a secret for her and Karen spends weeks fantasizing about their marriage, when the surprise is actually a horse that Brian is buying. One day Karen's mother visits her at school and tells her they will be getting a new sister/daughter, a five-year-old from Korea. The sequel, **Karen's Sister** (New York: Greenwillow, 1983), relates the story of the adoption of the new sister as well as Karen's mother's marriage to a man with three children. In a third title, **Karen and Vicki** (New York: Greenwillow, 1984), Karen learns to adjust to living in a large family and to get along with her new older stepsister, Vicki and a father. These humorous stories by a single adoptive mother use Karen as the narrator providing a fresh perspective on single-parent living and the acquisition of a family. Although single-parent adoptions of healthy Korean children are rare, this is one of the few older children's fiction titles which use an adopted Korean child as the protagonist.

191   Martin, Ann M. **Claudia and the Great Search**. New York: Scholastic, 1990. 151pp. (OCLC 21254039)
Thirteen-year-old Claudia Kishi, a U.S. born Japanese-American eighth grader, is convinced she is adopted because she is very different, in appearance and abilities, from the other members of her family. In addition, she is unable to find her birth announcement in the local newspaper and there are very few baby pictures of Claudia. These clues convince her she was adopted as an infant and her parents have never told her the truth. As part of her work with her friends in their babysitting club, Claudia begins sitting and tutoring Emily, a two-year-old adopted from Vietnam, and while learning more about adoption and adjustment, sees more comparisons to herself. When her parents confront her on her unusual behavior, Claudia tells them her fears and accuses them of lying to her. Better understanding her behavior, Claudia's parents tell her she is not adopted and explain the discrepancies Claudia sees. Claudia is reassured and relieved she is not adopted and continues working with Emily. Although Emily's adoption is presented positively, Claudia's fear of adoption and deception casts a negative image. This is #33 of the **Baby-sitters Club** series. For other stories about Emily, see Martin's **Kristy and the Mother's Day Surprise** (192) and **Karen's Little Sister** (070).

192   Martin, Ann M. **Kristy and the Mother's Day Surprise**. New York: Scholastic, 1989. 152pp. (OCLC 19637861)
Kristy, president of the Baby-sitters Club, has an idea to treat their mothers for Mother's Day. The Baby-sitters Club arranges to give the mothers a break from being moms by taking their young children to a carnival and on a picnic. Kristy, who comes from a large blended family, becomes excited when she learns her family may have a baby. Nothing else is mentioned about a new sibling until the day before Mother's Day, Kristy's parents announce they are adopting a two-year-old girl, Emily, from Vietnam and will pick her up at the

airport tomorrow.   Kristy, her brothers and sisters as well as the other members of the Baby-sitters Club organize a welcoming party for Emily. This fun story, #24 in the **Baby-sitters Club** series, incorporates sibling rivalry and a discussion of jealously prior to Emily's arrival, but also uses the new child as the bridge between the other two families that make up Kristy's new family. Emily is also featured in other **Baby-sitters Club** and **Baby-sitters Little Sister** books, particularly in **Karen's Little Sister** (070). Claudia's own story of the time she thought she was adopted is found in **Claudia and the Great Search** (191).

193   Martin, Ann M. **Yours Turly, Shirley**. New York: Holiday House, 1988.
         133pp. (OCLC 17649340)
Shirley, a dyslexic fourth grader, becomes the class clown to cover up her deficiencies. One evening her parents tell her they are adopting a three-year-old Vietnamese boy who will soon arrive. Shirley is overjoyed to be helpful to a little brother, until a phone call informs her parents their child, who is arriving in three days, is really an eight-year-old girl. Somewhat daunted at the notion of a sister so close in age, Shirley prepares to share her bedroom and teach her sister, Jackie, English. Jackie is placed in first grade since she knows no English, but learns so rapidly she is soon moved to a gifted third grade, while Shirley is still having great difficulty and accepts help from the Resource Room.   A name-calling incident positively cements the girls' relationship and the school year ends positively as Shirley wins an academic award for her composition on family. Although a cute story, there are a few unrealistic aspects such as a foreign-born eight-year-old's English improving so much in two months and the initial placement error.

194   Mayhar, Ardath. **Carrots and Miggle**. New York: Atheneum, 1986. 159pp.
         (OCLC 12550945)
When thirteen-year-old refined cousin Emiglia from London is orphaned and comes to live with the Ramsden farm family in Texas, everyone has a difficult time acclimating. Emiglia, nicknamed Miggle by five-year-old Cherry, believes physical labor is beneath her, while her cousin, tomboy twelve-year-old Charlotte, called Carrots, is not very sympathetic knowing they all have to pull their weight on the farm especially since their father's death. Carrots and Miggle experience conflict during their first meeting and slowly try to work out a relationship. Miggle eventually tries to integrate herself into the family and Carrots tries to be more understanding and empathetic. Some children at school frame Miggle by planting marijuana in her locker and Carrots comes to her defense to clear her of the charge. From that point, the girls are allies. When a letter arrives indicating that a wealthy California relative with an only child is willing to take Miggle so she does not have to suffer this hard life, Miggle chooses to stay with the Ramsdens where she feels needed and involved. Presenting a resolution to conflicting personalities and lifestyles, this story also provides good characterization.

195   Miles, Miska. **Aaron's Door**. Illus. by Alan E. Cober. Boston: Little,
         Brown, 1977. 46pp. (OCLC 2425323)
In an attempt to block out another rejection, Aaron locks himself in his bedroom at his new adoptive home.   He resents his younger birthsister

Deborah's easy adjustment and interprets it as betrayal. After allowing Aaron needed time and space, his new father breaks through the door to embrace his new son and together they join the rest of the family. The black and white sketchy drawings add to Aaron's stark, cold feelings, but contrast sharply with the warm, calm reassuring text. This is a beautiful story that acknowledges the pain and risk involved in forming relationships in adoptive families. The father's message carried out in a combination of strength and gentleness helps Aaron to move on with his life.

196   Mills, Claudia. **Boardwalk With Hotel**. New York: Macmillan, 1985. 131pp.
    (OCLC 1443538)
    Eleven-year-old Jessica has always known of her adoption, but after Brian and Julie are born to her parents, Jessica becomes increasingly convinced her parents do not love her as much as they love their birthchildren. Jessica sees proof of this difference in the way her parents treat her younger siblings, the way they emphasize their piano skills over her tap dancing and the fact that their new school pictures are on the mantle and hers is not. Jessica, who is to babysit for Brian and Julie this summer, becomes increasingly competitive with Brian and has a tendency to bully Julie. Feeling betrayed, Jessica feels even more left out during her grandmother's visit. She confronts her father about her worries and he does his best to comfort her and reassure her of their love. When the children play a game of Monopoly and Jessica, sensing she is loosing, throws a tantrum, upsets the gameboard and storms away. Her best friend, Isobel tries to help her see that perhaps she acted hastily. Brian thinks his parents like Jessica best and talks of going away to camp. The two siblings reconcile and plan the rest of their summer. This is a powerful story about adoptive sibling rivalry featuring a main character with a strong personality.

197   Miner, Jane Claypool. **Miracle of Time: Adopting a Sister**. Illus. by Vista III
    Design. Mankato, MN: Crestwood House, 1982. 63pp. (OCLC
    8171193)
    Teen-age Shirley is very excited at her ballet lessons because today her new five-year-old sister Kim is coming from Vietnam. During the first night Shirley is awakened by Kim's nightmare screams and sees her unresponsive behavior. Tiny, undernourished Kim remains listless, not talking or showing any emotion. Shirley, who had been anxious for her arrival, now finds herself alternating between feeling sorry for Kim and resenting her, then feeling guilty for her feelings. A doctor verifies Kim is effectively blocking out all the pain in her life and does not let herself feel anything. She suggests lots of love, good food and eventually, special help. Shirley's mother indicates since Kim has more problems than the family can handle, they may have to give Kim back to the agency. Shirley gets the idea to try dancing for Kim and while it makes no initial impact on Kim, when Shirley pretends a mistake and bumps the wall Kim allows a little smile. Shirley and her mother laugh and Kim shares another small smile with them. With at least one illustration on each two-page spread, this is a somewhat unrealistic story, but reveals the genuine efforts of a sibling in the adjustment of a newly adopted child.

198   Montgomery, L(ucy) M(aud). **Anne of Green Gables**. Illus. by M.A. and W.A.
        J. Claus. Boston: L.C. Page and Company, 1908. 429pp. (OCLC
        367111)
        Needing help on their Prince Edward Island farm, Green Gables, elderly
        Matthew Cuthbert and his sister Marilla decides to adopt an orphan boy from
        a Nova Scotia orphanage. They are surprised, however, when the child left for
        them at the train station is a high-spirited eleven-year-old redheaded girl
        named Anne. The Cuthberts take a liking to Anne and decide to keep her,
        but Anne has a hard-to-control temper and is an incessant talker giving new
        names to old, musing over daily occurrences and exercising her active
        imagination. While she finds a warm acceptance with Matthew, Anne needs
        to earn love and respect from Marilla by learning to behave appropriately.
        The book chronicles Anne's first five years in their town of Avonlea. When
        Matthew dies, Anne forgoes a scholarship to remain in Avonlea to teach
        school and help Marilla. A timeless, delightful, humorous, yet thoughtful story
        of an energetic young girl who changes the lives of those around her. Many
        editions of this story are available as is true with the sequels which include
        Anne of Avonlea (Boston: Page, 1909), **Anne of the Island** (Boston: Page,
        1915), **Anne's House of Dreams** (New York: Stokes, 1917), **Anne of Windy
        Poplars** (New York: Stokes, 1936) and **Anne of Ingleside** (New York: Stokes,
        1939).

199   Mulcahy, Lucille. **The Blue Marshmallow Mountains**. Illus. by Don Lambo.
        New York: Thomas Nelson, 1959. 128pp. (OCLC 2666801)
        After twelve-year-old Miguel and his eleven-year-old sister, Paquita, are
        orphaned, their peddler grandfather takes responsibility for them and they
        accompany him in his wagon on his summer round of peddling in New Mexico.
        While en route, they stop at a friend of Grandfather Juan's only to stumble on
        a mystery involving a painting stolen from a church. The trio continue their
        journey stopping at the next town where they meet with old friends who have
        a house for sale that Grandfather and the children would like to buy. They
        go on their way in hopes of earning enough money during the summer to pay
        the down payment. The travelers accept a painting as a gift that turns out to
        be the missing church painting. The reward money for the missing painting
        provides the down payment for the new home for Grandfather Juan and the
        children. Featuring Hispanic characters and with occasional black and white
        illustrations, this is an exciting mystery. The children deal with the grief of
        their mother's death in different ways, Miguel tries to be strong, while Paquita
        languishes and nearly looses her will to continue.

200   Murphy, Frances Salomon. **Ready-Made Family**. Illus. by Moneta Barnett.
        New York: Thomas Crowell, 1953. 174pp. (OCLC 4630569)
        The Kowalski children, sensible twelve-year-old Hedwig, angry and rebellious
        ten-year-old Peter and sweet six-year-old Mary Rose, whose mother has died
        and whose father has disappeared, reluctantly move to a foster home from the
        orphanage. Knowing only homes which took advantage of them or were
        abusive, the children are hesitant to join the Kennedys, their new foster
        parents, whom they soon call Mom and Dad. The children are delightfully
        surprised to learn how nice family life can be when they are wanted and loved.
        Hedy worries that Peter's oppositional behavior will force them to be moved,

but the understanding parents take it in stride and Peter grows to enjoy a good relationship with Dad. Hedy takes on a babysitting job to save money to pay for future orthodontic work, but she is fearful that Mom's mother does not like her, and is scared of being sent away. When relatives want custody of Hedy because they need child care help, the Kennedys and the authorities determine Hedy will stay with the Kennedy family as long as she wants to. Grandmother offers to pay for Hedy's braces and the two become friends. Although a little too pat, this is an interesting story, with occasional black and white drawings, of the differing adjustments of three siblings in permanent foster care.

201 Murphy, Frances Salomon. **Runaway Alice**. Illus. by Mabel Jones Woodbury. New York: Scholastic Book Services, 1951. 118pp. (OCLC 14709342) After her father marries a woman with a small son, they are on their way to get twelve-year-old Alice, when they are killed in a car accident leaving Alice and Charlie, the stepbrother she had never met, in an orphanage and later placed in foster homes. Alice runs away from her first foster home and is taken to a temporary home. The caseworker gives Alice a dime so that if she feels the need to run away again, she can call for help. Mrs. Potter, the new foster mother, makes it very clear they are interested in a boy so this is just temporary, until another placement can be found for Alice. However, having cooperative, helpful Alice around shows Mrs. Potter what she has been missing by not having a daughter. As the Potters grow fond of Alice, she also grows fond of them. Alice learns new self-reliance, makes a new friend and fears the day she will have to leave. Gaining a greater understanding of family, when she learns the Potters want to keep her, Alice suggests her little stepbrother Charlie be allowed to come as well. When he does, Alice is comfortable enough to return the caseworker's dime since she will not be needing it. This is a reassuring story of a anxious child who blooms in the right family. Also published under the title **A Nickel for Alice** (New York: Crowell, 1951).

202 Myers, Walter Dean. **Me, Mop, and the Moondance Kid**. Illus. by Rodney Pate. New York: Delacorte Press, 1988. 154pp. (OCLC 17733257) Recently adopted eleven-year-old T.J. and his younger brother, Moondance, remain good friends with Mop who still lives in the Catholic orphanage where they grew up. Mop wins a position as catcher on their little league baseball team in hopes of interesting the coaches in adopting her. The book covers the antics of the threesome and their team's efforts to beat a rival team. The hoped-for adoption and the big win culminate the story. While primarily an exciting baseball story, adoption is presented positively, albeit rather simply and naively.

203 Neilsen, Shelly. **Then And Now, Victoria**. Elgin, IL: David C. Cook, 1990. 105pp. (OCLC 21117596) Victoria Mahoney seems to be the only one in her eighth-grade history class who does not have an exotic historical figure to research. While cleaning her attic she finds a trunk of letters and photographs of her ancestors. She decides to do her report on her great-grandfather Mahoney who was an immigrant from Ireland. As Vickie works on her ancestor project, the Mahoney family is working on adopting a baby. Some of Vickie's friends do not like the idea of non-blood relatives in a family, but Vicki grows to understand little baby

Mahoney has as much to do with the past she has been studying as the future they will share together. Relying on their faith in God, the Mahoneys prepare for their baby. Rather than concentrating on a flashy historic figure, Vickie's choice of a simple, yet important family member teaches her much about herself and her family.

204   Nixon, Joan Lowery. **A Family Apart**. Toronto: Bantam Books, 1987. 162pp. (OCLC 15696832)
       In 1856 in New York City, the six Kelly children's widowed mother is unable to support them properly. Thirteen-year-old Frances Mary, the oldest child, must work a regular job with her mother leaving a younger child to mind the others. When brother Mike is picked up for stealing, his mother pleads with the judge and, out of love, agrees to give custody of the children to the Children's Aid Society to be part of the orphan train project. In so doing, the Kelly children leave New York under the care of the Society and travel to Missouri to be adopted by waiting families. When she hears boys get placed easier than girls, Frances Mary quickly changes clothes, cuts her hair and goes by "Frankie" so that she can more easily keep her promise to her mother that she and little Petey will stay together. When they arrive in Missouri, the Kelly children are separated into different families, with "Frankie" and Petey going to the same family that soon learns her secret. Further adventures of the Kelly children in the **Orphan Train Quartet** are found in **Caught in the Act** (Toronto: Bantam, 1988), **In the Face of Danger** (Toronto: Bantam, 1988) and **A Place to Belong** (Toronto: Bantam, 1989). This is a lively adventure story that also imparts factual information about the orphan train. See Magnuson's **Orphan Train** (473) for a fictionalized account of the first orphan train trip from New York.

205   Norris, Faith, and Peter Lumn. **Kim of Korea**. Illus. by Kurt Wiese. New York: Julian Messner, 1955. 157pp. (OCLC 1499349)
       When ten-year-old Kim Chung Wan is orphaned and there are no relatives to care for him, he is taken to an orphanage in Seoul during the Korean War. The living conditions are so bad, Kim runs away and lives in an abandoned English mansion vacated by its British owner. While there, he is befriended by Sergeant Len Minner who grows fond of Kim and wants to adopt him and bring him back to the States to his wife. Len is hospitalized for an injury, but tells Kim to stay where he is and he will come for him when he is released from the hospital. Kim's house is overtaken and he begins a lonely, yet daring journey to find Len. At a GI base, Kim bolts when he realizes they want to send him to an American orphanage until they can locate Len, but as he races away, Kim runs right into Len who has frantically been trying to locate him. Kim leaves with Len and they face their new life together. The occasional black and white drawings are often stereotypical. Although dated, this is an exciting adventure story of a brave Korean boy and his search for his new life and family.

206   Nystrom, Carolyn. **Mario's Big Question: Where Do I Belong?** Illus. by Ann Baum. Batavia, IL: Lion Pub., 1987. 44pp. (OCLC 14586532)
       Living in a large family that also includes some foster children, Mario is a ten-year-old boy who was adopted at age three. Although he feels he belongs in

the family, Mario becomes distracted as he thinks about his birthmother. Mario comes down to breakfast, helps feed the baby and realizes that his large mixed family includes such an assortment of children that no one really looks alike. On Wednesday's family night, the family discusses the similarities of being adopted by God and by a family. Later, he and his mom talk about Mario's birthmother and where he really belongs. His mom reminds him that even though she and his dad are not related they decided to become a family together. She also reminds him of his adoption story and that they consider him a gift from God. His parents give him a photo of himself with his birthmother along with a little lock of dark hair. Interspersed in the text are pages of explanations about adoption. The lively illustrations portray a busy multi-racial family with Mario presented as a Hispanic or mixed-race child. This is a realistic story tackling some serious issues for young readers. Another possible edition identified, but not located, is **Andy's Big Question: Where Do I Belong?** (Tring: Lion, 1987)

207   Paradis, Marjorie Bartholomew. **Too Many Fathers**. Illus. by Charles Geeg. New York: Atheneum, 1963. 198pp. (OCLC 1402290)
When Uncle Eliot, a famous writer, arranges to rent a resort cabin for the Alcott family for the summer, Stan, who worries Uncle Eliot is his birthfather, likes the idea, but he feels uncomfortable because he does not know how to swim, bicycle, or fish and is embarrassed to let people know. He plunges himself into his writing, which he fears may be inherited from his birthfather, and gets a part-time summer job to earn money for a typewriter. During the summer he gets to know several other young people including Connie Cranford, an only child who is adopted. He is drawn to her and their discussions about adoption make him all the more suspicious of his own heritage. While on an emergency trip for medication, Stan loses his boat in the approaching hurricane, but swims to safety, having taught himself. Stan confronts his parents on Uncle Eliot's preferential treatment of him and is told the truth that Uncle Eliot has always felt especially close to Stan since his deceased child would have been the same age. He has offered on many occasions to adopt Stan, including now, but his parents refuse. Relating a young boy's confusion, as he develops his own sense of worth. At one point in the story, Connie Cranford gives the erroneous impression large families do not adopt.

208   Parker, Richard. **Paul and Etta**. Illus. by Gavin Row. Nashville, TN: Thomas Nelson, 1973. 128pp. (OCLC 524211)
His mother dead and his father's whereabouts unknown, seven-year-old Paul Aintree now lives in a children's home and the Milfords, with only-child nine-year-old Etta, are interested in adopting him. After spending a few weekends with the Milford family, Paul accompanies them on a summer vacation where Paul and Etta vacillate between getting along and fighting making the vacation both a success and a disaster. Because Paul feels perhaps his behavior was unacceptable, he is surprised when the Milfords want him to join their family for good. Paul's caseworker announces Paul's father has come forward and wants to see Paul. Fearful of his father, and the love of his new family, Paul runs away, back to the children's home. Shortly thereafter Mr. Aintree, who had been in the Antarctic, arrives, meets his son and they begin a new

relationship. Milfords agree to continue fostering Paul and allow his father to live with them until he can establish himself and create a proper homelife for Paul. Occasional black and white sketches add to this unique story which details the 'courting period' of a placement before the child actually arrives in the home. The ending of the story, however, seems very unrealistic and unfeeling for the foster/adoptive family.

209   Parker, Richard. **Second-hand Family.** Illus. by Gareth Floyd. Leicester: Brockhampton Press, 1965. 120pp. (OCLC 9350696)
Orphaned Giles is placed in a new foster home with the Maxwell family. Although initially feeling awkward and uncomfortable, twelve-year-old Giles slowly attaches to the family first befriending sickly Mr. Maxwell and learning Mrs. Maxwell occasionally blows up, but cools off just as quickly. Life is most difficult sharing a bedroom with resentful teenage Martin, but Giles wins him over when he sets up a successful gig for Martin's rock band. When Mr. Maxwell is hospitalized for his tuberculosis, Giles is unable to remain with the family and is sent back to the children's home. Leaving them lets Giles realize how much he has begun to like the family. Soon after, the Maxwell family, with Mr. Maxwell out of the hospital, arrives at the home having made arrangements to take Giles home with them and adopt him. Chapters containing occasional black and white illustrations help portray England in the mid-1960s. Especially interesting is the variety of personalities in the family and Giles' ambivalent feelings and growing attachment.

210   Paterson, Katherine. **The Great Gilly Hopkins.** New York: Crowell, 1978. 148pp. (OCLC 3542211)
Known for her exasperating lying and unmanageability, eleven-year-old Gilly is sent to live at yet another foster home, this time with overweight and uneducated Maime Trotter who is also foster mother to seven-year-old William Ernest. Convinced her birthmother, beautiful flower child, Courtney, will soon come for her, Gilly is unwilling to invest in this new family and schemes to steal enough money for a bus ticket. Gilly's maternal grandmother, who had never knew about Gilly, arrives to discuss arrangements for taking custody of her. Gilly realizes the pleas to her birthmother have backfired and, although she would prefer to stay with Trotter, it no longer an option since there is a relative willing to care for her. Over the Christmas holidays, the estranged Courtney returns to her mother and daughter, but Gilly is devastated to learn her grandmother paid her to come back and that she plans only a two-day stay, not wanting to take Gilly with her. In tearful despair, Gilly calls Trotter who tries to help her accept the situation. In the end, Gilly is able to tell Trotter she loves her and to go peaceably home with her grandmother. Gilly, the main character of this Newbery Honor Book, is a strong-willed child, master of acting out her anger and frustration, who finds home and life is not as she imagined.

211   Perl, Lila. **Annabelle Starr, E.S.P.** New York: Clarion Books, 1983. 147pp. (OCLC 9323445)
Orphaned twelve-year-old Annabelle lives with her grandparents who also adopted Scotty, now eight years old. Convinced she has ESP, Annabelle becomes suspicious when a mysterious woman rents a room from her

grandparents. The woman keeps looking at shy Scotty who stays away from her. While cleaning the guest room one day, Annabelle discovers a photograph of a baby who looks remarkably like Scotty. Scotty becomes more fearful and runs away when he overhears Annabelle say the mysterious woman is probably his birthmother who has come to take him away. The day before the woman leaves, she apologizes for starring at Scotty and explains he reminds her of her son who has died, but would have been the same age. Annabelle, knowing the truth, finds Scotty and takes him home and calms his fears. An exciting story combining mystery, suspense and misunderstandings, there is also an added element of romance for Annabelle, her friend and her friend's mother.

212   Pfeffer, Susan Beth. **Just Between Us**. Illus. by Lorna Tomei. New York: Delacorte Press, 1980. 116pp. (OCLC 5889870)
As a subject for her mother's behavior modification class, sixth-grader Cass learns how to keep a secret. When her friend Robin confides in Cass her stepfather adopted her and she has not seen her birthfather in years, Cass is proud of her ability to keep the secret. Jenny, Cass' jealous other best friend, threatens to spread a rumor that Robin is adopted, but Cass is worried once Jenny begins the rumor Robin will think Cass told her secret. When Cass threatens her with another rumor, Jenny backs down and Cass agrees to help Jenny be kinder and Robin to be neater using the same behavior modification techniques her mother used with her. The reader is left with the impression the three girls will become better friends. The soft pencil drawings are well done, however the adoption angle of the story is weak and, unfortunately, its secrecy plays a big part of the story.

213   Platt, Kin. **Chloris and the Creeps**. Philadelphia: Chilton Book Co., 1973. 146pp. (OCLC 539738)
Embittered by her father's suicide, yet irrationally and unrealistically defensive of him, eleven-year-old Chloris is unable to move on with her life and sometimes successfully influences eight-year-old Jenny to have an equally negative outlook. Chloris is appalled when her mother marries Fidel Mancha, a happy, warm Mexican artist who wants to adopt the girls. When Chloris refuses to agree to the adoption, Fidel drops the petition until both girls are willing. Fidel remains calm and patient as he tries to win Chloris' trust, even when she barely acknowledges his existence. When Chloris sets Fidel's art studio on fire, but places the blame on Jenny, the family is devastated. Sarcastic as ever, Chloris sees a therapist and through drawing a picture of her birthfather, which she does with Fidel's help, Chloris learns as she accepts Fidel, the true image of her father emerges and the girls agree to the adoption. This is a powerful story of a troubled, resentful young girl's loyalty to an embellished past.

214   Rabe, Berniece. **The Orphans**. New York: Dutton, 1978. 184pp. (OCLC 3912929)
Twice orphaned ten-year-old twins Adam and Eva live in rural Missouri during the Depression. The twins' grandmother, G-Mama, is a spunky elderly woman who wants to keep them, but is outvoted by her daughters-in-law and the local sheriff, Erica. When the twins are sent to live with their mother's sister, she

will not agree to take them and they are sent to live in an orphan asylum until they convince the officials they have relatives who will take them. Sent back to G-Mama, who has been injured, the children manage the house and secretly try to nurse her back to health. Eventually Erica finds out and invites them all to live at her house until G-Mama is well. Erica becomes fond of the children and Adam, having made a pledge to Eva to get her adopted, discovers a legal loophole and approaches Erica to adopt them, keep her sheriff job and G-Mama could provide the daily care and supervision. They discuss the matter with a reluctant G-Mama, go to the judge and leave as a new family. This is a fun adventure story involving two spunky children and featuring an adoptive single mother.

215   Rankin, Carroll Watson. **The Adopting of Rosa Marie.** Illus. by Florence
          Scovel Shinn. New York: Holt, 1908. 300pp. (OCLC 17689387)
          Bosom friends, Bettie, Jeanie, Marjory and Mabel, all between eleven and fourteen years old, have their own life-size playhouse, Dandelion Cottage, and often borrow babies with whom to play. One day, Mabel borrows a dark-skinned baby girl, Rosa Marie, but when she returns, the baby's mother has disappeared. The girls hide the baby in Dandelion Cottage for five weeks until their mothers learn of her existence and she is taken in by an elderly couple. The girls have several humorous adventures throughout the year and plan to attend boarding school next year. The following spring, Rosa Marie's mother returns, admitting her mistake in leaving the baby for a new husband who abused her. She reclaims Rosa Marie and is helped to find a job so she can find a home and keep the baby. While a delightful turn-of-the-century story with classic illustrations, there are racist overtones such as "D.S.", the girls' code name for Rosa Marie, stands for "dark secret"; Mabel's mother telling her they cannot adopt the baby because she could not let her grow up with a little Indian continually at her heels; and the instant desire to play Pocahontas with Rosa Marie. This is the sequel to the author's **Dandelion Cottage** (New York: Holt, 1904).

216   Reeder, Red. **Clint Lane in Korea**. New York: Duell, Sloan and Pearce,
          1961. 208pp. (OCLC 1609101)
          While on a courier errand on his first day in South Korea to serve a thirteen-month stint in charge of a company near the DMZ after the Korean War, First Lieutenant Clint Lane, a former West Point football all-star player, finds himself in a local riot and meets thirteen-year-old orphaned Gim Cho-Bong whom the Americans call Jim-Joe. Lane and his wife want to adopt Jim-Joe, but clearing him for adoption is difficult and hampered by an abusive uncle. Jim-Joe has many dangerous adventures, including being kidnapped by a North Korean border-crosser and later by his uncle. With the help of military officials who admire Lane, he receives the permission to adopt and the necessary travel papers for Jim-Joe to leave Korea and the boy travels to join his new mother in the States. One of several books about Clint Lane, Reeder draws upon his own experience as a colonel in the military and combines an inside look at army life and the problems, at the time, of adopting a Korean war orphan.

217   Rich, Louise Dickinson. **Star Island Boy**. Illus. by Elinor Jaeger. New York:
            Franklin Watts, 1968. 154pp. (OCLC 436191)
        When eleven-year-old Larry, who has spent his life in foster homes as a State
        Kid, as he puts it, is sent to live on an island in Maine with several other
        foster children, he is suspicious why the inhabitants want so many additional
        children. Although he tries hard to not like them, he is easily drawn to the
        warmth and easy-going attitude of Aunt Emma and Uncle Joe, his new foster
        parents. He learns a lobsterman's way of life and finds himself liking it so
        much he runs away the day before he thinks he will be sent away. Uncle Joe
        and an old retired lobsterman find Larry stranded on another island and he
        learns that Uncle Joe and Aunt Emma have always planned to keep him
        permanently and he will become their new son. He also learns the island
        adults took in foster children to boost their juvenile population so they would
        not loose the island school. The book describes life on the island centered
        around lobstering. The family, school and community activities, as well as
        Larry's growing fondness of his new parents, are warmly described.

218   Roberts, Willo Davis. **Eddie and the Fairy Godpuppy**. Illus. by Leslie
            Morrill. New York: Atheneum, 1984. 125pp. (OCLC 9945053)
        Nine-year-old Eddie, who lives in the orphanage, is convinced no one wants
        to adopt him or have him as a foster child because he is ugly and gets into
        trouble. After suffering a broken arm, Eddie finds a puppy and believes it is
        a fairy godpuppy who will grant his wish of having a family. Trouble and bad
        times follow Eddie as his best friend leaves to be adopted and Miss Susan, his
        favorite orphanage worker, is leaving to be married. He considers running
        away, but then thinks it is a miracle caused by the puppy when Miss Susan and
        her fiance want to adopt Eddie. This is a humorous, adventurous story
        portraying the antics, fears and hopes of a young boy. The soft pencil
        drawings, almost one per page, are quite detailed.

219   Robinson, Thomas Pendelton. **Trigger John's Son**. New York: Viking Press,
            1934. 270pp. (OCLC 6869683)
        Twelve-year-old orphaned Trigger travels by train from Maine to Beechwood,
        Pennsylvania to join his new adoptive parents, the Smiths, whose only son
        recently died. Because of the distance involved, the Smiths will decided when
        they see Trigger if they really want to adopt him. Uncomfortable with the
        arrangement and wanting to make an assessment himself, Trigger leaves the
        train before it arrives in Beechwood and hops a freight train with the same
        destination. Once in Beechwood, he joins some boys, gets involved in a game
        of marbles which he wins and is befriended by Mr. England, an elderly rustic
        man who lets him live with him and arranges a meeting with Mr. Smith whom
        Trigger likes immediately. The next day he joins the Smiths and they try each
        other out. Trigger enlivens the Smiths' lives, much to the delight of Mr. Smith
        and the dismay of Mrs. Smith. Trigger maintains his activities with the boys
        as they help Mr. England, causes problems at school and truly becomes a
        Smith. Set in the horse and buggy days, this is a adventurous story of a
        spunky, animated young hero. The 1949 edition published by Viking has black
        and white illustrations by Robert McCloskey.

220   Ron-Feder, Galilah. **To Myself**. Translation of **MaOon Mishparhti** by Linda
       Stern Zisquit. Illus. by Irwin Rosenhouse. New York: Adama Books,
       1987. 133pp. (OCLC 16225381)
       Eleven-year-old Mike who had been living with a grandmother, goes to live in
       a well-to-do foster home where he is encouraged to make daily entries into a
       diary. The diary entries, often pointed and humorous, reveal his changing
       attitude and perceptions. The illustrations, usually one or two per chapter, are
       bold, yet sketchy, looking as if they have been drawn over corrugated
       cardboard resulting in the impression of a rubbing. This story provides a
       personal insight into the often confusing world of a foster child. Even though
       adoption is not part of the story, the depiction of foster care life which is often
       part of an adoptive child's past experience may be beneficial.

221   Sachs, Marilyn. **A December Tale**. Garden City, NY: Doubleday, 1976.
       87pp. (OCLC 3217928)
       Myra, a lonely little girl in an abusive foster home with her younger brother
       whom she dislikes, longs to be reunited with her father and other siblings in
       his care. Several times Myra attempts to get herself out of the foster home,
       but no one will help her. As an escape, Myra has imaginary conversations
       with Joan of Arc which give her the strength to find a way to help herself and
       her brother. This slim book offers a unique combination of realism and
       fantasy. Although not an adoption story, the description of and interaction in
       an abusive foster home may be significant to adopted children.

222   Scarboro, Elizabeth. **The Secret Language of the SB**. New York: Viking,
       1990. 129pp. (OCLC 20757335)
       Adam has the uncanny ability to sense when "SB" (Something Big) is going to
       happen. This time, his parents want his support and assistance while they
       temporarily house Susan, an eleven-year-old girl from Taiwan, until her new
       adoptive parents can take her. Adam, an only child, resents the intrusion,
       until slowly the two children begin to share some activities. Susan's hesitating
       English and comprehension causes a few problems, but Adam helps her with
       her reading so that she passes a reading test. Shyly, Susan plays soccer with
       Adam and his friends and becomes the best player. Adam and Susan share
       watching after-school TV shows and working on Adam's homemade ship. Just
       as the two become friends, the adoptive family is ready to take Susan.
       Although they vow to keep in touch, Susan's leaving is as hard on Adam as
       was the news of her arrival. While the adoption angle seems unusual, this is
       a touching story of the development of a special relationship and the role of
       temporary foster care.

223   Silman, Roberta. **Somebody Else's Child**. Illus. by Chris Conover. New
       York: Frederick Warne, 1976. 64pp. (OCLC 2623608)
       Fourth-grader Peter has a special friendship with his elderly bus driver,
       Puddin' Paint, but their friendship is strained when the driver makes a
       negative remark about adoption, not realizing Peter is adopted. During a
       winter storm, Peter helps Puddin' Paint find his two missing dogs and in
       working together, the two characters become closer and both gain a greater
       appreciation of adoption. Peter's parents and older sister are genuinely
       portrayed as they answer his questions about his adoption story and provide

support as he works through a difficult time. The black and white pencil drawings are detailed and lifelike offering support to the story.

224   Simon, Shirley. **Libby's Step-Family**. Illus. by Reisie Lonette. New York: Lothrop, Lee and Shepard, 1966. 191pp. (OCLC 1399809)
Libby Carlton, age thirteen, is as distraught as her future teenage stepsisters when her widowed mother decides to marry widower Sam Willis. After the wedding, the new family goes on a European vacation. As the girls work against cooperating, Libby meets Rosalie, a French girl, in Paris who does not like her stepmother or family situation. Rosalie goes to Florence with her grandfather and Libby meets her there where they learn Rosalie's stepmother is now offering to pay for dance lessons which are so important to Rosalie, without Rosalie having to sell her special book collection. All the girls realize their own misconceptions regarding stepparents and resolve to make a fresh start. The story ends with Libby anxious to return home to live in the Willis' apartment in New York. Illustrated by occasional black and white sketches, this story does a fine job of portraying the emotions involved as two families blend together.

225   Smith, Doris Buchanan. **Moonshadow of Cherry Mountain**. New York: Four Winds Press, 1982. 154pp. (OCLC 8430561)
For six years Greg, adopted by the Rileys when he was nine, has been an only child. At that time his parents gave him Moonshadow, a black Labrador retriever, to keep him company. Now his parents have adopted Clara, a nine-year-old girl who does not want to fit into their beloved mountain life, and Moonshadow is banished outdoors when Clara's allergy to dogs becomes apparent. In the meantime, Cherry Mountain begins to change as the land is developed and more people move to the area. The Rileys, but especially Moonshadow, are effected by the transformation. She is accused of being a cat-killer and threatened by the cat owners. While uneasy and often suspicious of each other, the families learn to live together and Clara becomes more acclimated to mountain life. The book tastefully presents the parallel stories of adjustment, integration and acceptance by Moonshadow and by Greg and Clara as they learn to live together and with the major changes in their lives. Greg's reaction to another adoptive sibling evolves from initial excitement, to resentment, and slowly, to acceptance.

226   Sommer, Susan. **And I'm Stuck With Joseph**. Illus. by Ivan Moon. Scottdale, PA: Herald Press, 1984. 124pp. (OCLC 10375688)
After several of her cousins' and friends' mothers have new babies, eleven-year-old Sheila is disappointed when her parents announce they are adopting a three-year-old boy, Joseph. Sheila's concerns are justified when he does not obey, mutilates Sheila's dollhouse family, purposefully breaks eggs when the children collect them from the hens and urinates and defecates at inappropriate times and places. Joseph takes much of his parents' energy and Sheila and her other siblings feel shunted aside. Seeming impossible to love, Joseph slowly learns new behavior, but not fast enough for Sheila. The book ends with Dad helping Joseph learn to be responsible for the eggs using an unconventional technique and Sheila resigned to knowing that attachment may indeed take a long time. Sheila, a Mennonite, often speaks to God wondering

what He has done to her. The lack of a pat, happy resolution makes this story of a young acting-out child and his effect on the rest of the family ring true. The parents do a good job of helping the other children understand Joseph's acting-out behavior.

227   Stahl, Hilda. **Elizabeth Gail and the Terrifying News**. Illus. by Kathy Kulin.
         Wheaton, IL: Tyndale House, 1980. 111pp. (OCLC 20779652)
         Twelve-year-old Elizabeth Gail is the foster child of Chuck and Vera Johnson who want to adopt her. Waiting for the necessary relinquishment papers to be signed by her abusive birthmother, Marie, Elizabeth is alarmed when she learns Marie has returned from Australia and is determined to regain custody of her daughter. The Johnsons use their Christian faith to try to convince Elizabeth she will stay with them, but her new caseworker sides with her supposedly now-reformed mother. Elizabeth first runs away then allows herself to bask in the Johnson family's faith and love, finds it in herself to forgive her mother and puts her fate in the Lord's hands. Marie and the caseworker come to get Elizabeth, but their plans are changed when Marie's mother unexpectedly arrives and gives enough character witness concerning Marie that the caseworker realizes her own error. Shortly thereafter, the Johnsons happily learn Marie has signed relinquishment papers freeing them to adopt Elizabeth. The occasional black and white drawings add to this story, #7 in Tyndale's **Elizabeth Gail** series, which provides a Christian perspective on adoption as well as an exciting story.

228   Stahl, Hilda. **Kayla O'Brien and the Dangerous Journey**. Wheaton, IL:
         Crossway Books, 1990. 126pp. (OCLC 22607954)
         After the death of their parents on a transatlantic, turn-of-the-century trip from Ireland, fourteen-year-old Kayla and her thirteen-year-old brother, Timothy, are left in the care of the Murphys who try to help the children get to the farm where they had planned to go to work. Instead, Mrs. Murphy betrays them, puts them in the care of the Children's Aid Society and they become part of the orphan train. Initially grief-stricken, Kayla once again turns to God and tries to make the best of the situation. Other children are adopted as the train makes it scheduled stops until only Kayla and Timothy and another little girl remain at the end of the line. The other little girl is taken immediately and then so are Kayla and Timothy, who had wanted to stay together. The children look on it as a miracle from God and gladly go to their new family. This book provides an exciting adventure story as well as a Christian perspective on living. This is the first book of a series featuring Kayla O'Brien.

229   Stahl, Hilda. **Sadie Rose and the Cottonwood Creek Orphan**. Westchester,
         IL: Crossway Books, 1989. 130pp. (OCLC 20899404)
         Twelve-year-old Sadie, a pouty, but spunky girl after the death of her father and her mother's recent remarriage, is still unsure of York, her stepfather, a devout Christian who has adopted the children. The children discover an orphan, Bob, stealing and later, when Sadie spends a few days helping widow Jewel Comstock, they see Bob and ask him to help. He reluctantly helps then disappears. When Sadie saves Bob from a charging bull, Bob confesses that he really is a she. Her name is Mary Elizabeth Ferguson and her family died

on the trip from Iowa to Nebraska. She moves in with Jewel, but Sadie wants Mary to come live with her family. The York family has a gathering the next day to build a larger house and to give York a real first name. The children shyly will now call him Daddy, and Mary, declining the York's invitation to live with them, decides to continue living with Jewel because she is needed. In this exciting frontier story Sadie, forever forgetting to live by Christian teachings, always keeps trying. This is one of the **Prairie Youth Adventure** series.

230   Stanley, Carol. **Second Best Sister**. New York: Scholastic, 1988. 188pp.
          (OCLC 17823792971)
Fourteen-year-old Meg feels shunted aside in her family since her parents' energy is focused on fifteen-year-old adopted sister Julie's swimming. Because Julie is an Olympic hopeful, her family moved to Florida so Julie can attend the best swim school. When an accident keeps Julie from swimming for some time, the sisters become closer and Meg learns her sister is feeling just as miserable as she is. She would prefer to give swimming less priority in her life, but feels she cannot let her parents down. Julie encourages Meg's drawing and an art teacher arranges for her art to be in a gallery showing. Meg finds herself confronting her father about her rejected feelings, but he cannot understand. Likewise, Julie finds the strength to tell her parents she wants the chance to decide for herself about swimming and needs a break possibly to change her priorities. Although their parents are confused by both girls, they are reluctantly open to changing. Julie gains some freedom and Meg comes into the limelight. While the parents are portrayed as rigid and blindly insensitive, the two girls work out a positive relationship instead of giving into appearances of favoritism.

231   Streatfeild, Noel. **Ballet Shoes**. Illus. by Richard Floethe. New York:
          Random House, 1937. 294pp. (OCLC 220674)
Over the years, on research trips, Professor Matthew Brown adopted three daughters, Pauline, Petrova and Posy, who live at his home in London with his niece, Sylvia. When the family does not hear from the traveling Great Uncle Matthew, Sylvia rents out some of the rooms to help manage costs. Two renters, retired professors, assume the responsibility for the girls' education, while another arranges dancing and acting lessons so that when they reach age twelve they will be able to get a license to dance and act for money to contribute to the household. Pauline enjoys the acting, Posy is a natural at ballet, but Petrova prefers mechanical interests. Pauline becomes employed first, then reluctantly Petrova, but after eight years, when funds become too low, Sylvia is forced to sell the house. Pauline signs a five-year Hollywood film contract, thereby securing the funds for Posy to go abroad to study ballet. Surprisingly, Uncle Matthew arrives home and decides that he and Petrova will find a small house near an airfield so she can pursue her dream. While not happy about leaving each other, the girls look forward to their new adventures. An intriguing story providing a behind-the-scenes look at theatre and ballet life, although an absent adoptive father is disturbing.

232   Streatfeild, Noel. **Thursday's Child**. Illus. by Peggy Fortnum. New York:
          Random House, 1970. 275pp. (OCLC 134052)

Spunky ten-year-old Margaret Thursday has lived with two spinster sisters supported by the money mysteriously left each year in the church for that purpose. When the money does not arrive, the rector sends her to an orphanage. She befriends a sibling group including fourteen-year-old Lavinia who gets her two younger brothers set in the orphanage, then takes a job with the intention of visiting the boys. Margaret continues to get into trouble until she and the two boys run away, work on a barge and then in a theatre. Benefactors of the orphanage, and Lavinia's employers, discover the orphanage's abuse, improve conditions and reunite the three children with their newly-found grandfather who wants all the children. Margaret declines the invitation to become the children's sister preferring to make her way as an actress. Occasional black and white sketches add to the story of a lively young girl with a great imagination. Interestingly, the children are performing **Little Lord Fauntleroy**, whose grandfather rightfully claims him, when the children's grandfather come to the theatre to claim them.

233   Swartley, David Warren. **My Friend, My Brother**. Illus. by James Converse. Scottdale, PA: Herald Press, 1980. 102pp. (OCLC 5677121)
Twelve-year-old Eric, who comes from a Christian family, is teased by Jon Simon because he is a Mennonite. Eric's father tell him Jon's parents died and he lives a troubled life with his aunt and uncle. When Eric approaches Jon with his new knowledge of his background, Jon angrily denies the situation. It is only when Jon spends the night at Eric's and Eric sees evidence of physical abuse that Jon opens up about his fearful living conditions. Although he promises not to tell, Eric confides in his father and a teacher who get Jon the help and protection he needs. When Eric has a chance to invite a friend for a church camping trip, he chooses Jon who then learns about the peace he can find with an active relationship with God. Jon is not happy as the oldest of many children in his new foster home and soon the caseworker looks into other arrangements for him. She approaches Eric's family who is willing to foster until they can adopt him. Occasional black and white pencil drawings add to this story of strong faith, close family and two friends who become brothers.

234   Swetnam, Evelyn. **Yes, My Darling Daughter**. Illus. by Laurie Harden. New York: Harvey House, 1978. 166pp. (OCLC 4000241)
Eleven-year-old Josephine remains distant and aloof not wanting to get close for fear of being sent away from her new foster family, the Jensens. Josephine pushes away their kind overtures and pretends to dislike them and their way of life. Slowly, she learns to accept them, finding particular enjoyment in having an understanding grandfather, but protects herself with a distant air when she gets too close. When Josephine learns her foster mother is pregnant, she runs away before the Jensens can send her away. When they find her, she tells them of her fears and they reassure they want her to stay, as well as the baby, and although they want to adopt her, it is her decision. The baby arrives and Josephine learns from baby Heidi that one can love another without being related. Now able to see that Mom and Dad Jensen really do love her, Josephine agrees to her adoption. This provides a good insight into the oppositional behavior of children who try not to bond, as well

as the slow breaking down of that behavior. In addition, this provides a positive image of the child's relationship with each parent.

235   Talbot, Charlene Joy. **An Orphan for Nebraska**. New York: Atheneum, 1979. 208pp. (OCLC 4495003)
In 1872, orphaned on a transatlantic voyage, eleven-year-old Kevin O'Rourke reaches America to learn his Uncle Mike is in jail. Kevin takes up with some newsboys and hawks papers to earn money for food. He discovers the Newsboys' Lodging House where he is sheltered, fed, schooled and given the opportunity to go west on the orphan train to be adopted. His uncle agrees with the plan and Kevin leaves for Nebraska where he is taken in by an unmarried newspaper editor, Euclid, or Yuke, as he is called. Kevin helps around the house and becomes a printer's devil, or helper. Kevin thrives in his new environment, but when he learns Yuke has a fiancee who is planning to arrive soon to marry him, Kevin feels he is in the way and plans to move further west. The day they are to meet the fiancee's train, she does not arrive, but Kevin's Uncle Michael, who is working on the train, encourages Kevin to join him. When a letter arrives telling Yuke his fiancee does not want to move west, he and Kevin decide to go west together instead. Other orphan train stories include Nixon's **A Family Apart** (204) and Magnuson's **Orphan Train** (473).

236   Talbot, Charlene Joy. **Tomas Takes Charge**. Illus. by Reisie Lonette. New York: Lothrop, Lee and Shepard, 1966. 192pp. (OCLC 302161)
When their widower father does not return home, eleven-year-old Tomas and his fourteen-year-old sister, Fernanda, who live in a Puerto Rican section of Manhattan's warehouse district, set up housekeeping in an abandoned apartment nearby in hopes their father will return soon. Fernanda, fearful of going out in public, manages the inside of the apartment, while Tomas finds food and does odd jobs to earn money to buy other supplies. Tomas befriends Barbara, an artist, who hires Tomas as a model and helps the children obtain proper care. Later, the Mallorys, the building superintendents who are fond of the children, take in the children and the landlord permits them to join two apartments to make the necessary room. Tomas and Fernanda learn their father was killed in an accident, but now have the Mallorys and a comfortable home within familiar surroundings. Occasional black and white illustrations add to this inner-city adventure story of a resourceful young boy.

237   Tate, Eleanora E. **Just an Overnight Guest**. New York: Dial Press, 1980. 182pp. (OCLC 6200275)
Nine-year-old Margie Carson lives with her older sister, Alberta, and her teacher mother and her often-absent long-distance truck driver father who insist on good grammar, cleanliness and proper manners. Margie's world is turned upside down when Ethel, a four-year-old biracial child, comes to spend the night. Ethel is a dirty, destructive, disruptive, neglected child who wrecks havoc on the Carson household. Margie has difficulty adjusting to Ethel, but begins to understand her more when she realizes Ethel has no toys or anyone who has ever taught her manners. When Ethel's mother does not return and has no plans to do so, the girls learn Ethel is their cousin and the Carson family decide to keep her. Resentful, Margie falls prey to the town gossip that

Ethel's mother is white trash and fears for her family's reputation and her own place in the family when it becomes evident Ethel is staying. Margie's father comes home to announce he has a new position requiring less travel and reassures Margie that Ethel will never take her place with him. Portraying a small town and a close black family, this story realistically presents the behavior and antics of a previously neglected child.

238   Taylor, Theodore. **Tuck Triumphant**. New York: Doubleday, 1991. 150pp.
        (OCLC 21376408)
        Fourteen-year-old Helen, the youngest Ogden, anxiously awaits the arrival of the family's adopted child, in the late 1950s, whom she fantasizes will be a cute baby, until he turns out to be Chok-Do, a six-year-old Korean child who is deaf, a fact Korea had kept from them. As the family deals with the grief and decision whether to keep the little boy, much to her surprise, Helen falls in love with Chok-Do becoming his defender and protector. Several dangerous incidents, however, reveal the seriousness of having a deaf child and the Ogdens have Chok-Do tested and decide on a distant residential school for the deaf. A summer vacation, with a near-death situation involving Chok-Do, gives the family new perspective and shows them the depth of their love for him. Plans change and Mrs. Ogden, a teacher, decides to take a leave of absence to teach Chok-Do so he can remain at home. Heroes in the danger situations are Helen's blind dog Friar Tuck and Tuck's seeing-eye dog who first appeared in Taylor's **The Trouble With Tuck** (Garden City, NY: Doubleday, 1981). One of the few books dealing with the adoption of a deaf child, this book deals with a family agonizing over the fate of an adopted child who was not what they expected. Unfortunately, the Korean adoption placement mix-up is suspect.

239   Tennant, Kylie. **All the Proud Tribesmen**. Illus. by Clem Seale. London: Macmillan, 1959. 159pp. (OCLC 19296327)
        Set on the islands between Australia and New Guinea, this is the story of the destruction of Firecrest, the island home of Miss Alice Buchanan and her adopted son, Kerri, a native islander, and their resettlement on the island of Malu. When Miss Buchanan and Kerri are instrumental in convincing the people to leave Firecrest saving them from a deadly earthquake, several members of the group are still frightened by the haunted reputation of their new home, Malu. Miss Buchanan helps Dr. Mason, a visiting scientist, and determines his native assistants are behind the trouble and convinces the Firecrest people to stay and make their new home. Due to the difficulties, Kerri misses the scholarship deadline date which would have allowed him to attend school on the mainland to further his education to help his people. Dr. Mason makes arrangements for his schooling, but Kerri has a difficult time adjusting to western clothes and behavior. Nonetheless, he makes a good friend, becomes successful in sports, but looks forward to his school break homecoming at which he is welcomed as a hero. While not a typical adoption story, this provides a storyline involving the blending of two diverse cultures and values.

240   Tripp, Valerie. **Changes for Samantha**. Illus. by Luann Roberts. Madison, WI: Pleasant Co., 1988. 66pp. (OCLC 18191011)

After the marriage of her wealthy grandmother, orphan Samantha goes to live in New York City in 1904 with her Uncle Gard and Aunt Cornelia. While there she finds her best friend, orphaned Nellie and her sisters, living in squalid conditions. The girls find a way to visit regularly, but when Nellie is chosen to be part of the orphan train, Samantha helps her escape with her sisters and they secretly live in the attic at her home. The housekeeper betrays the girls' secrecy to a surprised aunt and uncle who later decided to adopt all the girls to make one family. The book concludes with a six-page section looking at life in 1904. This is the final volume of the **Samantha, an American Girl** series. Others in the series by the publisher, but written by various authors, include **Meet Samantha** (1986), **Samantha Learns a Lesson** (1986), **Samantha's Surprise** (1986), **Happy Birthday, Samantha** (1987) and **Samantha Saves the Day** (1988). These are appealing in the same sense as Shirley Temple movies.

241   Van Stockum, Hilda. **Pegeen**. Illus. by the author. New York: Junior Literary Guild/Viking Press, 1941. 268pp. (OCLC 9422665)
Seven-year-old Pegeen, left alone in Ireland when her grandmother dies, is taken in by Father Kelly who writes to her American uncle in hopes he will adopt her. Father Kelly encourages Pegeen to write to Francie, a special friend, and he writes to the boy's mother who agrees Pegeen can stay with them until the uncle responds. Pegeen joins and tries the patience of the O'Sullivan family that grows to love her. Pegeen and the twins, seven-year-old Francie and Liam, are inseparable and enjoy many activities. When Father Kelly hears from Pegeen's uncle, neither the O'Sullivans nor Pegeen want to part, and when they learn the uncle is reluctant, the O'Sullivans seek to adopt Pegeen. Pegeen is portrayed, in words as well as in the frequent black and white illustrations, as a spunky resourceful girl who learns and enjoys the values of family life.

242   Ward, Jeannette W. **I Have a Question, God**. Nashville, TN: Broadman Press, 1981. 32pp. (OCLC 7495804)
Although aware she was adopted as an infant, eleven-year-old Sandi puzzles over the circumstances of her adoption, as well as her birthparents. The story relates several of Sandi's worries and her parents' handling of the situations. These situations include reasons birthmothers make adoption plans for children, the permanence of adoption, and mixed feelings when a sibling joins the family, especially an older adoptive child. Sibling rivalry is also addressed, as is the need for more information for adoptees. Frequent full-page black and white illustrations highlighted in blue add to the text. Written as if Sandi were speaking directly to God, the story is quite didactic.

243   Warner, Gertrude Chandler. **The Boxcar Children**. Illus. by L. Kate Deal. Chicago: Scott, Foresman, 1942. 156pp. (OCLC 5315767)
After their parents' deaths, four school-aged children, fearful of being sent to their grandfather whom they feel they should distrust, stay together finding an abandoned railway boxcar and turning it into their home. The resourceful children share many adventures as they live off the land and Henry's, the oldest's, earnings. The doctor Henry works for sees a notice in the local newspaper and realizes the four children are the missing grandchildren of a

local wealthy landowner, but keeps the children's secret until they build up faith in the old gentleman. When one of the children becomes ill, they move in with the doctor and learn the kindly wealthy gentleman they often see is their grandfather. They are delighted and move in with him in his grand house. Their grandfather buys the boxcar for the children and places in the backyard for their playtime enjoyment. This is the first of many stories in the **Alden Family Mysteries** series by the same author. The frequent black silhoutte illustrations add to this exciting, albeit unrealistic, survival story for young readers.

244   Warren, Mary Phraner. **Walk in My Moccasins**. Illus. by Victor Mays.
        Philadelphia: Westminster, 1966. 157pp. (OCLC 302856)
The Littlejohns become an instant family when they adopt a sibling group of five children ranging in age from one to twelve. The story chronicles the adjustments and activities of the children, Native American Sioux, with their new white parents. The family deals with racial taunts, attachment, learning new behaviors, learning Native American heritage and being part of a larger community. The scattered black and white drawings help tell the story. While seemingly a realistic portrayal of a transracial adoption, this title is the target of much criticism from Native Americans and others who claim it perpetuates stereotypes.

245   Welch, Sheila Kelly. **Don't Call Me Marda**. Illus. by the author. Wayne, PA:
        Our Child Press, 1990. 138pp. (OCLC 20933833)
Eleven-year-old only-child Marsha has mixed feelings when her parents, announce they are considering adopting a child, but she is upset when her parents tell her they are considering a handicapped child, possibly one who is mentally handicapped. After their homestudy is completed, the family is presented with a picture of Wendy, a pretty seven-year-old who is retarded. Looking like a normal child, Wendy behaves as if she is a much younger child, but with Marsha's mother's experience working with developmentally delayed children, her parents feel able to parent Wendy. Marsha is embarrassed by the younger girl's inappropriate behavior and fears what Wendy's presence might do to her friendships, especially with Mike at school. In the meantime, Aunt Laura, who has always been devoted to Marsha, tries to influence Marsha and her parents against keeping Wendy, but Marsha learns to be protective and caring of Wendy and soon begins to resent others' negative feelings toward her. The text, a combination of narrative and Marsha's diary entries, reveal Marsha's painful feelings, her slow change of heart and personal growth. Each chapter is preceded by a soft pencil drawing by the author/ illustrator who is an adoptive parent.

246   Wier, Ester. **The Loner**. Illus. by Christine Price. New York: McKay, 1963.
        153pp. (OCLC 302179)
A young boy without a name drifts as a crop picker with whomever he can hitch a ride. Although he has dreams of going to California, he keeps to himself, fearing authorities will discover him and send him to a children's home. One day he collapses and is found by a reticent old woman sheep herder who calls herself Boss. She takes him in, feeds him and eventually earns his trust and teaches him to work with the sheep. Using the Bible, they

name him David, after another sheep herder. David is befriended by Tex, the camp tender, and by Angie, the widow of Boss's son, Ben who was killed by a bear. Ever since his death, Boss has been trying to find and kill the bear. Boss and David endure the long, hard winter and David's confidence in himself grows. As a gesture of gratitude, David kills the bear that took Ben's life. When spring arrives, Boss and David move to the ranch with Angie and Tex who will soon be married. In this 1964 Newbery Honor Book, that features occasional black and white illustrations, David learns lessons of love, loyalty and responsibility which enable him to leave behind his loner way of life.

247   Winthrop, Elizabeth. **Marathon Miranda**. New York: Holiday House, 1979.
      155pp. (OCLC 4495398)
While walking her dog one day, Miranda meets Phoebe, a girl her own age who likes to jog. Phoebe, training for the city marathon, convinces Miranda to try it with her, both to build up her asthmatic lungs and to give the new friends something to do together. The girls' running distance increases with their friendship. Miranda is confused when Phoebe stops calling, but learns her parents have just told her she was adopted as an infant. Feeling betrayed and now unsure of herself, Phoebe withdraws. Feeling confused, Miranda goes on vacation to her grandfather's with the family and Margaret, a special elderly friend, whom Miranda learns had an adopted son who died young, accompanies them. Phoebe runs away and stays with Margaret in the guesthouse and finds consolation and support from the older woman and assistance in reuniting with her parents. When they all return to the city, Miranda and Phoebe compete in and finish the marathon. By the end of the story, both Miranda and Phoebe grow and learn to overcome obstacles. The notion of a child not knowing she was adopted seems outdated for a 1979 publication. It is also unusual that Miranda and her fourteen-year-old brother share the same bedroom.

248   Young, Jan. **Jellyfoot**. Illus. by Emil Weiss. New York: David McKay, 1964.
      184pp. (OCLC 1400418)
Only-child Lori Benson, who at twelve years old is one of two children living with as many families in an isolated section of the Sierra Madre country, desperately wants a horse. To alleviate Lori's suspected loneliness, her parents announce the pending arrival of Kit, a twelve-year-old foster sister, who will keep Lori company and busy. Kit and Lori have no use for each other and Kit uses her refined passive-aggressive behavior to alienate Lori. But as time goes by, the girls learn they can think of and execute some good ideas together. Although Kit plans to reunite with her birthmother whom she has fantasized into a remarkable young successful woman, her hopes are dashed when her aging overmade-up mother visits to say good-bye and that she does not want Kit with her. After an incident with their father's gun, Kit declares her bond to the family, is reassured she will remain with them and becomes more cooperative. Together Lori and Kit rescue a lost little boy and become heroes, as well as sisters. Similar to Smith's **Moonshadow of Cherry Mountain** (225) which also uses a secluded natural setting, an animal and a new child fearful of bonding.

Junior High Readers

249   Becker, Kayla M., and Connie K. Heckert. **To Keera with Love**. Kansas City,
          MO: Sheed and Ward, 1987. 170pp. (OCLC 17252536)
       This story is a personal narrative about Kayla Becker, who discovers that she
       is pregnant while a high school senior. The book relates her feelings and
       experiences as she continues her pregnancy and her decision to choose
       adoption. Becker focuses on her childhood and her dating years, the support
       of her family, as well as her relationship with the baby's father. Using an open
       adoption forum, Becker helps chose her baby's new parents and makes a
       positive plan for the baby girl, Keera. Told with such love and honesty, this
       book gives insight into the emotions of a young teenage birthmother.

250   Cohen, Shari. **Coping with Being Adopted**. New York: Rosen Pub. Group,
          1988. 126pp. (OCLC 16577638)
       Taking a close look at the feelings, attitudes and perspectives of birthparents
       and adoptive parents, as well as the adoptees themselves, Cohen provides
       readers a new approach to concerns about being adopted. She distinguishes
       between adoption-related problems and problems in which adoption can be
       used to confound and confuse. While providing valuable and needed insight,
       the text regarding fears, negative feelings and conflict may frighten some
       readers as it may be too self-descriptive to be comfortable reading. Several
       other titles are available in the **Coping** series; another of interest is **Coping
       With Stepfamilies** (New York: Rosen Group, 1985).

251   Craven, Linda. **Step-Families: New Patterns in Harmony**. New York: Julian
          Messner, 1982. 186pp. (OCLC 8709445)
       Each chapter in this book begins with a vignette of a specific teen and his/her
       problems with stepfamilies. The author covers such aspects of stepfamily
       living as the myths involved, family change and how to deal with it, roles and
       relationships within a stepfamily, fantasy versus reality, sibling problems,
       discipline issues and sexuality. The book concludes with a directory of
       organizations which may be helpful to members of stepfamilies, and a detailed
       index. Adoption by stepparents is covered in a sympathetic, yet provocative

manner. While this provides positive approaches to living within a stepfamily, the advice holds up equally well to families adopting older children. The suggestions and counsel concerning methods of and reasons for getting along, how to handle bothersome siblings, how to stay out of trouble, as well as advantages of living in such a situation, are noteworthy. Especially interesting and forthright is the chapter on sexuality which covers not only parental issues, but also incest, abuse and sexual attraction between siblings not genetically related. This is full of practical, down-to-earth advice.

252   Crook, Marion. **The Face in the Mirror: Teenagers Talk About Adoption**. Toronto: NC Press, 1986. 116pp. (OCLC 16052793)
Traveling across Canada, Crook interviewed forty young adoptees between the ages of thirteen and twenty-two and compiled the results publishing a work to explain adoption using the words and feelings of adoptees themselves. The book is arranged in broad chapters covering such topics as why a child is placed for adoption, why adoptive parents adopt, the roles of heredity and environment and the legal status of the adoptee. The overriding theme of the book is the adoptees' desire to know more about birthparents. Crook's book emphasizes the Canadian experience, but effort is made to make a United States connection. The book concludes with a bibliography, a copy of the questionnaire used for the book and a resource list where an adoptee can get help regarding adoption issues, including searching for birthparents. The term 'natural' parent, rather than birthparent, is used consistently throughout the book. The 1990 edition by the same author and publisher is called **Teenagers Talk About Adoption: The Face in the Mirror** . Although similar in purpose to Krementz' **How It Feels to Be Adopted** (258), the latter title is arranged by person rather than by topic.

253   DuPrau, Jeanne. **Adoption: The Facts, Feelings and Issues of a Double Heritage**. New York: Julian Messner, 1990. 129pp. (OCLC 20391191)
An update of the 1981 book by the same title, DuPrau divides her work into three sections. The first looks at adoption in a historical context providing a basis for, and examination and discussion of, present-day adoption practices. Special cases, such as the adoption of disabled, minority or other special needs children, are then reviewed. The second part of the book deals with the feelings of adoption, both from the point of view of the adoptive parents, as well as adoptees. The final section involves current conflicts regarding the rights of members of the adoption triad. The book concludes with a resource list of helpful organizations, a bibliography and an index. The personal examples and pieces of dialog add to this title's readability. There are several complaints that this was not revised enough to present an accurate contemporary picture of adoption. Complaints include inappropriate language used, limited adoptive situations covered and an incomplete index.

254   Gay, Kathlyn. **Adoption and Foster Care**. Hillside, NJ: Enslow Publishers, 1990. 128pp. (OCLC 20090637)
Describing how the child welfare system works and explaining the difference between adoption and foster care, this book shares some of the feelings of young people who have been adopted or who are in foster care. Gay also provides a brief history and covers both open adoption and transracial

adoption. Source notes follow the main text as does a brief bibliography, a list of helpful organizations and an index. Anecdotes give life to the text.

255   Glassman, Bruce. **Everything You Need to Know About Stepfamilies**. New York: Rosen Pub. Group, 1988. 64pp. (OCLC 18417606)
Using diary entries, Glassman focuses on the realities and possible perceptions of those realities, of stepfamily living. He describes different kinds of stepfamilies and their problems, always pointing out that there are strengths, as well as weaknesses, to any family situation. Using non-threatening language, Glassman discusses the need for fair and reasonable expectations for and by all members of the stepfamily. The book concludes with a glossary, a bibliography and an index. Adoption, cited in the index, is covered as an option in some stepfamilies. Since some issues in adoptive families are similar to those in stepfamilies, this could provide helpful information. This book is part of the publisher's series, **Need to Know Library**.

256   Hyde, Margaret O. **Foster Care and Adoption**. New York: Franklin Watts, 1981. 90pp. (OCLC 8031754)
Hyde thoughtfully presents an overview and explanation of the foster care system. Looking at various child welfare situations which make use of foster care, Hyde also depicts some of the problems and weaknesses of the system. She recounts a brief history of the foster system and then describes what it is like to move into foster care. Although the goal of foster care is to provide temporary care before children are placed back into their birth home or in an adoptive home, Hyde relates the emotional trauma suffered by children who remain in foster care for a long time, particularly with multiple placements. Hyde continues by looking at parents who are seeking to adopt children, as well as describing children who wait for adoptive parents. She also includes a section on the controversy over sealed adoption records. Using case studies to describe situations, Hyde portrays the current foster care system in a sensitive, albeit not positive, light.

257   Kalil, Kathleen Mary. **Adoption: Let's Talk**. [Dearborn, MI: Kathleen M. Kalil], 1990. 68pp.
This interactive workbook is designed to help adopted children and teens deal with their thoughts and feelings on being adopted. Written by a psychologist, each page features a question, then the question is answered in an objective, sensitive manner. Following Kalil's answer, she presents additional questions and space for the reader's own responses. Adoption concepts covered in this book include history and nationality, reasons a child is adopted, issues regarding birthparents, feelings and responsibilities of adoptive parents, an adoptee's responsibilities to adoptive parents, birthparents and self, issues revolving around searching for birthparents and finally, techniques for reaching out for emotional help and support. Appearing typewritten and photocopied on only one side of the paper, this is a useful resource to help adoptees answer questions and express feelings. Since this may be difficult to locate, the author encourages correspondence at P.O. Box 5594, Dearborn, MI 48128. Other activity-book approaches are Gabel's **Filling in the Blanks** (107) and Long's **It's Fun to Be Me** (066).

258   Krementz, Jill. **How It Feels to Be Adopted**. New York: Knopf, 1982. 107pp.
       (OCLC 8554310)
       Interviews with adopted children between the ages of eight and sixteen
       provided the basis for this book. Each of the nineteen chapters focuses on one
       child's experiences, feelings and thoughts on adoption. The chapters, which
       contain black and white photographs of the adoptees and their families, run
       four to eight pages long. These are very insightful accounts of young adoptees,
       compiled by a talented, empathetic writer. The account of twelve-year-old
       Carla is a grown-up version of the story told in Bunin's **Is That Really Your
       Sister** (002). Similar treatment, but including adult adoptees, can be found in
       Rosenberg's **Growing Up Adopted** (115).

259   Landau, Elaine. **Black Market Adoption and the Sale of Children**. New
       York: Franklin Watts, 1990. 128pp. (OCLC 20391461)
       Beginning with the adoption of Lisa Steinberg, Landau reports on the
       existence of black market adoptions which operate outside the law and usually
       involve large amounts of money and middlemen who take advantage of
       birthmothers wanting to make adoption plans for her child, as well as good-
       intentioned adoptive parents. Landau goes on to look at overseas situations
       and surrogate contracts. Using many photographs and stories of people caught
       in black market adoptions, Landau presents a harsh picture of the realities of
       unregulated adoptions and offers some solutions to the problems involved.
       The book concludes with source notes, a bibliography and an index.

260   Landau, Elaine. **Surrogate Mothers**. New York: Franklin Watts, 1988.
       128pp. (OCLC 17618157)
       Examining a relatively new factor in the adoption world, Landau presents the
       technical, legal, personal and ethical issues involved in surrogacy. Citing the
       controversial 1986 birth of Baby M, the daughter of surrogate mother, Mary
       Beth Whitehead and father, William Stern, Landau looks at the new
       technology which has influenced the different ways infertile couples can
       achieve pregnancy, such as in vitro fertilization, artificial insemination by
       donor and surrogate mothering. Sharing the experiences of real people, often
       in their own words, keeps this a lively insight into a current controversial topic.
       Particularly interesting are the unforseen legal situations developing where the
       rights of the child, as well as parents, are still confused. This work includes
       adoption by the non-surrogate mother, however, limits and problems
       associated with traditional adoption are mentioned as reasons that prompted
       the increased use in surrogates. Several photographs are included.

261   Le Shan, Eda J. **So You Are Adopted**. New York: Guidance Center of New
       Rochelle, [1960?]. 15pp. (OCLC 1418158)
       Designed by the Guidance Center of New Rochelle as a booklet for adopted
       teens and their parents, this describes the conflicting times often associated
       with adolescence and reassures readers most of their adolescent problems are
       not necessarily related to adoption. It also reinforces that families are bound
       together by love, rather than blood and that the teen years are the times to
       reassess one's life, values and direction. The booklet concludes by suggesting
       that sometimes adolescent problems may benefit from professional help. A
       bibliography of books relating to human biology, family relationships and

understanding one's self is also appended. While seemingly out of date, this slim booklet still has some concrete, worthwhile ideas.

262   McGuire, Paula. **It Won't Happen to Me: Teenagers Talk About Pregnancy**. New York: Delacorte Press, 1983. 234pp. (OCLC 8906637)
Each chapter of this book is devoted to an individual's story about an unplanned pregnancy. Several girls choose motherhood, some decide to have abortions and a few choose adoption. In addition to the fifteen chapters focusing on teens, there are four chapters each highlighting a professional who works with these girls. The book concludes with selected resources and an index. The stories and information provided are fresh enough for contemporary readers. Similar to Maxtone-Graham's **Pregnant by Mistake** (391) which is for older readers.

263   Nickman, Steven L. **The Adoption Experience**. New York: Julian Messner, 1985. 192pp. (OCLC 12022465)
Each of Nickman's seven chapters begins with a fictionalized account of a particular person involved in adoption then ends with a narrative commentary on the specific issues illustrated in the story. Aspects of adoption include searching for birthparents and the nature of relationships, adopting older children from neglectful situations, foster homes, awkward situations, fantasy regarding birthfamily, special worries and "ghosts" from the past that affect the present. Other topics covered are transracial adoption, adolescence, identity of an adopted child, disruption and help for troubled families and the perspective of the birthparents and their distress. Nickman concludes with a selected bibliography and an index. Although Nickman sees changing an adopted child's name, even foreign-born, as a sign of parents' lack of acceptance, this is remarkably clear, frank, readable and informative and touches on several issues.

264   Peebles, Katherine. **A Natural Curiosity: Taffy's Search for Self**. Illus. by the author. Louisville, KY: Learning House, 1988. 45pp. (OCLC 17321804)
This follows Katherine, or Taffy, as she is called, the second oldest of six children, as she and her brothers and sisters are removed from their parents' home for neglect and placed in foster and adoptive homes. While growing up, Katherine, in her cold adoptive home with her two younger sisters, holds on the dream of being reunited with her other siblings and parents. She begins her search while in her teens and later, Katherine is encouraged by her sister-in-law and earnestly searches for her birthfamily finding her older brother who leads her to the rest of the family, except for Sharon, the baby. Their reunions are tearfully joyful and the family members stay in touch resolved to continue searching for Sharon. First written for personal therapy, this story intermingles the story line and objective observations on grief, loss and identity. The few drawings by the author reveal childhood memories. Adoption and the child welfare system in general are negatively portrayed.

265   Powledge, Fred. **So You're Adopted**. New York: Scribner, 1982. 101pp. (OCLC 8170437)

Powledge, himself adopted as an infant, explores aspects of the adoption experience. Looking at the history of adoption, as well as some statistics and changes in adoption practices and attitudes, Powledge examines some common concerns and questions. He discusses the nature versus nurture controversy regarding an adopted person's development and looks closely at the notion of personal identity indicating an adoptive person's identity includes a few more facets than others. Powledge also covers the topic of searching for birth-parents, indicating searching does not have to be an actual physical search, but can also be a mental search of inner qualities which can result in the same peace of mind. Powledge concludes with a bibliography, a list of helpful organizations and an index. Citing relevant research, Powledge presents a readable, yet thorough overview of adoption for readers in this age group.

266   Rivera, Geraldo. **A Special Kind of Courage: Profiles of Young Americans.**
       Illus. by Edith Vonnegut. New York: Simon and Schuster, 1976. 319pp.
       (OCLC 1992096)
       Included in this collection of moving vignettes of eleven courageous young people who have faced various crises is the story of Tia Grant, a young Vietnamese polio victim adopted by a Colorado family during the Vietnam War. The brief story conveys the historical context, as well as the plight of Tia's birthfamily and how she became available for adoption. In the meantime, the piece also introduces Wendy and Duane Grant, the founders of an international adoption agency, who had already adopted one physically handicapped Vietnamese child and were wanting another. They were told about Tia and pursued her adoption welcoming the eight-year-old girl into their family in 1972. After a short time in the family, Tia underwent a series of operations so that she would be able to use crutches. Her abandonment issues were tested during the months she had to stay in the hospital, but she learned she could count on her new family. By February 1974, Tia was able to walk unassisted at the Denver airport to meet her new brother from Vietnam. A soft pencil drawing of Tia precedes her touching story. This selection is on pages 241-266.

267   Youd, Pauline. **Adopted for a Purpose: Bible Stories of Joseph, Moses, Samuel, and Esther.** Nashville, TN: Abingdon Press, 1986. 144pp.
       (OCLC 13268885)
       With separate chapters devoted to a different Old Testament biblical character, Youd tells each of their adoption stories. Joseph was sold as a slave by his jealous brothers, Moses was found by an Egyptian princess and his life spared, Samuel's mother gave him back to God to keep her word and Esther lived with her cousin, Mordecai, after her parents' death. Youd presents the notion that God's purpose for these people's lives could not have been achieved if they had not been adopted. She makes the connection that the same is true for people adopted even today. Each chapter is divided into sections of narrative followed by questions the reader is to ponder and answer. In this religious perspective of adoption, Youd relates that just as some people are adopted into families, we are all adopted into God's family. For readers looking for a biblical connection, many other stories of adopted biblical characters are available at all reading levels.

FICTION

268   Adler, C.S. **In Our House Scott is My Brother**. New York: Macmillan, 1980.
          139pp. (OCLC 5353141)
       Jodi's widowed father marries fun-loving Donna and they live together with
       Donna's son, Scott, who at thirteen is the same age as Jodi. The lifestyle
       change is difficult for Jodi as she deals with her stepmother's mood swings and
       desire to change things, as well as dealing with her stepbrother's selfish and
       uncooperative behavior. Just as Jodi begins to feel good about being in a
       whole family, much to Jodi and her father's surprise, Donna, who has a
       drinking problem, decides to leave with Scott. As with other stories about
       blended families, this book describes the pain and the joys of becoming a
       family.

269   Aks, Patricia. **The Searching Heart**. New York: Ballantine Books, 1983.
          150pp. (OCLC 10186672)
       A high school English class assignment on self-identity prompts Sally to search
       for her birthmother. While her adoptive mother is supportive, her adoptive
       father distances himself when Sally seeks his support. She uses a finding
       agency and rather quickly locates her birthmother, Delores, who has since
       married a wealthy man and has two small children. Delores welcomes Sally
       as they meet for lunch and invites her to spend a school break with them.
       There, Sally learns her birthmother has very little time for her, or her other
       two children, as her social life keeps her fully occupied. Experiencing Delores'
       lifestyle causes Sally to reassess her own and she joyfully returns to her
       adoptive parents who are eagerly awaiting her return. Somewhat melodramat-
       ic, this story is in the same vein as Lowry's **Find a Stranger, Say Goodbye**
       (305). The search aspects of this story are not very realistic.

270   Angelo, Valenti. **Big Little Island**. Illus. by the author. New York: Viking,
          1955. 190pp. (OCLC 1942793)
       Fourteen-year-old Lorenzo, orphaned by World War II in Italy, comes to the
       States to live with relatives in Manhattan, the "big little island." The author
       relates the happenings in Lorenzo's first year with his new family, his warm,
       loving aunt and uncle, his restless older cousin, Nick, his primping, teenage
       cousin Rosie, and his best friend, cousin Peter. The story gently tells of one
       life replacing another while not forgetting the past. Black and white drawings
       begin each of the chapters.

271   Armer, Alberta. **Troublemaker**. Cleveland, OH: World Publishing Co., 1966.
          191pp. (OCLC 1265993)
       When twelve-year-old Joe is sent to live with the Murray family as a foster
       child while his father is in prison and his mother is in the hospital, he
       discovers a new meaning of family. At the time he arrives, the Murrays have
       two younger adoptive children and an older foster daughter. Joe learns how
       to be part of a family team, but has much difficulty giving up an old habit,
       stealing. The Murrays, who would like to adopt him if he becomes available,
       try to help him by making him accountable for his behavior. When he steals
       he must work it off at the father's drugstore but, while there, steals more to
       run away, unsuccessfully, back to his mother. Visits by both foster children's

mothers provide insight into the original problems of the children and Joe slowly accepts his situation, gets control of his anger, but is torn between this new life and his life with his mother. Joe seems relieved when it is decided that Joe will remain with the Murrays for a while longer until his mother finds a new place and his father is released. This story imparts an exceptionally fine picture of a neglected child who has not learned even basic manners and customs and how he begins to incorporate a new sense of self and belonging.

272   Arthur, Ruth M. **Requiem for a Princess**. New York: Atheneum, 1967. 182pp. (OCLC 899165)
When, at age seventeen, Willow learns she is adopted, it distances her from her adoptive parents. She becomes ill and, instead of returning to school, goes to spend some recuperation time at a resort where she discovers a painting of Isabel, the beautiful Spanish adopted daughter of an ancestral owner of the home in the sixteenth century. Through a series of flashbacks, Willow experiences Isabel's life and as she pieces together the Spanish girl's life, she is better able to deal with her own. This is an exciting story, particularly with the parallel characters and story lines. Unfortunately, the thesis is based on the tragedy of not disclosing an adoption. Using a historical figure to help solve contemporary personal problems is similar to Sach's **December Tale** (221).

273   Ball, Zachary. **Kep**. New York: Holiday House, 1961. 207pp. (OCLC 1283248)
When only-child fifteen-year-old Kep accidentally kills his widowed father in a hunting incident, a preacher arranges for his adoption by a couple who have recently lost their only son to polio. The adoptive father is kind and warm as he helps Kep ease into his new life, however, the mother is cold and rejecting as she has not been able to work through the grief of losing her son. The turning point for the family occurs when Kep becomes ill and the mother finds it within herself to help the child here rather than grieve for the one who is not. Much use of nature and animals and another significant adult figure for Kep give this story additional depth. The preacher-arranged adoption is odd and his advice to Kep that he will help his new family by taking the place of the dead child is disturbing.

274   Bauer, Marion Dane. **Foster Child**. New York: Seabury Press, 1977. 155pp. (OCLC 2597364)
When her great-grandmother with whom she lives suffers a stroke, twelve-year-old Renny is sent to live with an experienced foster family, although she harbors the fantasy of living with the father she has never seen. The foster father, however, is a religious fanatic who engages in sexually inappropriate behavior with a confused Renny in the name of the Lord. Renny befriends a younger child, Karen, whose mother is hospitalized and whose father travels. To protect themselves, they run away only to learn Renny's great-grandmother is dying. Karen's father rescues Karen and Renny, reunites with his wife, wanting to adopt Renny, but only when Renny visits and talks with her comatose great-grandmother does she realize her parents, as well as her grandmother, are not able to care for her. She leaves with Karen's parents and in the Rawls' embrace knows they will care for her. A fascinating story

of how self-delusion and misguided Christianity help make a confusing situation.

275   Bawden, Nina. **The Finding**. New York: Lothrop, Lee and Shepard, 1985.
        153pp. (OCLC 11371681)
        Set in London, this is the story of Alex, eleven years old and living with his adoptive family, who was found as an infant in one of the sphinxes which guard the Cleopatra's needle on the Embankment of the Thames River. His manipulative grandmother causes a rift in the family and encourages a widowed neighbor to include Alex in her will because he resembles her daughter. When the woman dies, Alex is named to claim half of her estate. Because he fears it will change his life and relationships, Alex runs away and is taken in by some questionable characters who consider ransoming him. He is allowed to leave and returns to the sphinx where his family finds him. There is a fine character portrayal in this believable suspense story.

276   Beckwith, Lillian. **A Shrine of Rainbows**. New York: St. Martin's Press,
        1984. 122pp. (OCLC 10876710)
        When eight-year-old Thomas comes to live as the only child of Sandy and Mairi on the Hebridean island of Corrie, he arrives as a foster child with the intention of adoption. Thomas and his foster mother, herself an orphan, form a warm, caring relationship, however, Sandy is disappointed in the appearance and constitution of his new frail foster son and remains aloof. When Mairi becomes ill and dies, her loss devastates Sandy who is encouraged to continue his life by Thomas, who, while feeling he will have to go back to the orphanage, has been strengthened by Mairi's love. After another near tragedy, Sandy embraces Thomas as his son and proceeds with the adoption. This is a very moving story dealing with loss and becoming a family.

277   Benary-Isbert, Margot. **The Long Way Home**. Trans. from the German by
        Richard and Clara Winston. New York: Harcourt, Brace, 1959. 280pp.
        (OCLC 297237)
        Abandoned by his birthmother at a former school teacher's home, Christoph is befriended by a U.S. GI who wants to adopt him. The story recounts Christoph's life in the East German sector, his escape through the Iron Curtain at age thirteen and his eventual arrival in the States. Christoph lives with several families before he joins the GI's family already consisting of a homesick French wife, an Italian war-orphan daughter and a Korean-born son. The story concludes with the family adopting a French orphan and Christoph feeling as if he belongs. The legal status and process for these adoptions, as well as Christoph's relationship with the GI's family are rather questionable. It does provide an exciting international survival story.

278   Berckman, Evelyn. **Blind Girl's Bluff**. New York: Dodd, Mead, 1962.
        244pp. (OCLC 1433040)
        Adopted seventeen-year-old Angie is determined to find her birthparents. Her adoptive mother is supportive, but, she gives Angie mixed messages of love and concern, while Angie's adoptive father is openly against her searching. As the story continues, clues dropped by old friends provide Angie with enough information to verify her birthmother. As the mystery unfolds, Angie discovers

that her adoptive father is really her birthfather and learns the circumstances of her birth and the death of her birthmother. This is an exciting suspense novel based on the tragedy surrounding Angie's adoption.

279   Bradbury, Bianca. **Laurie**. New York: Ives Washburn, 1965. 172pp. (OCLC 1706694)
The first day of her senior year of high school, Laurie is shaken by the strong resemblance between herself and a new girl. Adopted as an infant, Laurie begins to have qualms about her own background as she hears rumors that the two girls are related. The distraction causes problems with her adoptive parents, friends and school work. Laurie's parents try to calm her fears and finally give her permission to contact her original adoption agency. Once at the building, Laurie realizes what family really is and decides to go home without keeping her appointment. While somewhat dated and advocating closed adoption, this provides a good story of a child's need to understand and accept her past.

280   Brown, Irene Bennett. **Just Another Gorgeous Guy**. New York: Atheneum, 1984. 223pp. (OCLC 9893858)
Hillary, age seventeen, is reluctant to be sent by her adoptive parents to help an elderly grouchy recuperating aunt at her Oregon inn for the summer. Hillary, who had been hoping for a romantic summer, has her spirits lifted, however, when she realizes that due to construction work, there are several young men in the area. She mistakenly thinks her parents are trying to get rid of her when actually they are planning to move to Oregon and are hoping Hillary likes it there. Hillary learns much about herself and that good looks are not necessarily the prime quality to look for in a boyfriend.

281   Bunting, Eve. **Surrogate Sister**. New York: J.P. Lippincott, 1984. 211pp. (OCLC 10696783)
When her widowed mother becomes pregnant as a surrogate mother, sixteen-year-old Cassie is embarrassed and angry. Following a lead from a gift from the prospective parents, Cassie is able to determine who they are, even though the information is supposed to be kept confidential. Cassie goes to their neighborhood and feels somewhat different after she has seen the people who will adopt her brother and knows they will be moving to another state. Feeling she is competing for Sam, a college-age boyfriend, with another girl, Cassie goes to seek birth control counseling only to decide beforehand she does not want a sexual relationship at this time. Coming to terms with her own decisions about the use of her body, she can somewhat better accept her mother's choice. In the end, while still not able to approve her mother's choice, Cassie is able to accept and support her. This is an interesting sibling perspective on the surrogate issue, while also providing an opportunity to examine one's own values regarding sexuality. Issued as a paperback under the title of **Mother, How Could You!** (New York: Pocket Books, 1986).

282   Campbell, Hope. **Home to Hawaii**. New York: Norton, 1967. 174pp. (OCLC 1092957)
Having just learned that she has a half-sister in Hawaii, seventeen-year-old Kim travels there to find her. Her father, who had been married once before,

had a child who Kim remembers playing with when the family lived in Hawaii, but never knew she was her sister. The sister, Malia, who remained in Hawaii to be raised by an aunt and uncle, is delighted to see Kim and the two renew their bond as friends and now, sisters. While in Hawaii, Kim, an only child, stays with a welcoming family where she learns about large families. There is much history and culture of Hawaii in this story, as well as references to music of the mid-sixties, however, the adoption angle of this story is weak.

283   Cheatham, K. Follis. **Life on a Cool Plastic Ice Floe**. Philadelphia: Westminster Press, 1978. 180pp. (OCLC 3844752)
When he is innocently involved with a friend who stole a car, fourteen-year-old Native American Danny is sent to live downstate in a detention center. Due to the lack of stability provided, the children are unable to live together with their grandparents. Although told he and is siblings will be together soon, the social welfare system seems to be working against that goal. Sam, at twenty-one, is too involved with larger Native American problems to be effective helping his own family and Danny tries to keep eleven-year-old Mary from being adopted by a white family who does not let her maintain her heritage or contact with her brothers. Out of desperation, Danny writes a letter to the judge that instigates an investigation resulting in the setting aside of Mary's adoption and her removal from the home. When the children's grandfather's health is in jeopardy, their hopes of returning to family are dashed. Portraying a strong case against the present social welfare system regarding Native American families, as well as transracial adoption of Native American children, this book also presents much Native American information and heritage. For a similar work that provides cultural background within a novel format, see Irwin's **Kim/Kimi** (296).

284   Clewes, Dorothy. **Adopted Daughter**. New York: Coward-McCann, 1968. 191pp. (OCLC 435773)
When her widowed mother dies, sixteen-year-old Cathy, adopted as an infant, is sent to live with her oldest sister, Dale, and her family. She commutes to her old school and during a train trip befriends a young filmmaker, Christopher. Cathy has difficulty adjusting to her mother's death and how she fits into her family with her much older siblings. In order to feel a sense of belonging, Cathy seeks out her birthmother. Dale, admits to Cathy that she is her birthmother and the two forge a new relationship as that mystery is solved for Cathy. Christopher helps Cathy find herself and make some decisions about her life and future. Cathy chooses to board at her school and spend holidays with another sister who now lives in the house where Cathy grew up. Set in England, the British title of this book is **A Girl Like Cathy** (London: Collins, 1968).

285   Coleman, Pauline H. **The Different One**. New York: Dodd, Mead, 1955. 244pp. (OCLC 2898052)
When high-school-sophomore Ella learns about heredity and genetics in biology class, she reasons that she must be adopted because she has blue eyes and her parents have brown eyes and she feels her siblings to be more confident in their abilities. Unhappy with herself in general, the story relates Ella's ups and downs with her family and friends as she struggles to verify her

adoption and learn about herself. When Great Aunt Ella comes to visit, her young namesake discovers in her a surprisingly unconventional, yet self-assured quality. A gift from Aunt Ella, a miniature of Ella's great-grandmother, shows another family member with blue eyes and Ella confronts her family to learn that she is not adopted. She is noticeably relieved and her family amused, quick to point out the positive attributes of adoption. This amusing story, with a very weak adoption angle portrays a typical middle-class, mid-1950s large family. Another story about a birth child who fears she is adopted is Martin's **Claudia and the Great Search** (191).

286   Corbin, William. **Smoke**. New York: Coward-McCann, 1967. 253pp.
  (OCLC 1287439)
Fourteen-year-old Chris is not able to accept his new stepfather, Cal. One day Chris discovers a fearful half-starved German shepherd, gains the dog's confidence, secretly seeks medical attention and befriends the dog which he names Smoke. He is afraid to tell Cal because he knows Smoke is probably responsible for the late-night attack on their chicken coup, but when the dog becomes very sick, Chris tells Cal so the dog can receive better medical help. To Chris' surprise, Cal allows him to keep the dog as long as Smoke stays away from the chickens and there are no responses to the newspaper ad he insists they run to seek out the dog's owner. When there is a response, before the owner arrives to claim the dog, Chris runs away with Smoke. When Chris is injured, he calls home, making peace with Cal, indicating he is ready to give up the dog, but learns Cal has purchased Smoke for him. Chris returns home, with a more mature attitude and an open mind towards his stepfather. This moving story of a boy's relationship with a new father, has parallels in the boy's relationship with Smoke as they learn to trust each other.

287   Derby, Pat. **Visiting Miss Pierce**. New York: Farrar, Straus, Giroux, 1986.
  133pp. (OCLC 13397006)
For a school project for his religion class, ninth-grader Barry, adopted as an infant, visits an eighty-three-year-old woman in a nursing home. The woman, Miss Pierce, has trouble focusing on the present and through her musings Barry, although initially cool to the idea, becomes involved in her past. Miss Pierce often mistakes Barry for her rebellious brother, Willie, who secretly married a house servant and had a child whom his mother made him relinquish to the nuns and have the marriage annulled because she wanted him to marry someone more socially prominent. Through these discussions Barry begins to comprehend other facets of his own adoption. Selected as an ALA Best Book for Young Adults, this emotional story features strong characterization and a young boy's insight into the notion of birthparents as real people.

288   Dickson, Marguerite. **Only Child**. Illus. by Genia. New York: Longmans,
  Green, 1952. 247pp. (OCLC 1667146)
High-school-junior and only-child Gwen Flint is confronted with many new feelings and adventures with the arrival of her two girl cousins from the country, Rozzie and Flip. When Gwen's father is injured, the family decides to save money during his recuperation, rents their Boston home and

temporarily moves to the country home left to Flip and Rozzie. Gwen discovers the old family homestead where her grandfather used to live finding a diary of a seventeen-year-old girl, who turns out to be an ancestor, and takes on the repair of the house and restoration of the garden. When the ownership of the house and property becomes an issue, Gwen fears she will loose it, but an old will clearly gives ownership of the property to her father and the project helps Gwen and Flip find a positive relationship and they learn they will enjoy being sisters. Occasional black and white drawings illustrate this story of a only child learning to be a part of a larger family, both practically and historically.

289   Duncan, Lois. **Stranger With My Face**. Boston: Little, Brown, 1981. 250pp.
          (OCLC 7577236)
       Seventeen-year-old Laurie has the feeling someone is spying on her and her friends accuse of things she has not done. Laurie realizes someone is impersonating her and senses someone who looks like her whose name is Lia. She confronts her parents to learn she, a Native American twin, was adopted singly as an infant. A new friend introduces Laurie to astral projection and proposes Lia is using it to contact Laurie. Using her belief in her Native American heritage, Laurie attempts astral projection herself several times and learns more about Lia, who is now in a mental hospital having killed her foster/adoptive sister in a fit of jealousy. When Laurie is out of her body, however, Lia slips into it not allowing Laurie to return. Using a healing turquoise pendant, Laurie drives Lia out, reclaims her body and later learns the real Lia has died in the hospital. While a poor adoption story, this is a gripping supernatural thriller. Out-of-body experiences are similar to George's **Grandma's Little Darling** (461).

290   Epp, Margaret A. **The Sign of the Tumbling T**. Chicago: Moody Press, 1956.
          125pp. (OCLC 18067305)
       On her aunt's deathbed, thirteen-year-old Linda learns her aunt actually knew her birthmother. Her aunt gives Linda a box with identifying information about herself, including her unknown birthbrother's name and the ranch she was born on. Linda, whose birthname is Luta, goes to live in the Alberta Rockies with her favorite teacher who lead her to accept Christ. When she meets a ranch hand, Bill, who is her seventeen-year-old birthbrother, the two form a close, quick bond and Luta helps him to claim Christ. In several mysterious thefts, Bill is set up as the culprit and eventually fired from the ranch. Luta, along with the ranch owner's son help solve the mysteries and find the real perpetrators. Bill and Luta, along with their new friends, plan to revive their birthhome ranch and discover gold on the ranch premises. This is not only a weak adoption story, but an equally weak Christian western.

291   Eyerly, Jeannette. **A Girl Like Me**. Philadelphia: Lippincott, 1966. 179pp.
          (OCLC 846969)
       When her friend Cass fixes her up with a blind date, high-school-senior Robin gets involved with a less-than-desireable fellow and is torn between him and her adoptive family. Later, Cass discovers she is pregnant and her father sends her to a home for unwed mothers, where she plans to have the child adopted. Robin's relationship with Cass forces her to look at the circumstanc-

es of her own adoption and she searches for her birthmother. This story is rather disjointed and the search for the birthmother is too pat, too simple and unrealistic. It does provide a vehicle, however, for a young person, adopted as an infant, the opportunity to approach the subject of adoption on a slightly more personal level.

292   Eyerly, Jeannette. **He's My Baby Now.** Philadelphia: Lippincott, 1977.
        156pp. (OCLC 2797795)
Sixteen-year-old Charles Elderbury learns a former girlfriend, whom he has not seen for some time, has just given birth to his child. When he finds out she has adoption plans for the baby, Charles, himself the child of an absent father, desperately schemes to find a way to keep the baby only to realize it is not realistic. While sometimes humorous, as well as serious, this is a look at teen-age parenthood from the perspective of the birthfather. Some readers may be offended by occurrences of sexual slang.

293   Garfield, Leon. **The Sound of Coaches.** Illus. by John Lawrence. New York:
        Viking Press, 1974. 256pp. (OCLC 848115)
When he is orphaned at birth at The Red Lion, a lodge in England, Sam is named and adopted by a coachman and his wife. They raise the boy teaching him the coaching trade which he takes over after his father is shot while on a coach run and is unable to continue his work. Departing from the routine, Sam has an accident on his first run and in anger, his father sends him away. With minimal bits of information Sam sets out to seek his heritage. A chambermaid, Jenny, befriends Sam, the two fall in love and they take up with an acting troupe which includes Daniel Coventry, who turns out to be Sam's birthfather. Confused, Sam joins the troupe and becomes an actor and Jenny is left behind. Sam attempts to sort out his life to incorporate Jenny, Daniel and his adoptive parents and friends whom he misses. One day the troupe plays at The Red Lion and Sam is happily reunited with his family and Jenny. While difficult reading, this is a dramatic story, complete with unexpected plot twists, by a master storyteller.

294   Goudge, Elizabeth. **A City of Bells.** New York: Coward-McCann, 1936.
        308pp. (OCLC 1887090)
Jocelyn Irvin, home in England after being injured in the Boer War in South Africa at the turn of the century, goes to visit his elderly grandparents in their small village and while there opens a bookstore in an abandoned building, formerly occupied by a writer, Ferranti. Also living with his grandparents are eight-year-old Hugh Anthony and Henrietta, a nine-year-old orphan whom the grandparents adopted. Jocelyn meets Felicity Summers, an actress on holiday, and the two become inseparable. Jocelyn happens upon some of Ferranti's manuscripts and completes one of his fairy tales much to the delight of Felicity, who arranges to stage the story as a play and to star in it. When a child star becomes ill, Henrietta takes her place in the play and enjoys the opportunity. Putting together clues, Jocelyn finds Ferranti, tells him his lover has died, but their daughter, Henrietta, is healthy and fine. Ferranti is aware of his incompetent fathering, but, Jocelyn, who is planning to propose to Felicity and become Henrietta's and Hugh Anthony's parent, offers Ferranti a place to live so that Jocelyn can offer the girl the stability of family life,

while Ferranti can offer her the artistic, vagabond life. This story provides an interesting adoption angle, while offering a delightfully detailed story of life in an Edwardian English cathedral town.

295   Hale, Arlene. **Nothing But a Stranger**. New York: Four Winds Press, 1966.
           169pp. (OCLC 899100)
The summer after her graduation from high school, Holly plans to write a series of feature stories on adoption for her father's newspaper. She learns some young married friends, unable to have children, have decided to adopt an infant and although Holly has not ever thought much about adoption, she proceeds with her research wanting to know more. She interviews not only her friends, but the social worker from their adoption agency, and an adoptive mother whose secretive attitude about her son's adoption bothers Holly. In the midst of her research, Holly learns, much to her outrage, that she herself is adopted. She estranges herself from her family and after the adoption agency agrees, Holly is granted access to her file where she learns that while her birthmother died, her birthfather is still living. She finds him on his deathbed at a veterans' hospital, sees a photo of her birthmother and receives a gift from him, but realizes that he really is a stranger. She returns home and soon forgives and reconciles with her family after writing the final segment of her adoption newspaper story. While a melodramatic adoption story, this also has elements of a typical teen family/social life.

296   Irwin, Hadley. **Kim/Kimi**. New York: Margaret K. McElderry Books, 1987.
           200pp. (OCLC 14412486)
Although high-school-junior Kim Andrews feels secure with her mother and adoptive stepfather, she wants to know more about her Japanese-American birthfather who died before she was born. She knows only his name and that her birthfather's family did not approve his marriage to her mother, so his family is not even aware of her existence. With the cooperation of her twelve-year-old half-brother, Kim leaves her home in Iowa to search for her father's family in Sacramento, California for one week. She is befriended by a Japanese-American family who lets her stay with them and helps her by teaching her about being Japanese-American: etiquette, attitudes and history. An older Japanese woman helps Kim, now called by Kimi, her Japanese name, find information on her father's incarceration as a child during World War II and helps to locate a current address and makes the initial contact with Kimi's birthaunt and grandmother. Although difficult, Kimi finds a cautious, but caring family that is willing to learn to accept her. Providing much Japanese-American history and heritage, this is an insightful, thought-provoking book. For a similar work that provides cultural background within a novel format, see Cheatham's **Life on a Cool Plastic Ice Floe** (283).

297   Jennings, John Edward. **The Golden Eagle: A Novel Based on the Fabulous
           Life of the Great Conquestador Hernando de Soto, 1500-1542.**. New
           York: Putnam, 1958. 253pp. (OCLC 1448737)
Based on the life of Hernando de Soto, this story relates his personal life as well as his military conquests. When he falls in love with his benefactor's daughter, he is sent from Spain to work in what is now Panama to separate the lovers. While in that area, he becomes involved with an Inca woman and

when the woman dies, de Soto promises to adopt her daughter and raise her. Upon returning to Spain, de Soto marries his first love, but his new Inca daughter is viewed suspiciously. Later, when de Soto's assistant falls in love with her, they unexpectedly travel together on the Florida conquest. A fascinating historical account that includes an adoption component.

298   Kjelgaard, Jim. **The Black Fawn**. New York: Dodd, Mead, 1958. 215pp.
       (OCLC 1398255)
       Now that he is old enough, Allan "Bud" Sloan is farmed out from the orphanage to a family to work and earn his keep. His new family, the Bennetts, are an elderly couple whose eleven children have grown and moved away. Gramps Bennett, while seemingly gruff, helps Bud learn the farming trade and appreciate nature, while Gram Bennett makes him initially uncomfortable since he is not used to being with someone so warm and good-hearted. The story relates how Bud hesitatingly becomes part of the family, through the work on the farm, fishing and hunting with Gramps and growing to care about the Bennetts. Although the story progresses seemingly without the benefit of adoption, the decision is made, to Bud's surprise and gratefulness, that the Bennetts will send Bud to agricultural college so that he can eventually take over the family farm. The comparison between himself and a fragile small fawn, which he finds early in the story and which later becomes a strong buck provides a visual parallel in this outdoor adventure story.

299   Klass, Sheila Solomon. **To See My Mother Dance**. New York: Scribner,
       1981. 154pp. (OCLC 7774715)
       Thirteen-year-old Jessica has wonderful fantasies about her birthmother who left on her first birthday to pursue a more bohemian lifestyle. When Jessica's father announces his impending marriage to Martha, Jessica's fantasies do not give Martha a chance. Adding to Jessica's problems is a self-centered, controlling paternal grandmother who is also against her son's marriage. As Martha attempts to exert her place in the home, Jessica engages in passive-aggressive behavior which thwarts any healing or future positive relationship. Martha, a lawyer, locates Jessica's birthmother and arranges for the two to meet and spend some time together. Martha and Jessica fly to California where Jessica's fantasies of a successful dancer for a mother fly in the face of the dazed, unfeeling woman she meets at the eastern religious commune who informs Jessica she is happy with the decision she made twelve years ago and wants nothing to do with her. Saddened, but more realistic, Jessica and Martha leave for home. This is a powerful story of fantasies blocking reality and of maintaining self-control.

300   Kropp, Paul. **Jo's Search**. Illus. by Heather Collins. Don Mills, Ontario:
       Collier Macmillan Canada, 1986. 93pp. (OCLC 16029199)
       Angry and rebellious, fifteen-year-old Josephine, adopted as an infant, snoops in her adoption file and discovers a letter and picture of her birthmother that she is to receive on her eighteenth birthday. Not wanting to hurt her adoptive parents, Jo deviously plots with her best friend, Kate, to locate her birth-mother. As an only child adopted by older parents who are now in their sixties, Jo feels that if she finds her birthmother all her problems will be solved. Playing detective in their Canadian hometown, Jo and Kate investigate

the hospitals, churches and soon discover identifying information and locate Jo's birthmother who warmly receives her. Jo informs her parents, who are more supportive than she supposed, and arrangements are made for Jo to spend some of the Christmas holiday with her birthmother and her family. During the trip Jo realizes who her "real" parents are and comes home a more mature, committed daughter. Detailed full-page pencil sketches accompany the story that realistically portrays a difficult parent/child relationship and underplays the difficulty in locating birthparents.

301   Leach, Christopher. **Kate's Story**. New York: Scholastic Book Service, 1968. 128pp. (OCLC 13081750)
Set in England, sixteen-year-old Kate is devastated by her father's death and is even more removed from her mother when she remarries and Kate learns that she was adopted as an infant. Angry, rebellious and unsure of her identity, Kate pursues a dying film star whom Kate thinks she resembles and later establishes a relationship with a favorite author. Defying her parents, she stays home while they go on holiday, is arrested for being part of a demonstration and is sent to a juvenile facility until her parents claim her. When given the choice of returning home to her family or attending a supervised school, Kate chooses the school. Written in response to an essay assignment for a class, it retains the flavor of an angry, confused young girl. A British edition, not located, was published in 1969 under the title **Answering Miss Roberts**.

302   Lee, Joanna. **I Want to Keep My Baby**. New York: New American Library, 1977. 166pp. (OCLC 3394942)
When fifteen-year-old Sue Ann discovers she is pregnant, her mother, who had been pregnant at age fifteen with Sue Ann, deposits her in a home for unwed mothers where she becomes friends with Rae Finer, a social worker who had also been pregnant as a teen. After the baby is born, Sue Ann's mother will not allow her to place the baby for adoption, but living at home with her meddling, newly remarried mother, stepfather and their two small children leads Sue Ann to go on welfare and find a shabby trailer for herself and the baby, Elizabeth. When that situation becomes dangerous, Miss Finer helps her find shelter at a half-way house for unwed mothers which allows Sue Ann to return to school and obtain a job, while Elizabeth is cared for. She continues seriously overworking herself until Chuck, the baby's father, appears and, instead of rescuing her, offers half of his paychecks. In a rage, Sue Ann harms Elizabeth and, fearful of herself, she has Miss Finer bring the adoption papers, realizing she is not able to raise Elizabeth after all. In the meantime, the book also relates the parallel story of the DeRedas, a childless couple who have been waiting to adopt a child, who are given custody of Elizabeth. Based on a TV movie, this is a touching story that dramatically portrays a resourceful, spunky, yet helpless child and her baby.

303   L'Engle, Madeleine. **Meet the Austins**. New York: Vanguard Press, 1960. 191pp. (OCLC 301308)
Following an accident, ten-year-old orphaned Maggy, spoiled and irritating, comes to live with the tightly knit, warm Austin family. The narrator, twelve-year-old Vicky, describes the humorous and frustrating events of this large family. Slowly, Maggie deals with her grief and settles into more agreeable

behavior. When the Austins seek a court decision on Maggy's future, the judge agrees she is to remain with the family, with the understanding her grandfather and Aunt Elena, a concert pianist, be made legal guardians. The children concoct a romantic plan that Aunt Elena and Uncle Douglas get married and adopt Maggie. While there is no real adoption in this story, the book is frequently found in such bibliographies. However, dealing with loss, the adjustments to family life and the forging of new behaviors and relationships certainly are common with adoption. Other titles in the Austin Family Trilogy which primarily feature the narrator, Vicky, include **The Moon by Night** (New York: Farrar, Straus and Giroux, 1963), in which Aunt Elena and Uncle Douglas have gotten married and adopted Maggy, and **A Ring of Endless Light** (New York: Farrar, Straus and Giroux, 1980).

304   Lifton, Betty Jean. **I'm Still Me**. New York: Knopf, 1981. 243pp. (OCLC 6861642)
When sixteen-year-old high school junior Lori Elkins receives an American History assignment to research her family tree she is bewildered because she is adopted. Believing her parents would not support her, Lori tries on her own to trace her birthmother and deceptively discovers her birthmother's name and the name of her adoption agency. While an adoption search support group cannot help her until she is eighteen, the law-student boyfriend of Lori's next door neighbor provides some help and Lori finds her birthmother, meets with her, learns about her own past and her birthmother's life and make arrangements to keep in touch. Lori's parents confront her, and although they cannot understand her need to know, they are kind and loving, offering to do what they can to help her. A fictionalized account designed for younger readers, this book presents Lifton's position for open adoption records. Her non-fiction works supporting the same are **Twice Born** (380) and **Lost and Found** (379). Readers are warned of a drinking episode and a few instances of Lori's sexual activities.

305   Lowry, Lois. **Find a Stranger, Say Goodbye**. Boston: Houghton Mifflin, 1978. 187pp. (OCLC 3650306)
As a high school graduation gift from her parents, Natalie Armstrong is given the time and the means to pursue her wish of finding her birthparents. Her parents and boyfriend do not understand her motivation, but are supportive as are her encouraging younger sister and maternal grandmother. Natalie's quest takes her back to the small Maine town where she was born and to a posh area of New York City where she meets her birthmother, now a famous model who shares an old diary that helps Natalie understand her origins. After meeting with her birthmother and learning of her birthfather's death, Natalie, with her need fulfilled, is ready to go on with her own life. While indulging in the fantasy of birthmother as a glorified person, this story by a well-known author provides sensitivity for this age group to a timely topic.

306   Magorian, Michelle. **Good Night, Mr. Tom**. New York: Harper and Row, 1981. 318pp. (OCLC 7875553)
During the Second World War, eight-year-old abused Willie is one of many children evacuated from London to the British countryside for safe-keeping. When he is turned over to Tom Oakley, a widower in his sixties who lost his

only child, Willie is fearful, anxious and suspicious and Tom is awkward and unsure of himself. The two forge a cautious, but caring relationship and Willie is transformed into a bright young schoolboy and chum. When Will's mother wants him returned to her, Tom is disturbed knowing her abusive parenting and later the police discover a near-dead Will locked under a staircase clutching a dead baby sister. Will is taken to a psychiatric hospital from which Tom kidnaps him and returning home to nurse him back to health around those who love him. In the meantime, Tom makes arrangements to adopt Will. After Will's best friend is killed in an air raid, Will grieves for all his losses and resumes his life with gusto. Although Will often behaves much older than his eight years, the author provides an emotional transformation of a small boy in a loving environment.

307   Means, Florence Crannell. **Us Maltbys**. Boston: Houghton Mifflin, 1966.
       250pp. (OCLC 1401235)
After a car accident which leaves Mr. Maltby unable to resume his regular job, the Maltbys decide to take in foster children to supplement their income. They take in five problem-laden teenage girls in addition to their two teen-age birthdaughters. The new girls reluctantly join the family, but soon find themselves caught up in the structure, consistency and warmth of their new home. All the girls test the rules and have adjustment problems with each other, but comfortably settle into their new life. The Maltbys decide to test the local ordinance against blacks by also taking in a black infant who has not been able to be placed elsewhere. Although some in town are shocked, most realize that little Jamie is just a baby and the ordinance no longer seems realistic. Some readers may object to the use of the words "negro" and "colored" in reference to blacks as well as the notion of fostering for the money. Although this is really a story of fostering, it provides an inside look at the adaptations and adjustments necessary when a small family adds older children. The emotions and episodes of both birthfamily members and the new members are similar to that of adoption. In addition, the parents are portrayed as warm, strong and caring.

308   Myers, Walter Dean. **Sweet Illusions**. New York: Teachers and Writers
       Collaborative, 1987. 142pp. (OCLC 13903360)
Myers presents a cast of characters, all friends involved with the same pregnancy counseling center, and devotes a chapter to each person. Written in the first person, each chapter relates concerns, problems and hopes of one of the friends. Each chapter ends with a particular situation and the reader is supposed to write the rest of the story. The characters, primarily a multiracial group of teens, deal quite frankly with pregnancy and the situations and choices it presents. Birthfathers, as well as birthmothers speak out as they continue with their lives, some keeping their babies, while other choose adoption. Also involving their own families and the reaction and support they receive from them, the characters handle their situations differently and with different results. The final chapter, which is a complete chapter, features one of the teen mothers seven years later when she contacts the counseling center to discover the director is one of her former pregnant friends. The two catch up and discuss their own lives and those of friends they knew earlier. Designed as a high-interest writing activity for young adults, Myers provides

a perspective on the feelings and concerns of a group of teens caught up in early pregnancy.

309   Myers, Walter Dean. **Won't Know Till I Get There**. New York: Viking Press, 1982. 176pp. (OCLC 8034944)
When fourteen-year-old Steve's parents tell him they are thinking of adopting a child, he has visions of having a small brother who will look up to him. Instead, his family initially fosters Earl, a thirteen-year-old with a criminal record. When Steve and Earl are sentenced to community service for defacing property, they work in a home for the elderly that is slated to close and while there learn about themselves, the elderly and the value of permanence. Written in the form of a diary, Steve relates his perspective on the summer, helping the six feisty seniors find a way to keep their home open. Earl, who has spent years in temporary homes, seems to relate to the residents' need for permanence. For the third time in his life, Earl's birthmother, even after meeting the adoptive family, refuses to allow his adoption. Feeling rejected, Earl willingly goes along with the judge's decision to give Steve's family permanent custody of Earl until he is eighteen. Featuring a black family in an inner-city setting, this story reveals the anxiety, anger and cautious joy that accompanies an older child adoption. The parallel story of the residents of the home provide an interesting contrast.

310   Nerlove, Evelyn. **Who is David? A Story of an Adopted Adolescent and His Friends**. Illus. by Miriam Nerlove. New York: Child Welfare League of America, 1985. 113pp. (OCLC 11755729)
David begins to question his adoption and although his parents are unable to provide as much information as he needs, they find an adoption support group, attending themselves while David attends sessions for teens. David meets other adopted teens and is relieved to learn they share some of the same fears, anxieties and anger he does. David has a growing relationship with Diana, his girlfriend, whose older sister resentfully has a baby living at home and begins to see that perhaps adoption is a good solution for some children. On his eighteenth birthday, at his request, his adoption agency makes arrangements for him to meet his birthmother, Susan, and he learns about his past, her life and realizes where he belongs. He also learns his birthfather does not want contact. This provides an inside look at adoption support groups for teens and a variety of responses to the issues involved. In addition, it is interesting to watch David's personal growth and progress as he reconciles his adoption. There is one scene in which David's father talks to him about being prepared for a sexual encounter and gives him a packet of condoms.

311   Neufeld, John. **Edgar Allan**. New York: S.G. Phillips, 1968. 95pp. (OCLC 291674)
When Reverend Fickett and his wife decide to adopt a two-year-old black child, Edgar Allan, the family reaction is mixed. While Michael, the twelve-year-old narrator, is proud, fourteen-year-old Mary Nell is hostile to the idea, and the younger children are unconcerned. The small California community does not accept the addition of Edgar Allan and expresses its dislike through a cross-burning on the Fickett's lawn, racial epithets aimed at the Fickett children, an ultimatum from the church board and calls from angry parents

when Edgar Allan is enrolled in preschool. Going against their better judgement, the Ficketts give in to the pressure and have Edgar Allan's adoption disrupted. Oddly enough, Mary Nell feels bad her parents acted on her anger and the church board wants Reverend Fickett to resign since he is not able to stand up for what he believes in. Michael feels betrayed by his father who, in the end, could not make the different parts of his life work together. The two resume their walks and learn to understand and accept each other. They discuss the possibility of trying another similar adoption when they move to their new parish. This is a sad story of how racial prejudice, and giving in to it, negatively impacts on the lives of so many people.

312   Okimoto, Jean Davies. **Molly By Any Other Name**. New York: Scholastic,
         1990. 276pp. (OCLC 21340229)
Seventeen-year-old Molly, an Asian girl who is the only child of a white professional couple in Seattle, becomes curious about her heritage when a class speaker discusses adoptees finding birthparents. She confides in Roland, a fourth-generation Japanese who is her best friend. He is not encouraging, but is supportive. Molly nervously speaks to her parents who are reluctantly supportive and begins proceedings using the services of a search organization. In the meantime, Karen, Molly's yet unknown birthmother has just moved to Halifax, Nova Scotia with her husband and ten-year-old son. Karen receives a call from the search organization and she agrees to meet, wanting to remove the lies from her life and Karen and Molly correspond and make arrangements to meet. Molly learns about her heritage, her birthparents and the circumstances of her birth. Karen, her husband and son have a successful reunion with Molly and her family at a park at the U.S./Canadian border. A contemporary book featuring a teenage Asian main character with a love interest is rare. This is a powerful story of choices and finding oneself.

313   Oppenheimer, Joan L. **Which Mother is Mine**? New York: Bantam Books,
         1980. 133pp. (OCLC 6340843)
Fourteen-year-old Alex, who has been in the foster care system since age four, has been fostered by the Dennis family since she was eight. Although she receives occasional letters from her birthmother, Alex's loyalties are with her foster family. She is shocked to learn her birthmother, Jill, plans to come to California for six weeks with the intention of getting to know Alex better and to regain custody. Although angry and initially resentful, Alex finds she actually likes her birthmother, but prefers to continue living with the foster family. The Dennis family, feeling somewhat violated, retains a lawyer and pursues Alex's adoption with her approval. Alex finds herself becoming fonder of Jill, yet does not want to cut the ties with the Dennis family who has provided her security. A court hearing allows everyone, except Alex, to present a point of view, but prior to the judge's decision, Alex arranges a private meeting with the judge and they compromise on a six-month delay for the decision. Alex will continue living with the Dennis family, Jill will attend college classes in the area and Alex will have time to sort out her feelings and needs. Although slightly contrived, this story provides a powerful insight into the conflicting feelings of a child torn between two sets of parents.

314   Pfeffer, Susan Beth. **About David**. New York: Delacorte Press, 1980. 167pp.
      (OCLC 601677)
      David is portrayed as a bright, but unhappy, restless, unsettled high school
      student who murders his adoptive parents and then commits suicide after
      mistakenly believing his mother is pregnant. The bulk of the story revolves
      around the aftermath as experienced by his friend, Lynn, as well as other
      friends. This is a particularly disturbing book, in addition to the basis of the
      story, because adoption is so negatively depicted. Through the words and
      thoughts of the characters, the author presents adoption as second best: an
      explanation that David's parents had worked on their fertility problem after
      David's adoption because they so badly wanted a child of their own; a
      statement regarding birthdays being hard for David because he was adopted.
      The adults, as well as the teens in this story, view adoption as a source of
      trouble and unhappiness. This is unfortunately a work by a popular, widely-
      read author whose realistic fiction is generally excellent.

315   Read, Elfreida. **Brothers By Choice**. New York: Farrar, Straus and Giroux,
      1974. 153pp. (OCLC 793477)
      Brett Forester, age fourteen, is sent to find his older adopted brother, Rocky,
      when he runs away after feeling continually belittled by his professor father.
      Brett finds Rocky living and working in a co-op community where he is a
      valued member. Although Rocky is happy to see Brett, he is reluctant to have
      him stay because while he was out of money he made a bad choice and now
      owes two drug dealers over seven hundred dollars. Brett decides to stay on,
      work and help Rocky pay his debt so they can go home together. When
      Rocky realizes Brett has given up a chance to go on a musical trip to Europe,
      he knows Brett considers himself his brother. The night before they are to
      leave, a co-op barn catches fire and in the confusion Brett is kidnapped by the
      dealers, Rocky pays them, then later Brett steals the signed drug deal which
      implicates Rocky. Instead of destroying the evidence, Rocky decides to take
      it home, tell his parents the whole story and perhaps they can begin a new
      relationship. The two are picked up by truckers and driven home where they
      are warmly received. A good adventure story adds to the message of what it
      means to be brothers and family.

316   Roth, Arthur J. **The Secret Lover of Elmtree**. New York: Four Winds Press,
      1976. 165pp. (OCLC 2121657)
      While pumping gas at his adoptive father's service station, highschooler Greg
      Yardley meets a man who turns out to be his birthfather offering him a college
      education and future in his lucrative business in the city. His adoptive parents
      want Greg to consider the offer seriously since they cannot provide him a
      comparable future. After much agonizing and several humorous and near-
      tragic events, Greg decides to stay in Elmtree with his family and work with
      his dad at the service station. Even though the basis of the story is far-fetched
      and the opening text is questionable as it refers to real parents, this is a
      melodramatic, yet humorous successful story. Greg's worrisome wondering
      and adolescent antics are a large part of the success.

317 Rowe, Viola. **Freckled and Fourteen**. Illus. by Jacqueline Tomes. New York:
 William Morrow, 1965. 223pp. (OCLC 6902611)
 Eighth-grader tomboy Rusty Eastman is the only girl and only redhead in her
 family of five children. Convinced she is adopted because she looks so
 different from the rest of her family, Rusty is nonetheless shocked when she
 discovers adoption papers in her parents' desk. She confronts her favorite
 uncle, Uncle Law, who verifies the fact for her and agrees to keep her
 knowledge a secret until after her eighth-grade graduation. On the evening
 of her graduation, her parents confess and apologize to her for not telling her
 sooner, but Rusty remains aloof and distant, unsure of her position with them.
 Instead of going with her family on their regular summer vacation, Rusty stays
 with Uncle Law as his housekeeper. During their separation, Rusty learns
 how much she really loves her family and when they return, she begins
 investing herself in them once again. Rusty becomes attracted to Sammy, the
 paper boy, and the two slowly, awkwardly begin a relationship. Rusty's parents
 assure her of their permanent love for her, she obtains a summer job with
 Rusty and, not-so-reluctantly, gives up her tomboyish ways. This book contains
 many sexist notions regarding the appropriate activities and looks of girls.

318 Shyer, Marlene Fanta. **My Brother, the Thief**. New York: Scribner, 1980.
 138pp. (OCLC 5946542)
 Fifteen-year-old Richard, whose mother remarried following his parents
 divorce, has been adopted by his stepfather. Twelve-year-old Carolyn, the
 daughter of the second marriage, is deeply disturbed when she discovers
 Richard and his friend, Flim-flam involved in stealing. Although Richard's
 parents become distraught over his behavior, when Carolyn tries to tell her
 mother of his stealing she disbelieves her. Not wanting to be a snitch, Carolyn
 tries to convince her brother to stop stealing and learns he wants to sell the
 goods to obtain money to go see his birthfather, whom he has not seen in
 years. Fearing she is learning his bad habit, Richard gets out of the stealing
 ring only to have Carolyn accused when the club manager finds her and a
 stash of stolen goods in their family's locker at the club. When the family and
 the police arrive, Richard confesses. Due to his good record the judge
 dismisses the charges against Richard, however, Flim-flam, who already has a
 record, is remanded to a minimum-security prison. Richard and his family
 attempt a new start and Carolyn wants no more secrets. Doing a good job at
 describing anger and self-hate, this is one of the few adoption stories to
 portray the serious acting-out of a disturbed teen and the unintentional cover-
 up of other family members.

319 Stahl, Hilda. **Teddy Jo and the Missing Family**. Wheaton, IL: Tyndale
 House, 1986. 119pp.
 After the death of their parents, fifteen-year-old Johnny, thirteen-year-old
 Abby and their ten-year-old sister Nan are separated and placed in different
 foster homes awaiting more permanent, but separate placements. The two
 girls find each other and the neighborhood children help look for Johnny and
 pray for his safe return. Thirteen-year-old Teddy Jo Miller, a budding artist,
 draws a picture of Johnny and they spend days secretly looking for him. In the
 meantime, unknown to the searchers, Johnny is living in the country next door
 to the Miller's grandfather who has befriended Johnny and is helping him with

his drinking problem by strengthening his religious faith. The children are brought together and the Miller's grandfather contacts the children's caseworker and arrangements are made to keep them together but, instead of going into another foster home, they will be adopted by Teresa and Stuart Hill, a young foster couple the children have come to know. This is #14 of the **Teddy Jo** series. A short, Christian mystery, this is rather unrealistic, but romantic.

320   Storr, Catherine. **Vicky**. London: Faber, 1981. 152pp. (OCLC 16555481)
When Vicky's birthmother died two days after she was born, Vicky was adopted by her birthmother's hospital roommate who had given birth to a daughter, Chris, the same day Vicky was born. Set in England, both girls are now sixteen and their mother has just died. After her death, Vicky's curiosity about her birthmother is enhanced when her adoptive father shows her the paperwork regarding her adoption as well as a lock of her birthmother's hair and a mysterious photograph of a young man. Vicky, her friend Stephen and Chief Detective Inspector Price help her to find and visit the teacher who had reported her birthmother as missing. The teacher fondly recalls her birth-mother and obviously recognizes the young man in the photograph, but does not disclose his identity. The relationship becomes clear, however, when the teacher's son, Victor, unexpectedly arrives during their visit. Now knowing her father, but making no overtures at this time, Vicky returns to her adoptive father and understands their special relationship. An interesting story of a British search and reunion, as well as of Vicky's relationship with her adoptive family. The character Vicky and her adoptive status first appeared in Storr's **The Chinese Egg** (London: Faber, 1975) in which she, Stephen and Chief Detective Inspector Price are involved in a search for a missing baby.

321   Strang, Celia. **Foster Mary**. New York: McGraw-Hill, 1979. 162pp. (OCLC 4493623)
Fifteen-year-old Bud, the narrator, was taken in by Aunt Foster Mary and Alonzo Meekin, who are also migrant workers. Others in the family include eight-year-old Benny and five-year-old Amiella. With no one providing proper care for him, seven-year-old Lonnie joins the family as well. Foster Mary wants a warm house, regular meals, no more traveling and for her children to become college educated. When Alonzo is named the caretaker of the Ransome's orchard it means they will not have to move as often following the crops. They are provided with a real house that Foster Mary makes very homey. The Meekin children have parts in the school Christmas play and are delighted when the injured Alonzo is able to be out of the hospital to see them perform on Christmas Eve. Bud realizes Foster Mary and Alonzo are like the people in the play; they take the little they have and share with those who have less. On their way home, helpful friends give Amiella a kitten and Bud a puppy, signs of permanence in their new home. A thoughtful story, set in Washington state, of a migrant family and community supporting each other.

322   Summers, James L. **The Iron Doors Between**. Philadelphia: Westminster, 1968. 209pp. (OCLC 471768)

When sixteen-year-old Vic, whose adoptive parents are no longer active in his life, is paroled following an eighteen-month stay in reform school, the Chapmans, an older couple with grown children, take him in as a foster son. With good intentions, the Chapmans attempt to provide Vic with a new chance and Vic becomes friends with good-hearted Raf and Millie Hunter, who come from a good family. Even with these friends, however, Vic is unable to drop his guard and deceptive pretenses, continuing to play off those he cares for and those who care for him. He becomes involved with a bad group and is caught by the police on several occasions. Apprehended for breaking and entering, Vic is released to the care of his foster parents who are at a loss to manage him. When he runs away the first time, the Chapmans take custody of him, but when he runs away again and steals another car, he is put into jail. When the Chapmans and Millie visit Vic, they sadly realize how much happier he is there. This is a disturbing story of a teen without a conscience who is unable to attach or get a hold of his own life.

323   Sykes, Jo. **Trouble Creek**. New York: Holt, Rinehart and Winston, 1963. 217pp. (OCLC 1402602)
After the death of his father and his mother's remarriage, sixteen-year-old Ten Holland is resentful of his new stepfather, Dick. Dick and Ten are hired to help Lantis Brighton find his son, Alvin, who never returned from a mountain hunting expedition last year. Dick and Ten take Lantis and his son, George, a brooding fellow who had also been on the hunting trip with his brother. The four are involved in a series of strange incidents and Ten discovers evidence of a large-scale poaching operation. They find Alvin's glove and knife, as well as several other clues which lead the members to their own suspicions regarding Alvin's fate. When Alvin's gun is found, a frightened, irrational George, who is unable to admit he thinks he killed his brother, appears willing to kill Ten to hide his guilt, but Dick returns and talks him out of it. With George's cooperation, the searchers find Alvin's body and determine George did not kill him, but find the carcass of the elk George really shot while thinking he shot Alvin. The mystery solved, the two pair of fathers and sons go off each with a renewed relationship. While an exciting adventure story complete with wild animals and a Western setting, this is also a story of a boy finding a relationship with his stepfather.

324   Talbert, Marc. **Dead Birds Singing**. Boston: Little, Brown, 1985. 170pp. (OCLC 11676144)
Seventh-grader Matt, whose father died several years ago, is the sole survivor of a drunk-driving accident which killed his mother and only sibling. He is taken in by his best friend's family who plan to adopt him. The story revolves around Matt's coming to terms with the accident and his own loss. It deftly portrays the grief, anger and sadness as Matt works through his emotions. Sometimes acting out his anger, Matt eventually faces this tragedy and finds his peace. A powerful story which pictures the new family as caring and fun as they try to help Matt ease into his new life.

325   Terris, Susan. **Whirling Rainbows**. Garden City, NY: Doubleday, 1974. 153pp. (OCLC 800563)

When her professor-parents travel during the summer, thirteen-year-old Leah Friedman, a half-Polish, half-Native American girl who was adopted as an infant by her Jewish parents, is sent from her California home to a girls' summer camp in Wisconsin to discover her Chippewa roots. Instead, Leah finds herself as a scapegoat and an outcast among the other campers who are unaware of Native American heritage. Leah's cousins who also attend the camp do not provide her solace. Harriet, a cabinmate, rarely speaks and Torie, a junior counselor, uses Leah and makes her the butt of many jokes. Leah feels very isolated, but works hard enough to be chosen as one of the eight campers to go on a four-day canoe trip in the wilds. Even though the other campers think little of Leah, she and Torie are the ones who find a faster way back to the camp when Liz, their staff leader comes down with the flu. Reticent Harriet clears Leah's name with the supervisors and Leah begins to realize the importance of developing the qualities within herself. She reestablishes contact with her parents a more mature person. In this interesting story of finding one's self, Leah is constantly being asked how it feels to be Native American, or Jewish or adopted as if they were separate parts of herself.

326   Trotter, Grace. (Nancy Paschal, pseud.) **Song of the Heart**. Philadelphia: Westminster, 1961. 218pp. (OCLC 4212993)
Twenty-one-year old Lonna, now a music major in her senior year of college, was adopted at age two by the Henderson family. Lonna has always been drawn to her music rather than boys, but is swept off her feet by Stanley, the young lawyer son of the Lowells who host a recital for her. They plan marriage and Lonna plans to tell Stan about her adoption, instead Lonna's younger jealous sister maliciously intervenes and Lonna is confronted on the day of her recital by Stan's mother who thinks too highly of family lineage to allow the engagement to continue. When he learns what happened, Stan reassures her he does not agree with his mother and still wants to marry her, but Lonna is too confused, moves in with a friend and seeks information regarding her birthfamily. The adoption agency provides her with the name of a birthaunt whom Lonna contacts and learns her birthgrandmother was a famous European singer. Embracing those roots, she continues with her summer musical performance. Stan's mother asks for her forgiveness, but Lonna's decision about Stan is made more difficult when a local benefactor proposes to finance a year's study in New York. Stan, however, is prepared to go to New York with her as her husband and the two reconcile. Rather dated with the notion of adoption being an obstacle to marriage, but a good story of sibling jealousy.

327   Viglucci, Pat Costa. **Cassandra Robbins, Esq.** Madison, WI: Square One Publishers, 1987. 176pp. (OCLC 15015740)
The biracial seventeen-year-old girl, in this book which was unavailable for evaluation, was adopted at birth by white parents. Although she realizes now that she is older she has flexible options for dating both black and white boys, she still wonders where she fits in.

328   Voigt, Cynthia. **Homecoming**. New York: Atheneum, 1981. 312pp. (OCLC 6447367)

On their way to see Great-aunt Cilla and perhaps to live with her, the four Tillerman children are abandoned by their mother. Responsible thirteen-year-old Dicey takes charge of brainy fourth grade brother James, slow, shy second-grader Maybeth and rambunctious first-grader Sammy. Not having enough money, they spend many tiring and dangerous days walking to their aunt's in Connecticut to learn she has died. Her daughter takes the children in out of a begrudging sense of duty, but when the children learn about their maternal grandmother, they go to Maryland in hopes of living with her. The children find an old bitter woman who resents the death and leaving of her husband and children and is not capable of making a commitment to the children. The children make themselves useful to the old woman and they suffer a rocky transition time before they realize they need each other. Grandmother softens and becomes responsible, freeing Dicey to resume her own life. Their story continues in **Dicey's Song** (New York: Atheneum, 1982) and **Sons From Afar** (New York: Atheneum, 1987). This is a powerful and emotional story of a spunky young girl and her self-resilient family as they find a place for themselves.

329   Weaver, Stella. **A Poppy in the Corn**. [New York]: Pantheon Books, 1960. 319pp. (OCLC 302728)
Set in England after World War II, this is the story of Teresa, a young French orphan girl whose first adoption, to a foreign correspondent for a British newspaper and his wife, fails and she is sent to live with and be adopted by her adoptive aunt and uncle. When Dr. Clare wins an research award and travels to America, his wife goes along with him, leaving the children in care of the family housekeeper, Tucker whose day excursion lasts weeks due to an accident. The teenage children, unable and somewhat unwilling to find another adult to stay with them, fend for themselves. When their cash runs low, Laurence gets a job as a hired hand and the girls get the meals and run the house and mind young Ben. Laurence and Anna are concerned when they learn Teresa is stealing from a local store and from neighbors. They are unable to confront Teresa, but it affects their relationship with her. Although there are strange happenings, the children find comfort, solace and assistance from the neighbors and Teresa finds a man who knew her birthfather. He confirms both her parents were killed by the Germans and helps Teresa look ahead to her future. While somewhat unrealistic, it does impart the sense of excitement of a survival story. The British title is **Sisters and Brothers** (London: Collins, 1960).

330   Windsor, Patricia. **Mad Martin**. New York: Harper and Row, 1976. 119pp. (OCLC 2331485)
Martin, an odd, solitary little boy, goes into foster care when his grandfather, with whom he lives an nonstimulating life, is hospitalized for an injury. In this large foster family, Martin learns about feelings and new ways of relating and behaving. Although not initially warm to these new ways, Martin begins to assimilate and enjoy himself. Fortunately, his grandfather also re-learns some interpersonal skills and the two of them begin a changed life together. The fascinating story of an emotionally-delayed child who has not learned mainstream manners and feelings parallels the experience of many children adopted at an older age from neglectful situations.

331   Woolfolk, Dorothy. **Mother, Where Are You?** New York: Scholastic, 1977.
      270pp. (OCLC 4227448)
After the death of her adoptive father, college sophomore Janet and her
roommate, Donna Rockford, an amateur detective, pick up some unsettling
clues that someone is out to get Janet. Now that her father is dead, Janet
feels more comfortable about searching for her birthparents as she feels she
cannot marry Dennis, her boyfriend without knowing who she really is. A
worker at the adoption agency surreptitiously provides them with leads which
enables Janet to search for her birthmother. There are several attempts on
the girls' lives as they pursue the search, but Janet is determined to continue.
The girls contact Janet's birthuncle who acts as a mediator between Janet and
her birthmother, Ellen, who warmly welcomes Janet and tells Janet her
birthfather was Donald Johnson, the cousin of Thomas Johnson, a state
legislator and adoption agency board member, making her the sole heir to the
Johnson fortune. When they confront Thomas Johnson, who stands to loose
out as the apparent heir, they realize he has been trying to eliminate Janet's
claim by being on the board of the orphan home and monitoring her
placement and hiring a hit man to kill her. The police take Johnson into
custody and Janet is reinstated as heir. One in the series featuring Donna
Rockford, this is an exciting mystery story which uses adoption as the key.

High School Readers

NONFICTION

332 **Adopting Children With Special Needs**. Patricia J. Kravik, editor. Riverside, CA: North American Council on Adoptable Children, 1976. 72pp. (OCLC 5884968)

A collection of short personal narratives by people involved in the adoption of special needs children, this book provides insight into the joys and the problems of parenting and living with these children. Divided into sections addressing different aspects of special needs adoptions, including a section written by children, the editor has compiled a collage of experiences which realistically describes living with and loving children who are emotionally disturbed, mentally handicapped, physically handicapped, as well as foreign-born, or in sibling groups. The book, which features many black and white photographs, concludes with a bibliography. **Adopting Children With Special Needs: A Sequel**, edited by Linda Dunn (Washington, D.C.: North American Council on Adoptable Children, 1983) is also available.

333 **Adoption Without Fear**. Edited by James L. Gritter. San Antonio, TX: Corona Pub. Co., 1989. 170pp. (OCLC 19355239)

Sixteen couples who have adopted through the same Michigan agency relate their experiences with open adoption. Several couples indicate their initial apprehension concerning the implications of an open adoption, but as they continue their story they describe a warm, positive adoptive experience. In his seven-page introduction, as well as the nine-page afterword, the editor, an adoption supervisor, thoughtfully explains his and his agency's changing perspective on open versus closed adoptions. A short bibliography and information on the Michigan Association for Openness in Adoption (see Appendix B) conclude the book. Interesting reading, this collection of narratives provides a refreshingly personal look at a relatively new form of adoption.

334 Allen, Elizabeth Cooper. **Mother, Can You Hear Me?** New York: Dodd, Mead, 1983. 208pp. (OCLC 9197093)

Cooper, a school psychologist, was adopted by her foster parents when she was fourteen years old. After the death of her adoptive parents, she decides to search for her birthmother. After nearly fifty years, Cooper discovers her birthmother, a deaf mute, living in an institution for the retarded. Cooper slowly forms a new relationship with her and her family. This is a moving story of one adoptee's reconstruction of her past.

335   Anderson, Ann Kiemel. **And With the Gift Came Laughter**. Wheaton, IL: Tyndale House, 1987. 165pp. (OCLC 17330089)
After several miscarriages, when Ann and Will Anderson realize they will not enjoy parenthood through birth, they consider adoption. Ann, a Christian inspirational speaker, is contacted by a pregnant listener who wants the Andersons to adopt her baby. The birthmother spends her last several months living near them and Ann is her Lamaze coach. Following the birth of a baby boy, the birthmother relinquishes rights and the Andersons have a son. Shortly thereafter, they are contacted again with a similar request and later are parents of another son. With a deliberate Christian perspective, the book shares the Andersons' joy and grief as they become parents. Sixteen pages of color photographs are a delightful addition. A revised and expanded edition of this was published by the same publisher in 1990 with the title **Open Adoption: My Story of Love and Laughter**.

336   Anderson, Rachel. **For the Love of Sang**. Oxford: Lion, 1990. (OCLC 21301420)
Although not available for evaluation, the pre-publication information indicates this concerns the transracial adoption of a handicapped child.

337   Anthony, Joseph. **The Rascal and the Pilgrim: The Story of the Boy from Korea**. New York: Farrar, Straus and Cudahy, 1960. 242pp. (OCLC 2199752)
An autobiographical account, this is the story of how self-determination enables a Korean orphan boy to come to the States and seek a new life. "Little Joe," after living in several orphanages, runs away and ingratiates himself to some GIs during the Korean War. Through their helpfulness and that of an American priest who becomes his guardian, "Little Joe" makes it to the U.S. in his early teens. He completes high school, begins college and gets married. This is an exciting story which graphically describes the life of a Korean War orphan and the thoughts and feelings of a child wanting a better life. Eight pages of black and white photographs are an interesting addition to the story.

338   Arms, Suzanne. **Adoption: A Hand Full of Hope**. Berkeley, CA: Celestial Arts, 1989. 436pp. (OCLC 18625398)
The revised edition of **To Love and Let Go** (New York: Knopf, 1983), this book looks at all sides of the adoption issue giving particular attention to the needs and experiences of the birthmother. Arms, having no direct ties to adoption herself, uses intimate stories of birthparents, adoptees and adoptive parents to impart the special nature of the adoption triangle and the advantages of open adoption. Concentrating on birthmothers who have

relinquished their children as newborn infants, Arms provides a serious look at the needs, problems and possibilities of modern adoption.

339   Baker, Josephine, and Jo Bouillon. **Josephine**. Translated from the French by Mariana Fitzpatrick. New York: Harper and Row, 1977. 302pp. (OCLC 3003854)
Following her death in 1975, Bouillon used notes she had written for the purpose and constructed a biography of his wife, Josephine Baker, the illustrious black entertainer. In addition to her remarkable European career and her later success in her native United States, Baker also has twelve adopted children from around the world. Referring to her children as the "Rainbow Tribe," the children, nine boys and two girls, represent a variety of ethnic backgrounds: Korean, Japanese, Norwegian, Venezuelan Indian, Arabian and Colombian, to name a few. As well as describing Baker's career, the book also concentrates on her personal life, including her several marriages and her children. Sixteen pages of black and white photographs enhance the life story of this exotic celebrity. A later biography is Phyllis Rose's **Jazz Cleopatra: Josephine Baker in her Time** (New York: Doubleday, 1989) which features thirty-two pages of illustrations.

340   Bain, Barnard E. **My One Hundred Children**. New York: Simon, 1954. 210pp. (OCLC 1671965)
Bain, the administrator of a children's home, describes the lifestyle and children, ages four through eighteen, of the orphanage. He provides some history on the Presbyterian Home in Lynchburg, Virginia, then continues by relating episodes and stories about the children beginning with the little girls, then the little boys, continuing with the teen girls and boys, then on to highlight specific aspects of the program. While adoption is mentioned and is always a consideration for available children, the focus of the book is on the life, education and moral training of the children while in the care of the home. Although dated, this is a good description of a children's home in the mid-1950s. There are also some timeless insights into the nature of foster children, as well as children in general.

341   Barley, Ann L. **Patrick Calls Me Mother**. New York: Harper, 1948. 227pp. (OCLC 494876)
Moved by the plight of war orphans after World War II, Barley, a single woman, travels to Europe to find a child to adopt. She spends several months in Holland, Belgium and France where she finds nine-month-old Patrick. The story relates, often humorously, her experiences as she locates a child, processes the paperwork to allow Patrick to exit France and be admitted to the U.S., as well as the joys and complications of motherhood at home. This is a unique story as there were very few single adoptive mothers in the mid-1940s. The story is light and humorous as it describes the activities of this naive, but well-intentioned mom.

342   Becker, John T., and Stanli K. Becker. **All Blood is Red--All Shadows are Dark**. Cleveland, OH: Seven Shadows Press, 1984. 153pp. (OCLC 12557017)

This is a collection of essays contributed by the Becker family on the subject of race and racial identity. Although most of the entries are written by Stanli or Tom (John) Becker, an interracial couple, there are others written by their oldest child, a birthdaughter, and their four adopted children, who represent various shades of skin color. The essays, which vary in length, describe episodes and attitudes relating to the importance of color as opposed to the importance of culture. One overriding issue concerns how to fill out government forms that ask for racial group. The Beckers claim they belong to the human race and some of their children are bothered there is no correct box for them to fill out. If they choose black, they are denying their white heritage, or vice versa should they choose white. Many examples of daily living situations are provided in which the Beckers' interracial lifestyle causes others to behave in a stereotypical fashion, for example, when a white woman tells one of the older black-looking Becker children to stay away from the white baby in the shopping cart, when the baby is a younger white-looking Becker child. The essays provide much thoughtful insight, as well as a challenge to how we perceive and deal with racial beliefs.

343   Begley, Vincent J. **Missing Links: The True Story of an Adoptee's Search for His Birth Parents**. Chevy Chase, MD: Claycomb Press, 1989. 202pp. (OCLC 20547605)
In his thirties, Begley was able, over a period of time, to find his birthmother's sister. Through his newly found Aunt Joan, Begley learns much about his birthmother, her family and eventually meets her. Their relationship takes root and she remains a strong part of Begley's family. The birthfamily is oddly reticent about Begley's birthfather and he later learns his father was a Catholic priest, who is now deceased. His attempts to meet his birthfather's family are met with patent denial. Providing a perceptive and sensitive approach, Begley portrays the journey of his search and reunion, as well as his worry and concerns about adoption.

344   Bell, Harry. **We Adopted a Daughter**. Decorations by Katharine Bernard. Boston: Houghton Mifflin, 1954. 181pp. (OCLC 1555158)
This light-hearted story describes the adoption and first years of two-year-old Barbara, the only child of her new parents. Describing her adjustments, developments and antics, Barbara's father, the author and narrator, tells a warm story of the family's life through sickness, celebrations and a family move across the country. The chapter opening illustrations are simple, but charming.

345   Berman, Claire. **We Take This Child**. Garden City, NY: Doubleday, 1974. 203pp. (OCLC 858244)
Examining different types of adoption, Berman presents separate chapters, each providing a case study approach. Following a general introduction, the author proceeds with the classic tale of a couple approaching an agency for a healthy white baby. Considering options, Berman continues by taking close-up looks at transracial adoption, the adoption of older children, adopting a handicapped child, single-parent adoption, adopting a foster child, intercountry adoption and independent adoption. She also provides a chapter describing a failed adoption. Concluding the book is a bibliography and a list of

organizations concerned with adoption. While somewhat outdated, much of the information is still accurate and presents a look at several different adoptive situations in one volume.

346   Bilow, Pat. **And Now We Are Four.** Plainfield, NJ: Haven Books, 1980. 163pp. (OCLC 7279391)
Having long provided week-end respite care for local foster children, the Bilow family, which includes two birthsons, decides to become a full-time foster family in the hopes of possibly adopting a child or two. Their placements include a seven-year-old girl named Jenny and later her six-year-old sister, Ann, part of a sibling group of five sisters, who thrive with the Bilow family. The adoption plans never materialize as the girls' birthmother regains custody. A later placement is a fourteen-year-old boy, Casey, who has more severe problems than the family can handle. After several episodes of running away, getting into trouble and finally trashing their home, alternate arrangements are made for Casey. The author provides a realistic insight to the day-to-day behavior of foster children who did not have a good start in life. It imparts much information, with a Christian perspective, on foster parenting.

347   Blank, Joseph P. **Nineteen Steps up the Mountain.** Philadelphia: Lippincott, 1976. 234pp. (OCLC 2331612)
Blank provides an inside view of the remarkable DeBolt family and their nineteen children, thirteen of whom are adopted and have varying physical disabilities. The adopted children include three Korean-Caucasian children, one whom is polio paralyzed, five Vietnamese, one full Korean child who had been blind, one black congenital quadruple amputee from the United States and one white child from the States who is spina bifida paraplegic and blind. A major part of the story is devoted to watching this child acclimate to the family and new environment. Intent on making their children functionally competitive within the real world, Bob and Dorothy DeBolt champion their children to achieve their potential, far beyond usual expectations. Black and white photographs are peppered throughout the book as individual stories of the children unfold. The descriptions of large family life are intriguing and depicted with a good balance between joy and despair. Especially noteworthy is the painful honesty regarding a near-disruption of a child who failed to attach to the family.

348   Booth, Nyla, and Ann Scott. **Room For One More.** Wheaton, IL: Living Books, 1984. 209pp. (OCLC 12668946)
This is the story of the Ann and Phil Scott family and the adoptions of fifteen children after the arrival of two birthchildren. Told with a Christian perspective, the book unfolds the story of how the children come into the family. Always willing to do God's will, the Scotts take children with problems and handicaps from all over the world and help them become family. The story tells of the family's joy for their successes, as well as their anguish and struggles during difficult times. While prayer healed some of their children, they also describe the pain of an adoption disruption. Ann Scott is associated with PLAN (Plan Loving Adoptions Now) in McMinnville, Oregon. The fourteen pages of black and white photographs are an added bonus.

349   Braithwaite, E. R. **Paid Servant**. New York: McGraw-Hill, 1962. 219pp.
        (OCLC 263346)
        Written by the author of **To Sir With Love**, this is the autobiographical
        account of his activities as a child welfare officer in England after he left
        teaching. Set in the late 1950s, Braithwaite, a West Indian, is hired to help
        with the foster or adoptive placement of children of color. Braithwaite
        attempts to find good caring homes for the children, regardless of the colors
        involved. Finding a home for four-year-old Roddy, who is half-white and half-
        Mexican, is difficult as Braithwaite's first choice of prospective parents decide
        the child is not black enough. His second choice of parents, who are excited
        to have Roddy, is turned down by his supervisors because they are Jewish.
        Through Braithwaite's diligence, Roddy finds a loving permanent foster home
        and other families find new ways to manage with their families. This is a
        fascinating look at adoption from the perspective of the caseworker.
        Braithwaite does a fine job of exploring the prejudice within the system and
        the balance of caring in such a job.

350   Brown, Christine. **Goodbye Patrick**. London: Arlington Books, 1973. 186pp.
        (OCLC 714870)
        After determining through preliminary testing that, although they have not yet
        conceived a child, they are not infertile, the Browns, both journalists, decide
        to adopt a child. Set in Scotland, the Browns approach a Catholic adoption
        agency, are approved for a child and within a year are given their first child,
        Michael, at seven days old. Overjoyed as typical new adoptive parents, the
        Browns adopt four more children, two boys and two girls, each of whom arrive
        as an infant or a toddler. Prior to their last adoption, the Browns move to the
        London area where they adopt their fifth child, a daughter, Kim who is half-
        Indian and half-Chinese, when Michael, the oldest child, is five years old. The
        story honestly and humorously relates the antics involved in the adoption and
        adjustment of this fast-growing young family.

351   Buchwald, Ann. **Seems Like Yesterday**. New York: Putnam: 1980. 220pp.
        (OCLC 5799684)
        Buchwald relates how in 1949 she moved to Paris, obtained a job as a publicity
        director with a French designer and met her future husband, the humorist Art
        Buchwald. She relates their unusual engagement, made more interesting by
        her Catholicism and his Judaism and their marriage in 1952. After learning
        they were not able to conceive, Art suggests adoption. When French doctors
        tell them they are ineligible to adopt a French child, they adopt sixteen-month-
        old Joel in 1954 from Ireland. Later, they travel to Spain where they adopt
        Connie, at almost two years old. A few weeks later their French doctor
        provides them with the opportunity to adopt a French baby. Two months later
        they welcome newborn, Jennifer. Within nineteen months the Buchwalds
        adopt three children whose ages are eighteen months apart. Having given up
        her job, Buchwald recalls adjusting to parenthood in one of Europe's most
        exciting cities, with her itinerant columnist husband. Full of name-dropping,
        this is a delightful book, which includes an on-going humorous commentary by
        Art Buchwald.

352   Cady, Frank. **We Adopted Three**. New York: Sloan, 1952. 250pp. (OCLC 1024318)
After complications from the birth of their son, Jeff, Frank and Betsy Cady learn they will not be able to have more biological children. They turn to adoption and, after a lengthy time, when Jeff is ten, receive two-year-old Jane. Seven years later the Cadys adopt again, this time receiving Susie at one day old and, less than a year later, three-day-old Sherry. The book accounts the adoptions processes, the children's antics and the family's activities and ideas all told from the proud father's point of view. While the attitudes regarding adoption have changed since the 1950s, this is an often humorous detailed description of typical adoptions of the time. Another similar, father-told story is Bell's **We Adopted a Daughter** (344).

353   Caplan, Lincoln. **An Open Adoption**. New York: Farrar, Straus and Giroux, 1990. 150pp. (OCLC 20754375)
Caplan presents a parallel commentary on the open adoption between birthmother, Peggy Bass, and adoptive parents, Lee and Dan Stone, as well as on the history of adoption in the United States, concentrating primarily on the recent unconventional open adoptions. Caplan follows Peggy, a college junior, and the baby's father, her boyfriend, Tom, from the time she finds out she is pregnant to well after the finalization of the baby's adoption by the Stones. Capturing the full range of emotions and activities of all parties involved and presenting objective information as well, Caplan reveals the debate within society over open adoptions. Concluding with a list of sources of information on adoption, this book, most of which originally appeared in the **New Yorker**, provides an insight into the questions faced by those involved in open adoptions.

354   Carney, Ann. **No More Here and There**. Chapel Hill, NC: University of North Carolina Press, 1976. 88pp. (OCLC 2072779)
Alternating between diary-like accounts of the adoption and adjustment of five-year-old Jake and informative passages regarding adopting an older child, this book provides a humorous, yet realistic and practical account of adopting a child over the age of two years old. The book presents a profile of a specific child then takes the reader through the pre-placement process, the actual placement, the honeymoon and reality phases. Sharing feelings as well as information, Carney imparts special advice on such topics as sibling rivalry, the outside world and pays particular attention to such special problems as running away, sex, the child's past, effects on the marriage and babysitters. Concluding with the little concrete signs of a child and family eventually investing in one another, Carney presents a valid look at how a child grows into a family.

355   Cherne, Jacqolyn. **This Encircling Chain**. Photographs by John Cherne. Maple Grove, MN: Mini-World Publications, 1985. 45pp. (OCLC 12806172)
Unable to obtain for evaluation, this is a book of poetry by an adoptive mother.

356   Chinnock, Frank W. **Kim: A Gift From Vietnam**. New York: World Publishing Co., 1969. 211pp. (OCLC 24695)

This book relates Chinnock's travels to Vietnam in 1966, despite discourage-ment from adoption workers and Immigration and Naturalization Service officials, to locate a child he and his wife can adopt. The author describes Kim's arrival, nearly two years later at about four years of age, and goes on to recount her first year in the Chinnock family. Sixteen pages of black and white photographs enhance the story. This is a very readable account of the search for a child and the family's rocky adjustment after Kim's arrival. Watching Kim's relationships with her brothers and parents, it is heartening to see her growing confidence.

357   **Chosen Children**. Compiled by Muriel B. Dennis. Westchester, IL: Good
          News Publishing, 1978. 150pp. (OCLC 4619522)
      Written by adoptive family members, this collection of essays recounts the joy, as well as the pain, in adopting children who are different and provides a Christian insight into adoption. Using heartwarming anecdotes, most essays feature a specific family's experiences with special needs adoption each citing their faith as the motivation to adopt and the strength to continue. Eight pages of black and white photographs featuring the families help bring them to life. The prologue features an essay on the Christian meaning of adoption and the final section of the book outlines the adoption process. Although essayists consistently use the terms "natural" parents and "children of their own," readers looking for a Christian perspective on special needs adoption will find this informative and comforting. Carolyn Nystrom, the mother of one of the featured adoptive families, wrote several prayers and thoughts on her experiences as a foster parent who eventually adopted some of her foster children in **Forgive Me If I'm Frayed Around the Edges** (Chicago: Moody Press, 1977).

358   Connor, Grace. **Don't Disturb Daddy!** Illus. by the author. Boston: Branden
          Press, 1965. 178pp. (OCLC 1073117)
      This story describes the antics of a childless couple living with the husband's father, as they adopt eight-year-old Ruthie, her nine-year-old brother and later their three-year-old sister. The father is usually a staid, removed, scientific type, while the mother is lively, imaginative and more involved with the children on a daily basis. The manipulative children soon determine the relationship between their parents and proceed to find ways of obtaining their objectives. While attempting to be humorous, this story is disturbing because of the lack of communication and cooperation between the parents. The father's behavior is often adolescent and the mother spends a good deal of energy trying to work around him.

359   Crawford, Christina. **Mommie Dearest**. New York: William Morrow, 1978.
          286pp. (OCLC 4114625)
      Crawford relates the disturbing account of her life as the oldest adopted daughter of single parent Joan Crawford. She reveals an alcoholic, abusive home life while maintaining a positive public image for her mother's career. Christina relates always wanting approval from her mother who was not able to give it. Instead, Christina lived under her mother's iron rule often suffering physical, as well as psychological consequences. Often left at schools for holidays and summers, Christina grew up wondering what she had done wrong

and in her teens began slowly to rebel. After leaving college, she gained more independence and in the later years of her mother's life, they obtained a semblance of a relationship. Joan Crawford died, however, leaving nothing in her will for Christina or her brother. Twenty-four pages of black and white photographs enhance the story. Receiving much play in the media, this is a grueling, graphic description of a tragic life. For another bitter celebrity adoption see Reagan's **On the Outside Looking In** (404).

360   Dahl, Judy. **River of Promise**. San Diego, CA: LuraMedia, 1989. 77pp. (OCLC 18833044)
Dahl, an ordained minister, describes the process, painful and joyful, of the adoption of two children as part of a lesbian couple. Dahl recounts her background and that of her lover, Terryl, describing the basis for their relationship and their desire to have a child. After trying donor insemination, the two eventually locate an adoption agency willing to work with them as two single parents. Their first adoption, an open adoption which places infant Noah with them, is disrupted when the birthmother changes her mind. After several other adoption possibilities fall through and other tries with donor insemination are unsuccessful, the two discover a willing international agency and are soon awaiting the arrival of a foreign-born infant girl. Prior to her arrival, the author learns of another domestic adoption possibility so they plan another addition to their family. Although the process takes many years, within in short period of time they each adopt a child. Interweaving the biblical story of Noah and many conversations with Dahl's god-figure, Gracie, this story presents the unusual adoption story of two committed women. Although with definite religious overtones, this is a rare account of a homosexual adoption.

361   Dorris, Michael. **The Broken Cord**. New York: Harper and Row, 1989. 300pp. (OCLC 19518477)
Adopted by Dorris in 1971 as a single parent, Adam, a three-year-old Native American child whose mother died of alcohol poisoning, is significantly developmentally delayed. Undaunted, Dorris, himself part Native American, determinedly sets out to teach Adam what he needs to know. Dorris eventually finds a school for Adam, but his learning problems causes tension both at home and at school. When Adam is six, Dorris adopts another Native American child, two-year-old Sava, and becomes more acutely aware of Adam's delayed development. While on a business trip to a reservation, Dorris sees some young boys who remind him of Adam and is told that they suffer from fetal alcohol syndrome (FAS). The book, a result of Dorris' research on his son's affliction, is a combination of personal narrative and readable, factual data on the medical condition caused by a drinking pregnant mother. The final chapter is Adam's own story, at age twenty-one, in his own words. Dorris shares a father's hopes, dreams and anguish eloquently. This, the first book on FAS for the general public, is a winner of the 1990 National Book Critics Circle Award.

362   Doss, Helen Grigsby. **The Family Nobody Wanted**. Boston: Little Brown, 1954. 267pp. (OCLC 670005)

Set in the 1940s and early 1950s, this is the story of a childless couple who want a child. Much to the husband's chagrin, the "one child" eventually becomes a houseful of children over the years as they adopt twelve "unadoptable", usually mixed-race, children. While somewhat dated and Pollyanna-ish, Doss relates the ups and downs of her family's additions and adjustments in a folksy, humorous, down-to-earth manner. Other versions of the Doss family story include **The Really Real Family** (105) and **A Brother the Size of Me** (155), both for younger readers.

363   Duling, Gretchen A. **Adopting Joe: A Black Vietnamese Child**. Rutland, VT: C. E. Tuttle Co., 1977. 98pp. (OCLC 3051733)
Reprinting letters and recounting anecdotes, this book describes the adoption of two-year-old Joe from Vietnam. It details Joe's introduction and acceptance into the Duling family which already had one adopted child from the States. It tells of Joe's arrival, his fear of thunderstorms, his first trip to the shoe store and most important, his gradual trust in his new family. The book concludes with an epilogue, a Prayer for the Children of Vietnam prepared by Father Robert Drinan, a medical guide for parents of Vietnam-born children, Vietnamese recipes and a lengthy bibliography. While a conglomeration of material, this is a fascinating little book that shares the realities of the first year of a foreign adoption. For a similar story see Eitz's **Dark Rice** (365).

364   Dusky, Lorraine. **Birthmark**. New York: M. Evans, 1979. 191pp. (OCLC 5126195)
Chronicling her childhood, education and professional career, Dusky, a reporter, relates the story of her relationship with a married man and the pregnancy she faced virtually alone. She gives birth to a baby girl in April of 1966 and reluctantly gives the child up for adoption. During the years after the baby's birth, Dusky becomes involved in adoption issues both on a personal and professional level. She begins to write about adoption and the plight of the birthmother, joins forces with Florence Fisher's group, Adoptees Liberty Movement Association (ALMA) (see Appendix B), works to change the laws regarding sealed records and follows many false leads to her birthchild. Continuing to write to her daughter via the agency which will hold the letters until the girl contacts them, Dusky wants her to know of her love and concern for her and that she would like to be some part of her life, but not take the place of her adoptive parents. Dusky shares a painful story in which the fears, dreams and hopes of a birthmother provide an often overlooked perspective on the adoption experience.

365   Eitz, Maria. **Dark Rice**. Illus. by Fred. L. Weinman. Waukesha, WI: Country Beautiful, 1975. 120pp. (OCLC 2090789)
The author, a single woman, herself an orphan from Germany, recounts her adoption of Jonathan, a two-year-old black-Vietnamese child. The story begins when the author first sees his picture and begins the process of bringing him to the States. The bulk of the book tells of his adjustment to his new life, trusting his new mother and learning about his new world, as well as the author learning to be a mother to her new little son. Relating anecdotes, the story dwells on their first years together and then planning for the adoption of Nicholas, a new little brother from Vietnam. The book begins with a sensitive,

heartfelt five-page letter to Jonathan's unknown American birthfather. Beautifully told, with one or two black and white illustrations per chapter, this story is a caring, sensitive portrayal of a foreign adoption. Compare this with Duling's **Adopting Joe** (363).

366   Fisher, Florence. **The Search for Anna Fisher**. New York: Arthur Fields, 1973. 270pp. (OCLC 654419)

Hailed as an important milestone in the adoption literature, this was the first widely-published story of an adoptee's search for her birthparents. Fisher, who eventually founded the Adoptees' Liberty Movement Association (ALMA), examines her erratic childhood and her adoption which she accidentally discovered. She continues by recounting her twenty-year search for her birthparents without benefit of legal assistance. Although her birthmother was not willing to allow Fisher into her present life, Fisher's birthfather and his family were genuinely accepting. Fisher relates the frustration and discouragement involved in tracking records to fulfill the need to know who she is.

367   Gay, Kathlyn. **The Rainbow Effect: Interracial Families**. New York: Franklin Watts, 1987. 141pp. (OCLC 14412982)

Looking at the special problems and joys of interracial families, Gay presents the view that such families, whether birth or adoptive, have much to offer the American way of life. Divided into chapters that look at such aspects as identity, dating, name-calling and prejudice, divorce and remarriage and support groups, there is also a separate section on transracial adoption. Based on interviews with interracial families, as well as research on the subject, Gay presents a well-rounded, objective view. Black and white photographs of interracial families and the words of the family members themselves give this book a very real quality. The book concludes with an index. Transracial adoption is portrayed in a positive light, with problems and limitations clearly identified. The support groups discussed in the final chapter will be quite useful.

368   Gediman, Judith S., and Linda P. Brown. **Birthbond: Reunions Between Birthparents and Adoptees--What Happens After**. Far Hills, NJ: New Horizons Press, 1989. 285pp. (OCLC 20619262)

Using personal narratives from hundreds of interviews with reunited birthparents and children, the authors have constructed patterns in the post-reunion process disclosing the commonalities of feelings, issues and behaviors among those who have chosen to be reunited. Gediman and Brown look at the history of adoption and reunion, as well as the facts and figures of adoption. They continue by examining the motivation for reunions and what happens once contact is made. They provide separate chapters for dealing with birthfathers, siblings, adoptive parents and a birthmothers network. Following the text are notes, a bibliography and a list of adoption, reunion and post-reunion resources. While there are many titles dealing with various aspects of search and reunion, this is a significant book as it explores a new area, the post-reunion experience.

369   Giddens, Lynn. **Eternal Inspirations**. Chapel Hill, NC: Amberly Publications, 1983. 118pp. (OCLC 11299638)

Giddens, adopted in 1952, recounts her family's background and life with a troubled adopted sibling. She covers the medical and emotional problems of her older adoptive brother from the time he was adopted as a possible terminal case, to his rebellious, drug-addicted adolescence and death. For medical reasons, as well for personal reasons, as a young adult Giddens sets out to locate her birthparents. After a search that took one and a half years, Giddens locates her birthmother, and although her birthfather is dead, she is welcomed by other family members. Giddens also locates some of her adoptive brother's birthfamily to let them know of his life and death. Although seemingly over-dramatic at times, this book presents both a tragic story of one young man's life, as well as the story of young woman's reclamation of her origins. In a companion volume which covers more general factual information on adoption, the author, under the name of E. Lynn Giddens, has written **Faces of Adoption** (Chapel Hill, NC: Amberly Publications, 1983).

370   Holt, Bertha, as told to David Wisner. **The Seed From the East.** Los Angeles: Printed by Oxford Press, 1956. 254pp. (OCLC 2564507)
Focusing primarily on the year 1955, this story provides a first-hand account of the family and activities which ultimately formed the Holt Adoption Program. After hearing about the plight of orphaned children in Korea, Bertha and Harry Holt and their six birthchildren decide to help by sponsoring several Korean orphans. Wanting to do more, Harry Holt travels to Korea to adopt eight mixed-race Korean children, all under the age of four. The book details the activities at home as well as in Korea as the family encounters difficulties in bringing the children to the States. The book continues by relating stories of family life at the Holt's after the addition of the eight children. Black and white photographs are a delightful addition to the book. A brief summary of what happened during the next fifteen years can be found in Bertha Holt's **Outstretched Arms** (Eugene, OR: The author, 1972). Both books emphasize the Christian basis for the family's actions.

371   Hulse, Jerry. **Jody.** New York: McGraw-Hill, 1976. 146pp. (OCLC 2213389)
When she is diagnosed with a grave illness, Jody needs to locate her birthparents for medical reasons, as well as for a sense of herself. Because she is hospitalized, her journalist husband takes on the search which needs to be completed in the eight days prior to her life-threatening surgery. Both the search and surgery are successful and Jody eventually establishes a relationship with her birthmother and twin birthbrother. The plot turns appear quick and uncomplicated, but the story also gives an insight into the feelings of other birthfamily members.

372   Hyde, Robert. **Six More At Sixty.** Garden City, NY: Doubleday, 1960. 190pp. (OCLC 1314901)
After raising their seven birthchildren, Hyde feels the urge once again to become an active parent. While his wife is not in total agreement initially, they both fall in love with and want to adopt the six Rodriguez children, Mexican Indian migrant children ranging in age from three to twelve years old. The four girls and two boys join the Hydes as a permanent foster placement and the book recounts their first year and a half as a family. With a unique

brand of humor, Hyde relates the adjustment, education and transformation of the children. The oldest child, Martha, so long accustomed to being in control as the parent-figure, has much difficulty finding her place in the family that she acts out her anger in unacceptable ways. She is temporarily put back in the juvenile facility where she runs away to Mexico and is unable to return to the U.S. This is a refreshing account of a large sibling group placement with pleasant, as well as unpleasant aspects of foster/adoptive parenting. Eight pages of black and white photographs enhance the story.

373   Ireland, Jill. **Life Lines**. New York: Warner Books, 1989. 358pp. (OCLC 18589631)
In this autobiographical account, Ireland relates the break-up of her marriage to David McCallum and her successful marriage to Charles Bronson. Ireland's two birth sons, Paul and Valentine and her adopted son, Jason, also became part of the growing Bronson household. Jason, adopted at birth, was a troubled child, but the extent of his problems did not surface until shortly after Ireland's dealings with cancer and her mastectomy when they learned twenty-two-year-old Jason was a heroin addict and suffered from hepatitis B. In parallel stories, Ireland reveals her father's struggle to live after a series of strokes and intermittently chronicles the life of Jason's birthmother whom she eventually meets. Ireland and Bronson try to help Jason through his recovery and relapses, and his birthmother tries as well, but through the end of the book he remains an alcoholic and addict. This is a frank, yet touching account of a woman simultaneously in the roles of mother and daughter unable to rescue those she loves.

374   Johnson, Jean McCraig. **Thoughts on Adoption**. Greensboro, NC: The Children's Home Society of North Carolina, 1978. 51pp. (OCLC 6675374)
These short entries provide thoughts by, to, or about those involved in adoption, grouped by topics such as biological relatives, foster families, adoptive families, other concerned adults, adult adoptees and thoughts in later years. The book presents short, no more than one page each, selections such as thoughts for an unmarried mother, for biological grandparents, for foster parents, for couples seeking to adopt, for the adoption caseworker, and thoughts of an unmarried mother, of a single person wanting to adopt, of an adoptee, of adoptive grandparents, of parents who adopted older children. It concludes with letters from and to biological parents. While championing for better access to more information, but not open adoption, the author presents myriad perspectives on the adoption experience.

375   Johnson, Joyce. **What Lisa Knew: The Truth and Lies of the Steinberg Case**. New York: Putnam, 1990. 302pp. (OCLC 20759498)
Recounting the events that led up to the death of six-year-old Lisa Steinberg in November 1987 and the subsequent court case which convicted Joel Steinberg, her adoptive father, Johnson recreates the dysfunctional and abusive Steinberg household which also included battered Hedda Nussbaum and unkempt baby Mitchell. Lisa, as well as Mitchell, was illegally adopted by Steinberg, a lawyer and Nussbaum, a former book editor, when they failed to file adoption petitions following the independent adoption placement of the

children. Johnson also focuses on the court case and the jury deliberations which eventually found Steinberg guilty of manslaughter in the first degree. Early in the proceedings, Nussbaum, herself apparently a victim of Steinberg's abuse, was cleared of charges and appeared as a witness for the prosecution. Although Johnson is not sympathetic with Nussbaum, she presents a chilling story of a tragic situation involving inappropriate adoption activities. For an account by Lisa Steinberg's birthmother read Michele Launders' **I Wish You Didn't Know My Name: The Story of Michele Launders and Her Daughter Lisa** (New York: Warner Books, 1990). Launders' book has also been published as **Don't Call Her Lisa** (New York: Warner Books, 1991).

376   Koons, Carolyn A. **Tony: Our Journey Together**. San Francisco: Harper and
      Row, 1984. 214pp. (OCLC 10322821)
During a week's missionary work in Mexico, Koons visits a prison where she meets nine-year-old Antonio who is left there after his mother abandoned him four years earlier under suspicious circumstances. Koons, a single woman, takes it upon herself to find more appropriate living arrangements for the boy; two years later she find herself adopting and bringing Antonio to the States. The book details her frustration in dealing with the Mexican legal system to free Antonio from prison, as well as the confusing process to allow him to immigrate. The heart-rending story of a difficult adjustment continues as Koons learns to be a mother and Antonio, now called Tony, works through past issues and tries to unlearn past aggressive behavior and uncooperative attitudes and become a son. The eight pages of black and white photographs enhance the often painful story.

377   Kornheiser, Tony. **The Baby Chase**. New York: Atheneum, 1983. 212pp.
      (OCLC 9646013)
After fighting infertility for nine years in their childless marriage, Kornheiser, a journalist, and his wife, Karril, are desperate enough to be caught up in a black market adoption after the prognosis for a successful adoption of a white infant is so negative. When they receive a call to participate in an independent adoption, described as "gray market," the Kornheisers are in a quandary. As much as they want a baby, they balk at the required $15,000 in cash and other hints that point to immorality and illegality. The couple is on an emotional roller coaster the next several weeks as they struggle with their emotions, as well as their rationality. They eventually decide not to go through with this particular adoption, but look forward to another adoption with a better sense of themselves. Often humorous and sarcastic, this is an intense, painful account of one couple's response to their infertility. International adoption is presented as a negative option.

378   Leitch, David. **Family Secrets: A Writer's Search for His Parents and His
      Past**. New York: Delacorte Press, 1984. 242pp. (OCLC 12809939)
Family Secrets tells the story of Leitch's relationship with Truda, his birthmother who contacted him after he mentioned her in his book **God Stand Up for Bastards** (London: Deutsch, 1973). First through letters, then phone calls and finally in person, Leitch begins to fill in the gaps of his past. At the birth of Leitch's son, he learns more about his birthmother's feelings about having him adopted. As Leitch's marriage dissolves, he continues with his

work and his relationship with Truda. One day, he receives a call from Margaret, his birthsister who was unaware of his existence, who informs him of Truda's death. Leitch and Margaret establish their relationship and after the funeral continue as friends. Margaret's story of her life and recollections are presented with a disturbing notion there may be yet another sibling. Continuing to go through Truda's belongings and talking to older friends reveal there is a younger sister, Linda Elizabeth, who was born when Margaret was eight and was likewise adopted. The book ends with the hope the three siblings will someday be reunited. Reading much like a detective story, this is a provocative story of secrecy, deception and one man's quest for the truth.

379   Lifton, Betty Jean. **Lost and Found: The Adoption Experience**. New York: Dial Press, 1979. 303pp. (OCLC 4494635)
Championing the right for adoptees to know their birth origins, Lifton presents an impassioned plea for openness. In the first section of the book, Lifton covers such topics as the adoption game in which everyone pretends the adoptee never had a life before the current adoptive home, the notion of adoptee as survivor and as a double personality, the "chosen baby" myth and the adoptee as an adolescent and as an adult. In the second part, Lifton provides information on the search for birthparents centering on such ideas as the decision to search, who searches, the usual stages of a search, the varieties of reunion experiences and what happens after contact is finally made. In part three, Lifton discusses such topics as telling adoptive parents about a search for birthparents, telling a child about his adoption, the notion of adoptive parents being "chosen" and the role of both birthmothers and adoptive parents. The book concludes with a list of rights and responsibilities for each member of the adoption triad, a directory of adoption search groups and an index. Lifton's hostile attitude in the beginning of the book subsides as the book ends.

380   Lifton, Betty Jean. **Twice Born: Memoirs of an Adopted Daughter**. New York: McGraw-Hill, 1975. 281pp. (OCLC 1288446)
Adopted during the 1930s, Lifton, a journalist, playwright and author, chronicles her search for her birthparents some thirty years later. Although Lifton finds her birthmother and engages in a long secretive and sporadic relationship with her, she discovers her birthfather has died. Filled with literary, historical and psychological allusions and quotations, this title, one of the first widely-published search accounts, was originally published for adults, however, it has found its way into many young adult library collections. Although depressing and somewhat melodramatic at times, Lifton provides a thought-provoking look into adoption and searching.

381   Lindeman, Bard. **The Twins Who Found Each Other**. New York: William Morrow, 1969. 288pp. (OCLC 31486)
Lindeman relates the story of Roger and Tony, identical twins, who are separated at birth and raised in different parts of the country in very different circumstances. As the boys grow older, they are occasionally questioned if they are the other person. Both boys know they are a twin, but they do not know each other's name or location until Roger is confronted with specific identifying information about his brother Tony and at age twenty-four, the two

brothers meet. The two live in close contact, sharing many similarities and, when they marry, a year apart, they are still inseparable, even living on the same street. The book begins with an introduction by a twin expert and a lengthy section in which the author discusses twin research. The last chapter consists of strikingly similar testing results for the twins and an unsuccessful effort by the author to have their birthmother meet with Roger and Tony. A fascinating book which meticulously describes Tony and Roger's similarities despite the circumstances surrounding their upbringing.

382   Lindsay, Jeanne Warren. **Open Adoption: A Caring Option**. Buena Park, CA: Morning Glory Press, 1987. 254pp. (OCLC 14188156)
Asserting that open adoption, which provides a degree of openness between birthparents and adoptive parents, is the best model to serve the needs of all members of the adoption triad, Lindsay provides readers with an inside view of the processes, the problems and the feelings associated with this relatively new approach to adoption. Lindsay effectively combines personal accounts with a smooth informative narrative which presents a warm and readable introduction to an alternative to the traditional closed adoption process. An annotated bibliography and an index conclude the book. This is a particularly helpful book that may alleviate fears as many agencies are now engaging in open adoptions.

383   Lindsay, Jeanne Warren. **Pregnant Too Soon: Adoption is an Option**. Illus. by Pam Patterson Morford. Buena Park, CA: Morning Glory Press, 1980. 204pp. (OCLC 6422370)
Calling upon her experience as a teacher in a teen pregnancy program, Lindsay shares the stories of several teens who found themselves involved in an early pregnancy. Often using the teens' own words, the book explores different aspects of parenting and adoption, always mindful that regardless of the age of the child, adoption remains an option for young parents who are unable to care for their children. Perspectives of adoptees and adoptive parents are also given. Lindsay does a fine job of combining factual information with empathetic personal accounts. Not only a good selection for pregnant teens, but also for teens who have pregnant friends or who are curious about how birthmothers may feel.

384   Lund, Doris Herold. **Patchwork Clan**. Boston: Little, Brown, 1982. 238pp. (OCLC 7999155)
Lund draws an intimate picture of family life in the Sweeney household as the family grows to include seventeen children, eight of whom are adopted from around the world. The children include four from Vietnam, seven birth-children, four black children and a blind Colombian Indian child. The book is arranged in three major sections each representing a block of time from 1975 to 1980. Peppered with black and white family photographs, the story chronicles the lives of several of the adopted children, particularly the Vietnamese children, and blends them into the family. The Sweeneys' story, while thoughtful and often humorous, remains honest and realistic, facing straight on the pain and anguish that often accompany adoptive families' adjustments.

385   McMillon, Doris. **Mixed Blessing.** New York: St. Martin's Press, 1985.
       247pp. (OCLC 12107654)
       McMillon, a mixed-race child born in Germany in 1951 who was adopted as
       an infant by a U.S. couple, details her life with her erratic and abusive
       adoptive mother. Feeling rejected by both her mothers, McMillon fabricates
       a glorified birthmother fantasy and eventually escapes her abusive life through
       education and her career. On becoming a successful journalist, McMillon
       takes up the search for her birthmother; finding her in Germany forces
       McMillon to put this mystery into perspective. Shortly thereafter, her adoptive
       mother faces a grave illness and McMillon, having a stroke of insight and
       understanding, begins to form a relationship with her. This is an engrossing
       story of an adopted abused child's confusion and terror, however, the story
       turns too quickly and without reasonable evidence to make the change of heart
       seem real.

386   McTaggart, Lynne. **The Baby Brokers: The Marketing of White Babies in
       America.** New York: Dial Press, 1980. 339pp. (OCLC 5239548)
       Posing as both an unmarried pregnant student and as a prospective adoptive
       parent, McTaggart researched first-hand this expose of black market adoption.
       McTaggart, a former newspaper managing editor, also collected documents,
       transcripts and conducted interviews with birthparents, adoptive parents and
       legal officials to aid in this work. In describing and examining specific
       individuals and activities, McTaggart attempts to expose the inadequacies of
       the legal adoption system, as well as the corruptness of the black market
       system. This is a very disturbing, albeit engrossing, rendering of shady
       adoption practices.

387   Mall, E. Jane. **P.S. I Love You.** Saint Louis, MO: Concordia Publishing
       House, 1961. 166pp. (OCLC 2061302)
       Mall, a minister's wife, describes their attempts to adopt which result in a
       string of foster children. When her military husband is assigned to Germany,
       they adopt five-year-old John and four-year-old Marie from a German
       orphanage, but prior to the children's arrival, they are asked if they would
       consider adopting Mitzi, a seven-year-old Japanese-American girl whose
       adoption is failing. Delighted, they welcome Mitzi and shortly thereafter the
       other two children arrive. Mall describes their first year together as the two
       small children learn English and American manners and as the five of them
       become a family. Combining the humorous with the more serious, Mall
       presents a realistic picture of their new international life. The family expands
       to include baby Carlton and an older East German refugee. Mitzi and her
       former adoptive family reconcile and she returns to them. Wanting one more
       daughter, Mall waits for her husband to concur and for the right child to be
       offered. Finally, they add ten-day-old Heide Jane. Although somewhat dated,
       this provides an inside Christian perspective to international adoption while
       in another country.

388   Marcus, Clare. **Who is My Mother? Birth Parents, Adoptive Parents and
       Adoptees Talk About Living with Adoption and the Search for Lost
       Family.** Toronto: Macmillan, 1981. 214pp. (OCLC 10947712)

After interviewing scores of people touched by adoption, Marcus presents a volume dedicated to explaining adoption, search and reunion using the words of the people involved. Topics addressed include the author's own experiences in tracing her past, deciding to search, the search itself, the reunion, what happens after a reunion and how professionals view adoption and reunion. A postscript advocates a future with open adoption records. Concluding the book is an appendix of reunion and information sources and a bibliography. As a Canadian publication, the author primarily concentrates on the adoption experience in Canada, however, the ideas, feelings and situations equally apply to the United States. Another book focusing on Canadian adoption, although for a younger audience, is Crook's **The Face in the Mirror** (252).

389   Margolies, Marjorie, and Ruth Gruber. **They Came to Stay**. New York: Coward, McCann and Geoghegan, 1976. 352pp. (OCLC 2091811)
Influenced by her reporting on orphans in Southeast Asia and despite all odds, Margolies, a TV reporter and a single woman, adopts a seven-year-old Korean girl in 1970 and a six-year-old Vietnamese girl in 1974. This story recounts her initial dealings and travels to find her children and then to work out details to bring them to the States. While both children go through very different adjustments, the co-author's trip to their birth countries reveals a wealth of information regarding their backgrounds. Eight pages of black and white photographs show the Margolies as they become a family. Sharing the joy, frustration, anguish and success of adopting and parenting older foreign-born children, this story is inspiring, particularly as it relates to single parents often thwarted by some traditional agency and governmental regulations.

390   Maxtone-Graham, Katrina. **An Adopted Woman**. New York: Remi Books, 1983. 365pp. (OCLC 8669641)
Maxtone-Graham, adopted at age two in the late 1930s, details her failed attempts to obtain information from her original adoption agency, her years of legal action and dealing with governmental agencies, all to piece together her past. Although the court and agency continue to fight her, Maxtone-Graham finds her birthmother and other birthfamily members. This is a hard-to-put-down book which clearly depicts the obstacles in the way of the adoptee searcher as well as provides a forum advocating open adoption records.

391   Maxtone-Graham, Katrina. **Pregnant By Mistake: The Stories of Seventeen Women**. New York: Liveright, 1973. 435pp. (OCLC 746153)
Using an interview format, each of the seventeen chapters of this book relates the story of a pregnancy. The women, some of whom were high school age at the time of their pregnancy, explain their feelings, options and decisions. Several of the young women chose adoption for their children. An adoptee herself [see (390) for Maxtone-Graham's own story], the author hopes these interviews will facilitate greater understanding and therefore, greater tolerance. While sometimes dated, many of the experiences sound quite contemporary. A new edition with index and new preface was published by Remi Books in 1990. Providing a similar treatment of the topic for younger readers is McGuire's **It Won't Happen To Me** (262).

392 Musser, Sandra Kay. **I Would Have Searched Forever**. Plainfield, NJ:
   Distributed by Haven Books, 1979. 144pp. (OCLC 5531246)
In 1954, at age fifteen, Musser surrendered an infant daughter for adoption.
Although she was advised to get on with her life and that she would have
other children, Musser has been unable to forget about her daughter. The
first part of this book is an autobiographical account of Musser's life and
search in 1977 for her daughter who, when found, is unsure of the kind of
relationship she wants with her birthmother. The second part of the book
contains testimonials regarding the need for information about surrendered
birthchildren. The third section of the book concerns itself with education and
legislation, highlighting Concerned United Birthparents' (CUB) (see Appendix
B) stand on adoption issues. The final section confirms the author's basis in
Christianity. A bibliography and a list of adoption activist groups primarily
geared toward search and reunion activities conclude this book in which the
author earnestly portrays the need for more humane adoption processes from
the point of view of a birthmother. Musser's post-reunion story continues in
What Kind of Love is This: A Story of Adoption Reconciliation (Oaklyn, NJ:
Jan Publications, 1982) in which she also details the growing analogy between
her adoption and Christian experiences.

393 Nason, Diane, with Birdie Etchinson. **The Celebration Family**. Nashville, TN:
   Thomas Nelson, 1983. 186pp. (OCLC 9895452)
Sharing the story of their six birthchildren and twenty-six adoptive children,
Nason reveals a family committed to their strong Christian faith and the call
to help others. Beginning with Nason's own childhood, the book relates
Dennis and Diane's early marriage, the birth of their first child, Mark, who
had many medical complications, and how the Nasons go on to adopt and give
birth to many more children. While the initial chapters of the book are
arranged somewhat chronologically, the other chapters are presented by topic,
peppered with family anecdotes. In dealing with domestic, intercountry and
transracial adoptions, physical and mental handicaps, including Down's
Syndrome, the deaths of two children and the estrangement of another, the
Nasons have maintained a keen sense of mission and faith. One chapter
focuses on the practical aspects of raising a large family. Eight pages of
photographs are included in this fascinating close-up look at a large adoptive
family.

394 O'Brien, Bev. **Mom, I'm---Pregnant**. Wheaton, IL: Tyndale House, 1982.
   127pp. (OCLC 9612915)
Told from the perspective of an unwed pregnant teen's mother, this story
relates the pregnancy of nineteen-year-old Sandy. Focusing first on her own
reaction to her daughter's pregnancy, O'Brien experiences her own anger, guilt,
bitterness and fear before she arrives at an acceptance of her daughter's
predicament. As abortion is never considered an alternative, Sandy chooses
to continue her pregnancy, works with a Christian counselor and, after much
thought and prayer, decides adoption is the best alternative for the baby.
Other chapters include discussions and thoughts on marriage as an option for
pregnant teens, the role of the baby's father and investigating alternatives.
The book concludes with a bibliography. With biblical text interjected
throughout, this book provides an interesting combination of personal

narrative, information and opinions regarding legal, social, medical and emotional aspects of teen pregnancy.

395   Palmer, Frances. **And Four to Grow On**. New York: Rinehart and Co., 1958.
        222pp. (OCLC 1652593)
Wanting to adopt their children sight unseen, the author and her husband first became the parents of Joe, age eight, and his sister, Ruth, age five; then a few years later, Tom, age seven and his sister, Beth, age five. The story, sprinkled with parental insight, chronicles their adjustments with anecdotes that trace the growth of the children's attitudes and behaviors. As the children grow up, they slowly acquire their parents' values. Despite the publication date, this is still a very readable story with a Christian perspective.

396   Patrick, Michael, Evelyn Sheets, and Evelyn Trickel. **We Are a Part of
        History: The Story of the Orphan Trains**. Santa Fe, NM: The Lighting
        Tree, 1990. 152pp. (OCLC 21558824)
Providing a brief, yet personal history of the Children's Aid Society orphan trains of the late nineteenth and early twentieth centuries, the authors highlight the major organizers, the children, as well as some of the criticism and flaws of the program which carried over 150,000 children west and south over a period of seventy five years. The authors portray the squalid child welfare situation in New York City which prompted the Reverend Charles Brace to organize the first orphan train and describes train trips and the process involved. One chapter features four years of correspondence between representatives of the Children's Aid Society and a couple in Missouri as they attempt to gain custody of three siblings. Also included are short biographies of people who had been orphan train children. The book concludes with a bibliography and has reproductions of documents and black and white photographs. A fictionalized account of the first orphan train is found in Magnuson's **Orphan Train** (473); other orphan train stories for younger readers include Nixon's **A Family Apart** (204) and Talbot's **An Orphan for Nebraska** (235).

397   Pedersen, Maia. **At Sixes and Sevens**. New York: World Publishing
        Company, 1969. 191pp. (OCLC 113311)
Pederson chronicles the first year following the adoptive placement of six-year-old twin girls into their large family. Arriving during the summer while the family is vacationing at its cottage in the Adirondacks, the twins bring their poor southern grammar and lack of trust to the family. The two girls and six-year-old Timmy effectively become triplets and provide fun, as well as stress, in the family. Because their past activities have been so limited, school and the family attempt to find and fill the gaps in the girls' education and experience. Overjoyed at the court finalization, the girls, realizing they are really in their forever family, relax, and more confidently stake their claim in the Pedersen family. Filled with anecdotes, the story realistically portrays the fun, joy and pain involved in an older child adoption. One of the few books on the adoption of twins, it is interesting to note the girls' different reactions during the adjustment period.

398   **Perspectives on a Grafted Tree**. Compiled by Patricia Irwin Johnston. Illus.
        by Diana L. Stanley. Fort Wayne, IN: Perspectives Press, 1983. 144pp.
        (OCLC 9532918)
        A collection of poems relating to adoption, this volume reflects thoughts of all
        members of the adoption triad.   Opening with Kahlil Gibran's essay "On
        Children," the book features a seven-page introduction to the work then is
        divided into eight sections of poetry under the headings "Beginnings and
        Endings," "The Grafting," "Reactions," "Attachment," "Motherspeakings,"
        "Identities," "Reflections" and "Benediction."   The book concludes with
        suggested reading, resource lists and an author index.   A very touching book
        describing all aspects of the adoption experience encompassing the joy as well
        as the pain.   The black and white illustrations provide a charming counterpart
        to the text.   This is a rare book of poetry on the subject of adoption.

399   Piepenbrink, Ruth.   **Forever Family: Our Adventure in Adopting Older
        Children**.   Huntington, IN: Our Sunday Visitor, 1981.   128pp.   (OCLC
        8303057)
        When their birth son was nine, the author and her husband finally achieve
        their goal of adopting a child when they heartily accept siblings, Ann, age
        seven and Joe, age four, to complete their family.   The author tactfully
        describes the family's adjustment and the children's slow, but growing
        realization this family is permanent.   Years later, the family adopts six-year-old
        overweight, but undernourished Sherry; and three years later they add five-
        year-old Chris.   In subsequent years the family adopts three-year-old Eve who
        had suffered burns in her birthfamily and later still, go on to adopt three more
        children coming from even more severe situations.   The book relates the
        family's activities, as well as the special problems and their solutions.   Told
        with a good degree of honesty, a dose of humor and a Christian perspective,
        this presents a realistic look at preschooler and older child adoptions.

400   Piester, Ruby Lee.   **For the Love of a Child: The Gladney Story: 100 Years
        of Adoption in America**.   Austin, TX: Eakin Press, 1987.   230pp.
        (OCLC 19010878)
        As a centennial tribute to the Texas adoption agency, the Edna Gladney
        Center, this book presents the history of the agency, as well as accounts of
        Gladney adoptees, birthmothers and adoptive parents.   Beginning with
        assisting orphan train children find appropriate homes in Texas in the 1880s,
        continuing by offering a maternity home for unwed mothers and subsequently,
        adoption services for the mothers who chose that option, the Gladney Center
        has responded to the prevailing needs of those involved.   While strongly
        against unsealing adoption records and altering the confidentiality require-
        ment, the Gladney policy affirms openness in terms of being open and frank
        with the adoptee.   Many pages of black and white photographs of children and
        families give the impression of a family scrapbook while sharing the philosophy
        of an agency with a long-standing reputation.

401   Powell, John Y.   **Whose Child Am I? Adults' Recollections of Being Adopted**.
        New York: Tiresias Press, 1985.   127pp. (OCLC 12927462)
        Prior to the stories of five adults who recall their own adoption, Powell
        provides historical and research background regarding the adoption experi-

ence. As a by-product of his doctoral dissertation in which he researched adults who had been adopted as older children, Powell presents a summary of his findings and the actual stories of five individuals. These people represent a variety of socio-economic backgrounds, as well as a variety of situations which initially made them available for adoption. They recall their memories of first meeting their adoptive parents, their lives prior to adoption, their emotional and real ties to birthfamily members, the struggles to gain their identity and their thoughts and ideas on how adoptive placements should be made. Fascinating reading, Powell relates the impact, negative and positive, of adoption on children old enough to be aware of what is happening to them.

402   Prentice, Carol S. **An Adopted Child Looks at Adoption**. New York: Appleton-Century Co., 1940. 222pp. (OCLC 1706391)
Adopted at age five when her widowed mother was dying of tuberculosis, Prentice went to live with two older single women. Old enough to remember the transition, Prentice relates her fears, concerns and memories stating she was always her birthmother's child. Other chapters concern safeguarding the mother, safeguarding the child, a fairy tale approach to adoption, heredity versus environment, motives for adoption and the challenge of the underprivileged child. She concludes with a manual for adoptive parents and a bibliography. Although perhaps appropriate for the time of publication, this book contains many outdated notions regarding adoption.

403   Quinlan, Joseph and Julia, with Phyllis Battelle. **Karen Ann: The Quinlans Tell Their Story**. Garden City, NY: Doubleday, 1977. 343pp. (OCLC 3259340)
After three miscarriages and the birth of a stillborn child, the Quinlans adopt a baby, Karen Ann, who is a sickly infant. Shortly before her twenty-first birthday, Karen and a friend move into their own apartment and during a party on April 15, 1975, Karen is taken to the hospital when her friends are unable to revive her. She is diagnosed as being in a coma although the doctors are unable to determine its cause. After ten days in the Newton Memorial Hospital, Karen is transferred to another hospital where she remains comatose. Realizing the severity of their daughter's condition and the brain damage already suffered, the family requests Karen be taken off life-support systems and be allowed to die. The family's request, made in consultation with their religious advisors, is turned down by hospital personnel and is eventually taken to the state Supreme Court which supports the family's wishes and Karen is left to die with dignity. (The book follows the Quinlan's story up to this point. Karen eventually died on June 11, 1985). Twelve pages of black and white photographs add to the heartbreaking story of the family's grief and faith.

404   Reagan, Michael, with Joe Hyams. **On The Outside Looking In**. New York: Kensington, 1988. 286pp. (OCLC 17659348)
Reagan, adopted as an infant, was three years old when his parents, Ronald Reagan and Jane Wyman, divorced. Always afraid he will not live up to his parents' standards, yet always seeking their approval and attention, Reagan begins acting out his anger and frustration as a school boy. Since he is never held responsible for his behavior, it escalates and at age fourteen, when his

mother finds him too difficult, he goes to live with his father, his new wife, Nancy, and their two children. He does not feel he belongs there either, as he never has a bedroom, sleeping instead on couches. As he grows up, Reagan, still irresponsible, marries and divorces, never seeing the child he fathered. He later marries a woman who helps him clear up his misconceptions and resume a normal life. He later discovers a half-birthbrother who helps him to fill in his past. While the book describes the tensions and fears of a lost child, it is disturbing story, often repetitive and confusing, presented in a quasi-chronological manner. For another tragic celebrity adoption story told by the child, see Crawford's **Mommie Dearest** (359).

405   Redmond, Wendie, and Sherry Sleightholm. **Once Removed: Voices From Inside the Adoption Triangle**. Toronto: McGraw-Hill Ryerson, 1982. 136pp. (OCLC 11804915)
After interviewing several adoptees, birthparents and adoptive parents, the authors present an inside view of the perspectives of each of these groups, especially as they relate to searching for birthparents or birthchildren. The stories of four adoptees are presented first, followed by stories about adoptees and genetic disorders. In the second section, one set of adoptive parents is highlighted and then reminiscences of three birthmothers are shared. The book concludes with methods for searching for birthparents in Canada. This section discusses terminology, addresses of provincial government offices of interest to adoptees, a list of Canadian support and discussion groups and basic information on search methods and sources. The authors, both adoptees, seek to give consideration to the emotional and intimate involvement regarding searching. While working on this book, Sleightholm contacted her birthmother and a postscript describes the reunion.

406   Register, Cheri. **"Are Those Kids Yours?": American Families with Children Adopted From Other Countries**. New York: Free Press, 1990. 240pp. (OCLC 21592305)
Wanting to identify some of the ethical issues raised by international adoption and to show how they are played out in the daily lives of adoptive families, Register, herself the adoptive mother of two Korean-born children, gathered the stories of members of many adoptive families and attempts to interpret them. Incorporating interviewees' own words at every opportunity, Register looks first at the children in need of families and then at the families searching for children. She looks at how the two are matched and how they slowly become family. In separate chapters Register looks at how families tell their adoption stories and the racial/personal identity of children adopted from abroad. In another chapter Register initiates the subject of searching for international birthparents. The book concludes with a bibliography and a detailed index. Enhanced and personalized by her own experience and the words of the interviewees, Register provides a readable, thought-provoking book looking at the nature of intercountry adoption.

407   Rigert, Joe. **All Together: An Unusual American Family**. New York: Harper and Row, 1974. 167pp. (OCLC 841321)
After the birth of their daughter, Marie, Joe and Jan Rigert adopt six-year-old Linda, Jan's adoptive sister, when their mother dies. Over the next several

years, they adopt six multi-racial infants. The book relates how the Rigerts pursue the adoptions, providing stories concerning each of the children and their adjustments and personalities, and examining the family's motivation for adopting transracially and multi-racially. In addition, Rigert discusses daily life, vacations and special problems, such as relatives, neighbors, siblings and school. He also covers more philosophical notions regarding being part of a multi-racial family. Included are eight pages of black and white photographs of the family. Although this is slightly dated, the concerns, feelings and problems Rigert covers are timeless. He tells his story with light humor, as well as great warmth and insight. Rigert also relates the family's trip to Europe in **Europe on Eight Kids a Day** (Minneapolis: Dillon Press, 1971).

408   Rogers, Dale Evans. **Dearest Debbie**. Westwood, NJ: F.H. Revell, 1965.
         62pp. (OCLC 1378576)
Taking the form of a letter, Rogers writes to her Korean-born daughter, Debbie, who has died. Debbie, a Korean-Puerto Rican adoptee, joined the Roy Rogers family at the age of three. Nine years later while on a church trip to an orphanage in Mexico, Debbie is killed in a bus accident. In the letter her mother relates memories of Debbie's life with the Roger's family. Gaining strength from her Christian faith, Rogers fondly recalls Debbie's arrival, adjustment and integration into the family. Focusing specifically on the few days around Debbie's death, Rogers tells about Debbie's twelfth birthday, a trip she made with some friends, the fated trip to Tia Juana, the funeral arrangements and the funeral itself. She then shares some of the letters, poems and other correspondence sent by well-wishers from across the country. Interspersing biblical quotations and religious poetry, Rogers presents a touching spirited, yet sorrowful look at a the life of one small girl. Other books by Rogers concerning their family life include **A Salute To Sandy** (409), **To My Son** (Westwood, NJ: Revell, 1957) and **The Woman at the Well** (Old Tappan, NJ: Revell, 1970).

409   Rogers, Dale Evans. **Salute to Sandy**. Westwood, NJ: F. H. Revell, 1967.
         117pp. (OCLC 1426729)
At age five, Sandy, a mildly brain-damaged boy with a background of abuse and neglect, is adopted into the Christian Roy Rogers and Dale Evans family, and although he is not as advanced as his age would have him, the family helps him and he grows in strength and confidence. Much to his parents' surprise, when he is older, Sandy is accepted by the U.S. Army, begins training and is ordered to Germany just before becoming engaged. In a moment of weakness, Sandy forgets his Christian upbringing and goes along with the other soldiers on a drinking binge and is dead by morning. In memory of their son, Dale and Roy Rogers volunteer to perform for the USO in Vietnam. Every other chapter tells the story of Sandy's life with the Rogers, while the opposite chapters relate the Rogers' experiences in Vietnam. Sixteen pages of black and white photographs enhance the story which includes many biblical references. Other books by Rogers concerning their family life include **Dearest Debbie** (408), **To My Son** (Westwood, NJ: Revell, 1957) and **The Woman at the Well** (Old Tappan, NJ: Revell, 1970).

410   Rose, Anna Perrott. **"The Gentle House"**. Boston: Houghton Mifflin, 1954.
           177pp. (OCLC 1072660)
       After Rose's experiences described in her **Room for One More** (411) and after
       the death of her husband, she became a teacher to an eleven-year-old Latvian
       orphan who had come to the U.S. Andris has survived the Russian bombing
       of his orphanage, as well as a series of D.P. camps, but he is so emotionally
       disturbed and of doubtful intelligence that his placement, as an only child of
       a wealthy family, does not succeed. After several other disastrous placements,
       Rose takes him in and slowly helps restore his mental health. Rose details
       Andris' problems, behaviors and adjustments with a good deal of sincerity.
       Although she is often able to muster humor when describing an incident, Rose
       is not sentimental. Through trial and error the family learns to understand
       what is behind Andris' behavior and they are better able to cope with the
       situations he presents. While published some time ago, this stands out as one
       of the few books which deals honestly and directly with the seemingly
       irrational physical and emotional behaviors often present in battered children.
       Duling's **Adopting Joe** (363) makes several references to this book.

411   Rose, Anna Perrott. **Room For One More**. Boston: Houghton Mifflin, 1950.
           272pp. (OCLC 18388481)
       In addition to their three birthchildren, the Rose family takes in three older
       permanent foster children, one of whom has polio. Providing anecdotes, Rose
       chronicles family life with their six children telling how the family adds three
       children, the kinds of questions and comments they get, how their home is
       arranged to accommodate the six children, pets the family acquired over the
       years and school problems and solutions. Rose describes the problems and
       successes of each of the children and of the family. Told in a very comfort-
       able, conversational manner, Rose presents episodes of wise parenting and
       childlike insights. While not an adoption story, the family decided against
       adoption for financial reasons, the experiences of this permanent foster care
       situation are similar enough that this book often shows up on lists of adoption
       books. The author's subsequent experience with the arrival of an eleven-year-
       old Latvian boy is chronicled in **"The Gentle House"** (410).

412   Ryan, Kristapher. **From We to Just Me: A Birth Mother's Journey**.
           Winnipeg: Freedom To Be Me Seminars, 1990. 82pp. (OCLC
           21678111)
       Ryan, a single mother, recounts the story of her decision to find an adoptive
       home for her two young sons, then ages five and one, after realizing her
       unhappiness with parenting. Interspersing quotes from scholars in adoption
       and other fields, Ryan unfolds her personal account of finding acceptable
       adoptive parents for an open adoption, the process of relinquishing her sons,
       helping her older child to accept the situation and adjusting to her new life
       without them, all the while explaining her feelings and motivations. The book
       concludes with a list of references cited. Ryan presents a painful, yet clear-
       sighted picture of a responsible decision.

413   Ryan, Marguerite. **Adoption Story: A Son is Given**. New York: Rawson
           Associates, 1989. 231pp. (OCLC 18106566)

When New Yorkers Maggie and Jeremy Ryan privately adopt Christopher, the infant son of an illegal, unmarried El Salvadoran domestic in California, they are devastated to learn the birthmother, Angelina, wants the baby returned to her. After a bitter court battle in which Angelina is given custody of Christopher, a decision supported by upper courts, Angelina moves to New York and she and Maggie undergo joint counseling to assist in Chris' transition, but he is never ready to leave the Ryans. The Ryans adopt another son and Jeremy is hospitalized with a heart condition that draws the couple closer together, but Chris remains with them, with Angelina as a regular visitor, almost part of the extended family, through the end of the book when Chris is seven. This is a heartbreaking story, including many actual court episodes, of the pain and love of two sets of parents and an unconventional solution to their situation.

414   Salkmann, Victoria. **There is a Child for You**. New York: Simon and Schuster, 1972. 221pp. (OCLC 514782)
After the birth of their three children, the Salkmanns decide to add a child to their family through adoption, specifically a waiting mixed-race child. The book relates in detail the homestudy process, as well as their own exploring and growing during the process. When the Salkmanns are finally approved for placement, infant Joey is placed with them providing a quandary for all. Although Joey's birthmother, who is white, claims the father is black, Joey is fairer than all the rest of the Salkmanns. The family bonds with Joey quickly, but they remain confused about how they are to deal with sharing a black heritage with a child they are not sure is black. Their own caseworker is unsure of Joey's real heritage and shows them pictures of other children with similar appearances and documented backgrounds. The book relates the family's activities, joy, worries and involvement in transracial adoption and offers the personal challenge to all to adopt waiting children.

415   Sanders, Patricia, and Nancy Sitterly. **Search Aftermath and Adjustments**. Santa Ana, CA: Patricia Sanders and Nancy Sitterly, 1981.   62pp. (OCLC 13152335)
Based on the premise that the search for one's birthparent or birthchild is not an end in itself, but rather a new beginning, Sanders and Sitterly provide several short essays on the feelings, options, relationships, problems and joys of the new insight gained from searching. They discuss such ideas as the fantasies of the searcher, the honeymoon period of a new relationship after reunion, as well as the subsequent down-to-earth period, the painful feelings when rejection is part of the search, the confusion of what to call each other and the myth of the chosen child. They also cover the feelings of the adoptive parents, promises made and broken and keeping their existence a secret. This contains thoughtful essays on another aspect of searching. The authors themselves are adoptees who have found their birthparents and are active in searching.

416   Sandness, Grace Layton. **Brimming Over**. Minneapolis: Mini-World Publications, 1978. 300pp. (OCLC 4474712)
Sandness, left a quadriplegic after she was stricken with polio while in college, chronicles her early life, her marriage and their subsequent adoptions beginning in 1963 with the adoption of Cindy, a four-year-old Korean-

Caucasian girl with mild cerebral palsy, then three-year-old Jennifer with polio. Despite the problems and details involved with Grace's condition as well as the children's health, the family goes on to adopt several additional disabled and minority children including Kim, a troubled black-Korean teenager who caused the family much grief and heartache. Twenty pages of black and white photographs help to make this a memorable book. In addition to living a full life against the odds, Sandness portrays a family adoption story in a realistic manner, sharing the good and happy, as well as the sad and hurt involved. Other books by Grace Sandness include **Beginnings** (Maple Grove, MN: Mini-World Publications, 1980) which features vignettes of challenged children finding adoptive homes gleaned from Grace's own experience as an adoption counselor; **The Loving River** (Dayton, MN: Balance Beam Press, 1983) which presents Grace's prose and poetry inspired by marriage, adoption and parenting; **Commitment: the Reality of Adoption** (Maple Grove,MN: Mini-World Publications, 1984) which provides short stories of special needs children and the families that adopt them.

417   Schaefer, Carol. **The Other Mother: A Woman's Love for the Child She Gave Up**. New York: Soho Press, 1991. (OCLC 21678405)
Although unable to evaluate personally, this book is about a southern birthmother who, eighteen years later, searches for and finds the son she gave up for adoption when she was nineteen years old.

418   Schwartzbaum, Avraham. **The Bamboo Cradle: A Jewish Father's Story**. Jerusalem: Feldheim Publishers, 1988. 248pp. (OCLC 17804511)
While on a Fulbright Fellowship to Taiwan in 1972, Schwartzbaum finds an abandoned baby girl in a railway station. After turning the newborn over to the authorities, the childless Schwartzbaums take special interest in the child, obtain custody, adopt her and take her back to the States with them. The Schwartzbaums, wanting to give their daughter, Devorah, a Jewish education, embark on a reclamation of their Jewish heritage by embracing orthodox Jewish life. The bulk of the book focuses on the family's activities as they strengthen their faith and go on to give birth to four sons. The Schwartzbaums go to Taiwan on another Fulbright when Devorah is still small and also spend a sabbatical leave in Israel where they eventually move in 1983. The book concludes with selections from Devorah's diary from 1983 to 1987 and a glossary of terms. As there are very few accounts of Jewish adoptions, this book, which includes sixteen pages of black and white photographs, as well as reproductions of letters and documents, is interesting from a religious heritage perspective as well as for its insights into an unusual intercountry adoption.

419   Sheehy, Gail. **Spirit of Survival**. New York: William Morrow, 1986. 407pp. (OCLC 13186239)
This engrossing story chronicles the author's involvement with Mohm, a ten-year-old Cambodian orphan, from their first meeting at a refugee camp in Thailand where Sheehy, an American journalist, was covering a story on the plight of the Cambodian refugees, through the legal and political battle to bring Mohm to the U.S., during Mohm's adoption by Sheehy and their adjustment and new life together. This well-known author of **Passages** (New York: Dutton, 1976) and **Pathfinders** (New York: Morrow, 1981) has written

a moving account of the struggles of one child to regain a life and a family. Adding even greater insight, Sheehy has interwoven Mohm's own thoughts and words, accent and all, into the story. In addition to several pages of photographs, the book also includes source notes and an extensive index.

420   Silber, Kathleen, and Phylis Speedlin. **Dear Birthmother: Thank You For Our Baby**. San Antonio, TX: Corona Publishing, 1982. 192pp. (OCLC 9255913)
Citing four myths of adoption concerning the feelings of a surrendering birthmother, the purpose of secrecy, the memory of birthparents and the motivation to search, the authors present ideas and practices which can help eliminate the myths from the adoption experience. Calling for open adoptions with communication between the birthparents and adoptive parents and using many examples of actual letters to illustrate their approach, the authors challenge those involved in adoption to change the status quo. In addition, the authors provide a new definition of adoption and introduce new language and grammar to describe the adoption experience. The book concludes with a short bibliography. While providing specific ideas how to change current adoption practices, this book is also significant for the correspondence between birthparents and adoptive parents which is interspersed throughout the book to illustrate ideas in the text. Silber went on to describe the long-term impact of open adoption in **Children of Open Adoption and Their Families** (San Antonio, TX: Corona, 1990).

421   Smith, Doris D.   **A Limb of Your Tree: The Story of an Adopted Twin's Search for Her Roots**. Smithtown, NY: Exposition Press, 1984. 158pp. (OCLC 11333159)
After the death of her twin brother due to kidney problems, Smith, who had been adopted as an infant with her brother, pursues the identity of their birthparents in hopes of learning pertinent medical information beneficial to her and her children. Encountering legal and bureaucratic roadblocks, Smith is turned down by the courts, misled by a psychic, but discovers the helpfulness of ALMA (see Appendix B) in beginning her search on her own. Assisted by people in California where she was currently living, as well as by others in her birth state of North Carolina, she is eventually able to find her birthmother and her deceased birthfather's family. Reunions with both sides of the family are joyous, as well as informative and although her mother will not divulge Smith's real identity to her current family, Smith enjoys continued relationships with all family members.   Through a paternal birthaunt, Smith learns of extensive inherited kidney problems, thereby achieving the primary goal of her search. Copies of actual documents, newspaper articles and letters accompany the text of this account. This book, published by a vanity press, reveals a great love of her own family, her adoptive family and her new-found birthfamily.

422   Standiford, Debi. **Sudden Family**. Waco, TX: Word Books, 1986. 163pp. (OCLC 13455895)
Relating the story of a couple's adoption of two Vietnamese teenage boys, one a polio victim, this book presents alternating chapters in which family members tell the story from their own viewpoints. Not personally examined, this book

with a Christian perspective, recounts the boys' journey from Vietnam, to a resettlement camp in Thailand, and to their new home in the United States.

423   Steven, Hugh. **Kim: "I Will Make Darkness Light"**. Irvine, CA: Harvest House, 1975. 152pp. (OCLC 3328721)
        Kim, blinded at age five during the Korean War, is adopted in 1957 at age ten. Relating her early life, Kim tells how the Holts [see Bertha Holt's story in **The Seed From the East** (370)] discover Kim and arrange for her adoption to the States. Always a spunky child, Kim arrives in her new home very shy and frightened, however, her personal qualities help her succeed. Discovering Christian faith, Kim gains strength in her endeavors eventually graduating from Indiana University with a major in music. Having always been musical, Kim pursues a graduate degree in music with the goal of becoming a concert vocalist. After winning a Fulbright scholarship, Kim realizes, while studying music in Vienna, she would rather become a religious singer, but not before returning to Korea to meet with her birthfather and sister. Although her adoptive family does not always agree with her decisions or goals, they remain supportive of her. This is an inspiring success story, which includes some especially good reminiscences of Kim's arrival in the States, of a stubborn and determined handicapped Korean-born adoptee who found strength through Christianity.

424   Stingley, James. **Mother, Mother**. New York: Congdon and Lattes, 1981. 219pp. (OCLC 7576491)
        Stingley, a newspaper journalist, is contacted by his birthmother who introduces him to a wealthy lifestyle, far different from that of his somewhat estranged adoptive family. As his birth story slowly unfolds, Stingley learns his deceased adoptive father is also his birthfather. After an almost incestuous affair with his birthmother and a series of blackouts, Stingley comes to terms with both of his mothers and himself. Stingley's character vacillates between gullible weakness and strong self-confidence, all the while exhibiting the struggle he endures to know himself.

425   **They Became Part of Us**. Edited by Barbara Holtan and Laurel Strassberger. Maple Grove, MN: Mini-World Publications, 1985. 191pp. (OCLC 13126123)
        This collection of writings is by adoptive families who are members of Families Adopting Children Everywhere (FACE) (see Appendix B). Running from two to six pages long, the selections are divided into five categories: building families, bringing them home, arriving in twos and threes, adopting older children and unpleasantly close encounters. Black and white photographs are sprinkled throughout this book that tells the stories of adoptive families in their own words. The purpose of the publication is to inform would-be adopters, the general public and social workers about various types of adoption and the feelings and experiences of those involved. Similar in scope and content to **The Unbroken Circle** (428).

426   Thompson, Jean. **The House of Tomorrow**. New York: Harper and Row, 1967. 179pp. (OCLC 264058)

Using a diary format, this story relates the experiences of a young college student who admits herself to a Salvation Army home for unwed mothers. Going under the fictitious name of Jean Thompson, the narrator, in first person, provides a moving account, from first admitting she is pregnant, deciding adoption for the baby and having the baby. This is an emotional story, which clearly portrays the joy and anguish of a birthmother. Thompson eventually arrives at a decision for what would now be called an open adoption.

427   **A Time to Search**. Henry Ehrlich, editor. New York: Paddington Press, 1977. 232pp. (OCLC 2929603)
Each chapter in this book is a personal account of an adult adoptee searching for birthparents. While their situations vary, the adoptees share the need to search and find their origins. The authors describe their backgrounds, the process they used to search, as well as the outcome of the searches. The book begins with an introduction in which the editor discusses sealed adoption records and traces the history of that practice. Concluding the book is a chapter with adoptive parent interviews and another with birthparent interviews. The term "natural parent" is consistently used rather than "birthparent." While not an adoptee himself, Ehrlich became interested in adoptees' search for birthparents when he worked for Adoptees' Liberty Movement Association (ALMA) (see Appendix B).

428   **The Unbroken Circle: A Collection of Writings on Interracial and International Adoption**. Edited by Betty Kramer. Minneapolis: OURS (Organization for a United Response), 1975. 466pp. (OCLC 1983323)
Usually no longer than eight pages long, each essay, letter, or portion of this book provides valuable insight into interracial and international adoptions. The book begins with a section on general information, then proceeds with a section on Korean adoptions, orphanages, Vietnamese adoptions and Columbian adoptions. Each of the country sections include such information as vocabulary lists, recipes, descriptions of the adoption process, as well as personal stories. Also included in its entirety is a thesis done on the adjustment of foreign-born children in Minnesota. A sequel, also edited by Betty Kramer, featuring a greater number of family-written accounts, is **Carry It On: A Collection of Writings on Interracial and International Adoption** (Minneapolis: OURS, 1978). Although the factual information in these titles reflect the time period in which they were published, the narrative accounts, similar to those found in the **OURS Magazine** (now published by Adoptive Families of America--see Appendix B) are still valid, positive sources of family adjustment information regarding interracial and intercountry adoptions.

429   Valenti, Laura L. **The Fifteen Most Asked Questions About Adoption**. Scottdale, PA: Herald Press, 1985. 219pp. (OCLC 11533544)
Valenti has identified the fifteen most asked questions regarding adoption and has devoted separate chapters to answering each question. Topics covered include who is available for adoption and why, why there are so few babies available for adoption, who can adopt, what is a homestudy, what is foreign adoption, how long it takes to adopt, what is an adoption support group, what are the costs involved in adoption, what about friends and relatives who are

against adoption, relationship between foster and adoptive parenting, why there are so many kinds of adoption, how to determine the right child for the right family, what should an adopted child be told, open versus closed adoption records and what kind of support is available after an adoption. Valenti also incorporates addresses of helpful organizations and a selected bibliography.   Using specific examples of people who have experienced adoption, as well as professionals in the field, Valenti has gathered a wealth of information regarding the current state of adoption.   Clear, practical and straightforward, Valenti's work is a valuable and thoughtful resource.

430   Viguers, Susan T. **With Child: One Couple's Journey to Their Adopted Children**. San Diego, CA: Harcourt Brace Jovanovich, 1986. 226pp. (OCLC 12372446)
After a long, painful struggle with infertility, Ken and Susan reluctantly look at the possibility of adoption as a means of parenthood.   After a dashed private adoption, they remain childless for several years. Learning of others' success, they pursue a South American adoption, but the paperwork proves to be troublesome and waiting for news is difficult. When they are approached with another private adoption, this time handled through a well-respected lawyer, they become the parents of Nicholas, a healthy U.S.-born Chinese baby.   Delighted at parenthood, Ken and Susan happily tackle the new activities, much enthralled with their new son. When Nicholas is four months old they receive a referral picture of a three-month-old Colombian infant who becomes their daughter, Ruth. Viguers ends the book with an epilogue that describes their position on "real" parents and their children. Although Ken and Susan wind up supporters of adoption, the beginning of the book makes adoption seem a second-best option.   In the prologue, Viguers admits this evolution in thinking as part of their growth. Alternating chapters tell the story from Susan's perspective, then Ken's.

431   Walker, Leslie. **Sudden Fury: A True Story of Adoption and Murder**. New York: St. Martin's Press, 1989. 394pp. (OCLC 19885672)
In 1984, seventeen-year-old Larry Swartz, adopted at age six, the first adopted child of Bob and Kay Swartz, calls the authorities to report his parents are dead.   For the next fifteen months, Larry, as the prime suspect, sits in jail while his lawyers try to piece together his past. The lawyers obtain access to Larry's sealed adoption records and use the information about his abusive past as part of his defense.   In addition, the lives of Bob and Kay Swartz are recreated to provide the family background which presented a puzzling mixture of intelligence and commitment to children along with stern discipline and religious zeal. With reputations of saints or villains, depending on the source, the Swartz family also adopted Michael, six months older than Larry and later Anne, from Korea. Larry is ultimately convicted of killing his parents and is serving time in a prison where he will receive the treatment he needs. Eight pages of black and white family photographs are included in this book which is a confusing account, with chapters out of chronological order, of a troubled child and his family.

432   West, Helen Louise. **Adopted Four and Had One More**. St. Louis, MO: Bethany Press, 1968. 94pp. (OCLC 431776)

In the 1950s when they discover they are not able to bear children, West and her Presbyterian minister husband, Clyde, are devastated when their first adopted child, Courtney, dies within the first six months of his life. Shortly thereafter, a baby girl, Clydea, is placed with them and they anxiously, but hesitatingly, resume their parenting activities. They go on to adopt infant Althea and shortly thereafter, four-year-old Curtis whom the courts have removed from his birthfamily. In 1963, after fourteen years of marriage and much to their surprise, the Wests learn they are pregnant and Helen gives birth to a baby girl, Annetta. When she is eighteen months old, Annetta survives a severe reaction to some medication in which she nearly dies. Sweetly, one of the Wests' adoptive children is eager to learn if the family can adopt Annetta so she won't miss out on what the older children have. Separate chapters are devoted to each child, as West describes their life, circumstances and adjustment with a Christian perspective. Some readers may object to the use of the word "negro."

433   Wexler, Susan Stanhope. **The Story of Sandy**. Indianapolis, IN: Bobbs-Merrill, 1955. 155pp. (OCLC 2583347)
When his parents are killed, Joe and Sukey, unable to have children, take in ten-year-old Tommy, but never legally adopt him. He marries when he is older and, after the birth of their second child, Tommy's wife Mary realizes how delayed Sandy, their first child, is. When a doctor labels him an imbecile, Mary wants rid of Sandy so the new baby can grow up normally. Tommy asks Joe and Sukey to take in Sandy. They are given legal guardianship and reluctantly promise not ever to mention him again to Tommy and Mary, even if they feel they have to give him up. Joe and Sukey take in three-year-old Sandy who is withdrawn and unable to engage in normal toddler activities. The family employs a series of helpers to assist in Sandy's care. Frankie, Sukey's niece, who is a social work student, becomes involved with the family as does her professor, Dr. Carey, who guides Sandy's emotional development and education. The story ends when Sandy is nine and is coming to terms with both sets of parents. While this is an emotional, enduring story, times have changed enough to make the references to a black family helper as "Mammy," as well as references to imbeciles and Mongolian idiots seem rather jarring.

434   Wheeler, Kathryn. **Tanya: The Building of a Family Through Adoption**. New York: North American Center on Adoption, Child Welfare League of America, 1979. 36pp. (OCLC 6088129)
The Wheelers respond to a waiting-child column in a Chicago newspaper featuring Tanya, a cute active verbal six-year-old girl with a bone disease and are selected as Tanya's parents. After a few weeks of visiting, Tanya, who has more severe physical problems than originally described, moves in with the Wheelers and they experience a six-week honeymoon. Wheeler describes their sometimes supportive, sometimes disapproving and insensitive, scenes with doctors, child care workers, teachers and family. Tanya's physical condition which limits her activities is discouraging and the discrepancy between her test results and apparent abilities make appropriate education difficult to determine. After the family doctor warns them of Wheeler's husband's need for a warmer climate, the family moves to Tucson where they must reconstruct medical and educational support for Tanya. Tanya has a stormy bonding

period with her family, but time and effort on the family's part enhance the process. Even though this is a short book, it describes so well the adoption of a physically handicapped special needs child. Wheeler chronicles not only the educational and medical adjustments necessary, but also those within the family unit.

435   White, William Lindsay. **Journey for Margaret**. New York: Harcourt, Brace, 1941. 256pp. (OCLC 1311185)

White, a war correspondent, travels to London during the Second World War prior to the United States' involvement and while there covering war-related stories, also takes the opportunity to adopt a child. The agency he approaches identifies two children for him, but he is encouraged to have them evaluated at Anna Freud's care center which specializes in war-traumatized children. The children, cheerful four-year-old John and frightened three-year-old Margaret, are transferred to the center and remain there for a time. Alternating chapters about covering the war and the progress with the children, White recounts the destruction of war and his will to build a family. Margaret's testing shows her to be bright and healthy. Although John's testing reveals a much younger child emotionally, a warning of possible problems, White decides to adopt both children. His limited return transportation, however, forces him to choose only one child, Margaret, who rejects him until, on the plane, she momentarily senses she might lose him. Then she clings to him the rest of the way home where they are met by his wife. While most of this book relates his experience with the war while in London, this presents a heartbreaking story of two children during the war.

436   Whitehead, Mary Beth, with Loretta Schwartz-Nobel. **A Mother's Story: The Truth About the Baby M Case**. New York: St. Martin's Press, 1989. 220pp. (OCLC 18558874)

In her own words, this is the story of Whitehead's life, how she entered into the surrogacy contract with Bill and Elizabeth Stern and the subsequent custody battle when she realized she was unable to give the child up. Combining her words, media accounts, court transcripts and tape recordings, Whitehead chronologically reconstructs her story. As the court custody trial drags out, Whitehead reveals shady legal practices and the Sterns are awarded custody; an immediate adoption by Bill and Betsy Stern takes place and they take little Melissa home. Whitehead's parental and visitation rights are terminated, until the New Jersey Supreme Court restores her parental rights and a schedule of shared custody and visitation is worked out. This compelling story, with strong emotions and several demonstrations of hostility, includes eight pages of black and white photographs.

437   Whitt, Anne Hall. **The Suitcases**. Illus. by Richard Thompson. Washington, D.C.: Acropolis Books, 1982. 184pp. (OCLC 8709012)

In this story based on her recollections, Whitt tells how she, then a scrappy six-years-old, and her two sisters, are taken to a Catholic children's home without explanation. After another orphanage placement in which the girls learn of their mother's death, and two unsuccessful foster placements, the girls are taken to a temporary foster home with the Nye family that has one infant daughter. Fortunately, their one-week stay turns into forever as the family and the girls grow to love one another. Anne is eventually able to let go of her anger and become her own person with the love and support of her family. In later years, Anne relates the death of her mother and the activities of their own families. Although formal adoption is never mentioned, the experiences as wards of the state, life in several institutions and homes and finally belonging to a family follow adoption patterns. Anne's story, most of which is set in North Carolina during the Depression, is told eloquently with the perceptive memories of childhood.

438 Williams, Jett, with Pamela Thomas. **Ain't Nothin' as Sweet as My Baby: the True Story of Hank Williams's Lost Daughter**. New York: Harcourt Brace Jovanovich, 1990. 338pp. (OCLC 21482870)

Six days after the death of country singer Hank Williams, a baby girl was born to his mistress who surrendered her to Hank's mother. The birthgrandmother raises the baby, Cathy, for two years until she is placed into public care and adopted into a mentally unbalanced family. When Cathy is twenty-one, her parents inform her she has inherited some money from Hank Williams' mother. Putting clues together and making a deliberate search, Cathy, who renames herself Jett Williams, locates significant people from her past who help her learn she is Hank Williams' daughter. When she learns she was not left anything in his will, Keith Adkinson, a lawyer who later becomes Jett's husband, agrees to help her legally prove paternity. Fighting the legitimate heirs, Jett learns her birthfather actually wrote a contract indicating his support and plan for his baby daughter. Winning the paternity court battle allows Jett to claim her heritage and place in her father's life and will. A five-page list of characters precedes the book and a twelve-page chronology concludes it. Sixteen pages of black and white photographs portray Jett and her families throughout the years. Although this is a powerful book describing a long, bitter journey to discover and claim her heritage, adoption does not fare well.

439 Williams, Pat and Jill, with Beth Spring. **Twelve-Part Harmony**. Old Tappan, NJ: F.H. Revell, 1990. 205pp. (OCLC 21328909)

After Pat and Jill Williams work to save their failing marriage, they go on to add to their biological family by adopting two preschool sisters from Korea, then twin Korean boys and later, three brothers from the Philippines ultimately ending up with twelve children. The book relates each adoption, taking care to explain the situation the children were being adopted from, as well as the family situation the children were joining. Interspersing anecdotes regarding their daily lives as well as information regarding foreign adoption, the authors present an inside look, with a Christian perspective, at parenting a large family. The epilogue recounts their recent activities as foster parents. The book features eight pages of black and white photographs of the family and concludes with a bibliography and a list of helpful organizations. This is somewhat similar in approach to Nason's **The Celebration Family** (393).

440 Winter, Marjorie. **For Love of Martha**. New York: Julian Messner, 1956. 191pp. (OCLC 1499185)

Six months after five-year-old Martha joined the Winter family, they learned she had been illegally placed through what is being called a baby mill. Now, eight months later, her second cousin, Mrs. Fenwick, arrives at their home wanting to take her away. Mrs. Fenwick seeks a writ of habeas corpus, but the Winters try to fend off the possibility of being served with the legal papers that will allow their daughter to taken from them. When Mrs. Fenwick agrees to dismiss her concerns if the birthmother signs a relinquishment, the Winters' lawyer works to legalize the adoption. Over a year later, with the birthmother located and the correct papers signed, the Winters go to court for their finalization hearing. A gruff judge disputes much of the gathered information, but to the Winters' surprise he signs the final order of adoption and the relieved family goes home. Winter provides a heartbreaking and messy picture of an unfortunate adoptive situation, but one that ends happily for the child and adoptive family.

FICTION

441   Adam, Ruth. **So Sweet a Changeling**. London: Chapman and Hall, 1954.
       222pp. (OCLC 13141056)
       Alma and Bernard Morris are the recipients of a baby girl when her flighty, unstable birthmother gives her to them without legal benefit. Over the next year the birthmother continues to reclaim the baby periodically only to return her to the Morrises. When they are unable to work out legal arrangements to keep the child, they go into hiding but are discovered. When the birthmother becomes pregnant by her new husband she relinquishes the baby to the Morris family. Set in England, this is an agonizing account of a child caught between caregivers. It reveals the discrepancy between the rights and responsibilities of birthparents

442   Andrews, V. C. **Heaven**. New York: Poseidon Press, 1985. 440pp. (OCLC
       12313242)
       Ten-year-old Heaven Leigh Casteel's father is cruel to her and not her four brothers and sisters, because Heaven is the child of his first wife who died when Heaven was a baby. When his current wife leaves him, Heaven's father sells the children for five hundred dollars each and Heaven goes to live with a flashy couple, leaving her home and Logan, the only boy she has ever liked, and travels with Cal and Kitty, who wants Heaven out of revenge against her birthmother whom she hated for stealing Heaven's father from her. Cal is kind and gentle, but ineffective, while Kitty's unbalanced mental state makes her unpredictable. Often abusive to Heaven, she treats her more as domestic help, while Cal fills in the fatherly, protective role Heaven has always wanted. Years later when Kitty becomes ill, Cal takes sexual advantage of Heaven, who is very confused. After Kitty's death, Heaven, at age sixteen, leaves and begins her search for her birthmother's family. Sequels to this story include **Dark Angel** (New York: Poseidon Press, 1986), **Fallen Hearts** (New York: Poseidon Press, 1988), **Gates of Paradise** (New York: Poseidon Press, 1989) and **Web of Dreams** (New York: Pocket Books, 1990). Some readers will object to the sexual references and physical violence in this book by a popular author.

443   Bawden, Nina. **Familiar Passions**. London: Macmillan, 1979.   160pp.
      (OCLC 5164011)
After dinner on their thirteenth wedding anniversary Bridie Starr's husband,
James, tells her he is leaving her. She leaves instead and goes to be comforted
by her adoptive parents. As Bridie spends time coming to grips with her
present and planning her future, she delves into her past and finds her
birthmother. She learns that her birthmother is a dear friend of her adoptive
parents and further learns, still to her adoptive mother's ignorance, that her
adoptive father is also her birthfather. Bridie, keeping the secret, meets a new
man and goes on with her life. The theme of adoptive father as birthfather
is similar to that in Berckman's **Blind Girl's Bluff** (278) for younger readers.
Some readers may be offended by the occasional sexual references and
episodes.

444   Bishop, Sheila. **A Speaking Likeness**. London: Hurst and Blackett, 1976.
      185pp. (OCLC 16378640)
After the death of her husband, Diana Pentland is concerned about her future
and that of her three-year-old daughter. She comes upon an ill young girl,
Eliza and takes her home to discover she is pregnant and ready to deliver.
After the baby boy is born, Eliza wants nothing to do with him and makes
legal and financial arrangements through lawyers for Diana to adopt the child.
Delighted with her new son and relieved she is financially secure, Diana goes
on holiday to Brandham castle. There she, as well as others, discovers that
her son has the same minor disfigurement as Henry, the heir to the castle.
While rumors are floating around the castle, Diana encounters Eliza, who is
Henry's sister who lives at the castle and learns her son was fathered by
Henry's cousin. She also learns Henry's father, the viscount, is not a lawyer
as she had thought and agrees to marry the viscount knowing he is the
grandfather of her son. While this has a large confusing cast of characters, it
is a typical gothic romance.

445   Blackmore, Jane. **The Other Room**. London: Collins, 1968. 222pp. (OCLC
      460484)
Set in London, this book tells the parallel stories of two couples who do not
know each other. Robert and Carla are an established married couple who
have been wanting a child, but have not been able to, and Simon and Mandy
are a teenage unmarried couple who have a child out-of-wedlock. The story
reveals the problems Robert and Carla encounter as they come to terms with
their infertility, while Simon and Mandy's growing problematic romantic
relationship leaves them with a child. When Robert and Carla approach and
adoption agency, it is Simon and Mandy's infant daughter who is placed with
them. At the six-month court hearing to finalize the adoption, Mandy and
Simon unexpectedly arrive wanting their baby back, a request which is within
their right. The court rules in their favor and they gain custody. Robert and
Carla are devastated, but the experience brings them closer together as they
await their next adoptive placement, a son. While the parallel story idea is
interesting and effective, the characterization and plot line seem artificial and
the characters lack dimension.

446   Brooks, Terry. **The Sword of Shannara**. Illus. by Greg and Tim Hildebrandt.
            New York: Random House, 1977. 726pp. (OCLC 2946061)
        Told in the fashion of Tolkien's **Lord of the Rings**, this is the story of Shea,
        the half-human, half-elfin adopted son of an innkeeper, who must pursue the
        quest of a magic sword to save all mankind from the forces of evil. The two
        other titles in the Shannara trilogy are **The Elfstones of Shannara** (New York:
        Ballantine, 1982) and **The Wishsong of Shannara** (New York: Ballantine,
        1985). This is an engrossing, entertaining epic fantasy featuring the heroics of
        a "mixed" adoptee.

447   Byrd, Elizabeth. **The Search for Maggie Hare**. London: Macmillan, 1976.
            207pp. (OCLC 2615725)
        Adopted at age ten into a wealthy Victorian Edinburgh family, Dorothea, now
        nineteen, has just suffered the death of her last living adoptive parent. After
        seeing a photo in a newspaper, Dorothea goes undercover and slips into her
        old life of drunks and prostitutes to find Maggie Hare and her lover, a mass
        murderer, whom she believes to be her birthparents. Pretending to her house
        staff that she is on holiday, Dorothea lives in squalid, dangerous conditions
        until she discovers and verifies her birthparents.   A romantic story is
        interwoven as she meets Edward who plays a surprising role. A fascinating,
        gothic, yet campy search story of a Victorian woman concerned about her
        heritage to determine her suitability for marriage and bearing children.

448   Carter, Mary Arkley. **A Member of the Family**. Garden City, NY: Double-
            day, 1974. 232pp. (OCLC 796903)
        After the accidental death of their only child, John and Ellie Thacher adopt
        a baby boy arranged through their family doctor.   Confidentiality is not
        maintained and the birthfather turns out to be the teenage boy next door, who
        is devastated when he realizes their new baby is really his son. A few years
        later the Thachers adopt again, this time going through an agency to maintain
        confidentiality. They adopt a twenty-two-month old girl, but, prior to court
        finalization, the birthmother wants to regain custody. After loosing the legal
        battle, the Thachers flee out of state with the children during the appeal.
        They receive information regarding the birthfather's past and return to
        Massachusetts where the court decision is reversed and the Thacher family is
        intact. An involved story, told in the first person by John Thacher whose
        soliloquies are painfully eloquent, this realistically presents not only the
        feelings of the adoptive parents and extended family, but also those of the
        birthparents as well.

449   Carter, Mary Arkley. **Tell Me My Name**. New York: William Morrow, 1975.
            238pp. (OCLC 1255154)
        During an impromptu anniversary party for themselves, Emily McPhail sees
        a young woman she thinks is one of Porter's, her husband's, students, but
        learns that Alexandra is the birthchild she gave up for adoption seventeen
        years ago. Alexandra, passed off as Emily's niece because Emily's family does
        not know about her, moves in with the McPhails and provides comfort, fear
        and panic in the family. When her real identity is uncovered, Sara, as she is
        now called, breaks down and tells the McPhails that she just recently

discovered she was adopted and was driven to find out who she really was. The McPhails contact her adoptive parents, and Sara, whose adoptive name is Janie, is tearfully united with her adoptive parents whom she thought had betrayed her. The book concludes with both Emily and Janie thinking straighter and with a clearer understanding of who they are and what they want. This is a heartbreaking story of the pain a family feels as the mother hides a guilty secret and the relief and strength to the family as she is released from the shame.

450   Cecil, Henry. **Fathers in Law**. London: Michael Joseph, 1965. 220pp. (OCLC 4583568)
Childless, Bill and Mary Woodthorpe adjust to their infertility and adopt an infant boy. Anxiously waiting through the mandatory three-month time period until the adoption is finalized, the Woodthorpes go to court and leave relieved that their family is now legally intact. They begin to worry anew, however, when they are blackmailed by a man who claims to know the child's birthfather, a prisoner in jail, who was never informed of his rights. Unfortunately, the Woodthorpes' successful blackmail lawsuit does not end their anxiety as the birthfather is released from jail, locates the birthmother and they petition the court to regain custody of the boy, now three years old. After an arduous court battle, the judge rules to let the child remain with his adoptive parents. Set in England, this is story provides an unusual combination of drama and humor. In an interesting fashion, much of the text deals with the British legal system and the courtroom scenes.

451   Chatterton, Ruth. **Homeward Borne**. New York: Simon and Schuster, 1950. 312pp. (OCLC 1445776)
In the late 1940s Pax Lyttleton, without the knowledge of her husband-soldier still in Europe after the war, brings a Polish, probably Jewish, refugee child, eleven-year-old Jan, to the States with the intention of adopting him. During a flashback sequence, Pax allows religious differences to thwart a romance, Jake is Jewish, and later marries Jake's best friend, Robert Lyttleton and they have a son. In an unconscious effort to allay her guilt for feeling she has betrayed Jake, her true love, Pax fosters Jan, who suffers greatly at the hands of his boarding schoolmates who learn he is Jewish. Feeling he does not belong, he runs away home to Pax and meets Robert, returned from the war with racist and anti-Semitic attitudes. Pax asks Robert for a divorce so that she can adopt Jan and provide him the chance he needs in life. This is a dramatic, powerful story which aptly describes the confusion, fear and helplessness of a small child who finds himself in an unwelcome country. The black servants's dialog is written in southern black dialect.

452   Conway, Laura. **Moment of Truth**. New York: Saturday Review Press, 1975. 159pp. (OCLC 1735303)
When a rare letter arrives from her long-estranged older adoptive sister, Fanny, Bronwen is summoned to her deathbed where she learns that Fanny is not really ill. She feigned illness so that Bron, who has always adored her elder, although deceptive, sister, would come to London to act as a companion for her twelve-year-old daughter, Ellen. The lies continue until Fanny secretly runs off to be married and is killed leaving Bron and Ellen, who contact

Ellen's estranged father, Jeremy. He takes over legal matters and learns that Fanny's lies kept him from his Ellen. As the three grow to care for each other and build a new life together, Bron confesses that Fanny was not her birthsister which frees her to marry Jeremy. Although this is a strange adoption theme, it is an intriguing story.

453   Covington, Vicki. **Gathering Home**. New York: Simon and Schuster, 1988. 240pp. (OCLC 17726852)
Eighteen-year-old Whitney, adopted as an infant by a left-wing minister and his wife, becomes involved in her father's political campaign. Set in Alabama, Whitney is concerned when the media focuses closely on her family and is prompted to find her birthfamily. When a social worker provides the opportunity, Whitney obtains the information she needs and makes an initial contact with her birthfather in New York who has been looking for her. Although her birthmother never responds, Whitney begins to correspond with Sam, her birthfather and learns about his ten-year live-in friend, Aaron, and Sam's mother who still lives in Alabama and is delighted to have a grand-daughter. The political campaign, against two ministers, turns nasty and Whitney's father has to balance political aspirations and personal responsibility when the Latin Americans involved in the sanctuary movement become targets. After her father loses the election, Whitney meets Sam and Aaron and they go to visit her new grandmother. As Whitney is coming to terms with herself, so is Sam as he wrestles with the idea of moving back to Alabama. This is a engaging book with full-bodied characters including very supportive adoptive parents who also have their own lives and concerns.

454   Cray, Dorothy. **Escape From Yesterday**. London: Collins, 1970. 254pp. (OCLC 103393)
Set in England, single Fenella agrees to watch over her adopted precocious eight-year-old niece while her parents go to the States on business. Belinda's presence and that of Martin, an English professor and summer guest in the cottage next door, change Fenella's views on life and the future as the threesome share summer activities, conversation and companionship. Belinda is extremely sensitive about being an adopted child, feeling as if she does not really belong anywhere and feels more so when her mother becomes pregnant on their trip. Martin learns from an old flame that an old romance resulted in a child who was placed for adoption and that Belinda is probably his child. The death of a mentally impaired neighbor helps teach Belinda she has a place and that the new baby will be part of her too. Martin and Fenella learn they are not as cold and as isolated as they appear and decide to marry by the end of the story. While a deeply psychological tale, the character of Belinda is quite unrealistic as her vocabulary and style of language seem much beyond that of an eight-year-old.

455   Deland, Margaret. **The Awakening of Helena Ritchie**. Illus. by Walter Appleton Clark. New York: Harper and Brothers, 1906. 357pp. (OCLC 756654)
A turn-of-the-century story of Helena Ritchie, a shy, withdrawn young widow who agrees to adopt a small boy named David. The minister arranges and oversees the placement which progresses smoothly until it is uncovered that

Mrs. Ritchie is not really a widow and the man she has been seeing is not really her brother. Upon the death of her estranged husband, Mrs. Ritchie gives up marriage instead of David, when her fiance issues an ultimatum. The scandal causes Mrs. Ritchie to give up David as well and he stays with the minister as he tries to help reform her. When she decides to leave the town, the minister sees that David, who has grown to love her, goes with her. Their story continues in Deland's **The Iron Woman** (New York: Harper and Brothers, 1911). Representative of the time, illustrated plates, one in color, decorate this book which is difficult to follow and is based on earlier lifestyles. References to house servants as niggers are disturbing.

456   De Vries, Peter. **The Tunnel of Love**. Boston: Little, Brown, 1954. 246pp.
(OCLC 789999)
When Augie and Isolde Poole are unable to conceive and decide to adopt a baby, they list their friends and neighbors, Dick and Audrey, who have four children, as character references. Uncomfortably, Dick knows about Augie's infidelity and the child his lover is carrying. Through a series of events, and because of the interest in matching parents and child, the adoption agency unknowingly places Augie's child with Augie and Isolde. As the baby grows older he looks more like Augie; eventually the truth comes out and Isolde turns Augie out of the house. Distraught and realizing how much he loves Isolde and the baby, Augie remains in a New York hotel until Isolde calls him home to let him know she is pregnant. The two reconcile and continue a monogamous life. Dick is the humorous, sarcastic narrator who vacillates between making puns and being romantic. This is a delightfully droll story, but some readers may object to the extramarital affair.

457   Drummond, June. **Thursday's Child**. London: Victor Gollancz, 1961. 255pp.
(OCLC 13920691)
Childless, Sophy and Luke Ranald contact an adoption agency and once accepted as prospective adoptive parents, wait and prepare for the arrival of their requested child, an infant boy. In the meantime, as the parallel story reveals, Frances Baldury, at twenty-one, becomes romantically involved with Nigel Inness and becomes pregnant. She decides to have the baby and with pressure from her parents and no support from Nigel, to give the baby up for adoption. Frances goes to live with a maiden aunt and remains there until after the birth of the baby, Ian. Not wanting too much time with baby, Frances cares for him a few days and then releases him to the adoption agency that places him with the Ranald family where he is a long-awaited joy. Later at a party, she encounters a contrite Nigel who wants to marry her, but her feelings of betrayal are too strong and she rebukes him, but the evening convinces her she wants her baby. She exercises her right to regain custody, contacts the adoption agency and they make the necessary arrangements. The Ranalds are devastated, but know they will receive another child. Frances moves to her aunt's once again and begins her new life with Ian. Set in England, this is a story of strong-willed women and their relationships.

458   Dwyer-Joyce, Alice. **Reach for the Shadows**. New York: St. Martin's Press, 1973. 192pp. (OCLC 858428)

Alexa O'Driscoll learns on her eighteenth birthday that she is an adopted child. Her father and her governess share the history they know, that she is the child of her late mother's sister, Lucinda, who was killed by her insane husband and that she is from Thwaitston, England. Having fallen in love with Fergus, her brother, now cousin, Alexa runs away to escape him because of the feared insanity in her background. She leaves Ireland and travels to England, changing her appearance and taking on a false name, to discover the truth of her birth and adoption. Alexa find the people of Thwaitston friendly, but so superstitiously caught up in the events of her past that they will not speak of them. Still in love, Fergus follows her and, when he finds her, joins her in her search and learns of a discrepancy in birthfathers. Now freed from the feared genetic insanity, Alexa is free to marry Fergus. Although the adoption angle is far-fetched, this is an exciting gothic mystery complete with hidden mansions, eccentric townspeople, as well as eerie and romantic subplots.

459   Edwards, Lenora F. **Somebody That Nobody Knows**. Hicksville, NY: Exposition Press, 1977. 40pp. (OCLC 3623767)
At the age of twenty, Lisa discovers she was adopted and because she does not know her real heredity decides to pursue a career instead of romance. She lies about her educational background and becomes a successful model. In spite of her earlier decision, Lisa becomes romantically involved with Bob, the man who hired her and, although she is uncomfortable with his sexual aggressiveness and refuses his advances, she remains in a relationship with him. He takes her home to his family where his mother confides in Lisa that she had a child out-of-wedlock in the same city and about the same time that Lisa was born. Lisa decides her love for Bob is greater than her need to find her birthparents or to discover if she is Bob's sister. She decides that not knowing her background is now an advantage rather than a disadvantage. Using stilted characters, dialogue and situations, this novella is unrealistic and insensitive, particularly as it relates to adoption. Some readers may be offended by several sexual scenes.

460   Fitzgerald, Tom. **Chocolate Charlie**. Port Washington, NY: Ashley Books, 1973. 253pp. (OCLC 590954)
David Dezengremel, a twenty-eight-year-old white cynical bachelor lawyer decides to change his life and approaches an adoption agency to adopt a son. The agency assigns Judi, an equally brash individual, to his case and they proceed with a very unusual homestudy. Charlie, a rambunctious black three-year-old, is placed with David and both have an immediate and humorous indoctrination to family life. Charlie introduces David to childhood, which he claims he never experienced and David introduces Charlie to family. David experiences dirty diapers, temper tantrums and the stares and problems associated with an interracial family. When David goes against company policy and agrees to defend an indigent woman, he is fired. By invitation, David sets up a private law office in the office of his new unconventional doctor/friend and continues his law practice. Charlie becomes sick and in a panic David calls the doctor who, after hearing Charlie's symptoms, directs them to the closest hospital. Charlie is diagnosed with Eastern Equine Encephalitis and to David's grief and agony, nearly dies. The sequel, **Chocolate Charlie Comes Home**, (New York: Warner Books, 1978) continues

their life together as David seeks legal finalization. Readers are warned about bad language and sexual references.

461   George, Stephen R. **Grandma's Little Darling**. New York: Kensington Publishers, 1990. 320pp. (OCLC 22658380)
Twelve-year-old Nora, placed for adoption with the Johnson family, has been in three different children's homes and six other placements since her family's death six years ago. Willing to be more cooperative in this family, Nora finds herself liking Freida and Carl Johnson and her new nine-year-old brother, Buddy. As a former orphan, Freida has good insight into Nora's feelings and behavior. Carl's visiting mother appears to be sickly, but Nora learns she is a threat to her life because, unknown to anyone, Grandma's body has been invaded by an ancient Egyptian lifeform that transports itself from body to body to sustain its own life. The Invader successfully takes over Nora's young body and Nora is transported into Grandma's body. The book details Nora's attempts to regain her own body, the discovery that recently-deceased Grandpa was also aware of the Invader and the Invader/Nora's adjustment to the family. When she sees no other option, Nora, who now has a slight ability to invade other bodies herself overtakes her young caseworker's body just as Grandma's body dies. This is an exciting body-snatching horror story. Duncan's **Stranger With My Face** (289) also uses astral projection.

462   Helprin, Mark. **Refiner's Fire: The Life and Adventure of Marshall Pearl, a Foundling**. New York: Alfred A. Knopf, 1977. 373pp. (OCLC 7735021)
Having epic qualities, this is the story of Marshall Pearl who was born to a Russian Jewish woman on an illegal immigrant ship as the travelers were trying to escape to Palestine. Marshall is cared for by nuns and is sent to the United States where he is adopted by the wealthy childless Livingstons. Always restless, Marshall travels the world as a affluent youth, attends Harvard and continues to travel to the Great Plains, to Charleston, to the Alps seeking adventure, finally going to Israel. With almost natural abilities in warfare, Marshall seeks himself, womanizes, engages in great adventures and tries to find a real home. Beginning in the 1930s with Marshall's young parents and ending with the October War this is a large work with strong images and characterization.

463   Hill, Grace Livingston. **Partners**. Philadelphia: Lippincott, 1940. 216pp. (OCLC 6577306)
Homeless and jobless after the death of her employer, twenty-year-old orphaned Dale Hathaway seeks refuge in a ramshackled rooming house and finds a temporary job in an office. She keeps to herself, while longing for Christian companionship. Shortly before Christmas, Dale loses her job and George Rand, a fellow roomer who is also a loner, comes to her for help when he discovers an abandoned infant at the entrance of the rooming house. The two take care of the baby, report him to the police and provide the now-dead birthmother with a proper Christian burial. George, a well-off newspaperman, finds better accommodations and engages a nurse and doctor to help the sick child. As Dale and George care for the baby, they soon realize they care for each other as well and as they pray together the baby becomes stronger.

When George returns from a business trip, they declare their love, get married and make arrangements to adopt the baby. In the meantime, Dale is notified of a unknown trust which will provide her with several thousand dollars on her twenty-first birthday so the young family will be financial secure. While a contrived story with a decided Christian emphasis, this is a heartwarming story of a child bringing parents together.

464   Hoffman, Louise. **A Quiet Passion**. New York: St. Martin's Press, 1975. 190pp. (OCLC 1338977)
Susan Graham coincidentally obtains a position as a nanny at Delwyn Castle, the same household her birthdaughter, Penny, was adopted into. There she meets Penny's sickly adoptive mother, Meredith, who is too drained to offer five-year-old Penny any love, and her adoptive father, Giles, who is warm, loving and doting. Susan is surprised to encounter Tony, her ex-husband and Penny's father, who as Meredith's cousin now works on the estate. Although not chronically ill, Meredith becomes sicker and more withdrawn, yet refuses any psychological help claiming a family curse is working to kill her. Unwittingly, Penny reveals to Susan that her father is using hypnotism to guide Meredith's illness and Susan learns that he is planning to murder her. Befriended by Sam, a psychiatrist assigned to the case, Susan comes to terms with her own feelings of loneliness and falls in love with the doctor. After the escape and death of Giles and with Meredith's expected termination of parental rights, Susan and Sam plan to marry and adopt Penny. Although a far-fetched storyline, the characterization and intricate sub-plots make this an exciting thriller.

465   Hutton, Malcolm. **Tara**. London: Hale, 1984. 176pp. (OCLC 11347937)
Telling the parallel stories of Tara King, who was adopted as an infant and that of her birthmother, Vicki, during World War II, this book traces Tara's search for her past. Finding little comfort or information from her adoptive family, Tara leaves home at age eighteen to search for her birthparents. Set in London, she obtains a job at a solicitor's office and pursues her search to learn the mother listed on her original birth certificate is really her aunt. Her birthmother's story tragically reveals Tara was conceived after her birthmother's soldier-husband was declared dead. When it was discovered that he was alive as a prisoner of war, Vicki moved in with her sister, had the baby, then her sister Mary registered the baby as her own so that no one, including the prisoner-of-war husband would know Vicki had a baby. When Tara was just a few months old, both Vicki and her sister were killed in bombing raid. Tara was immediately put up for adoption by her grandmother. It is the grandmother whom Tara eventually finds and forms a close relationship. Difficult to locate, there is a soap-opera quality to this book which also contains several sex scenes.

466   Jacob, Naomi. **Strange Beginning**. London: Robert Hale, 1961. 288pp. (OCLC 3828217)
Rosie Power is an impulsive young British girl who lies about her age to obtain her first musical acting job. At the same time, she meets Roddie, an unemployed actor she helps get a job, and he becomes her lifelong best friend. Rosie is charming and while still in her teens marries caddish Horace Barrett,

who, admitting bigamy, leaves her to go to America after the death of his wife, leaving Rosie his eight-year-old son, Horace. Reluctantly, Rosie adopts the boy and with Roddie's help finds good schools for him to attend. Rosie falls in love and marries the Italian Conte de Paravenda, leaving her stage career to become his Contessa and is devastated when the Conte is killed in an auto accident. In an attempt to save a sickly baby, she buys the baby from some gypsies, searches for his parents, then legally adopts the boy she names Stefano after her late husband. Years later, the unscrupulous young Horace Barrett falsely sets mother against son and Stefano leaves, becomes a waiter and then travels to England where he unknowingly interviews for a waiter job with Rosie's father who helps him not only right the situation with his mother, but find his childhood sweetheart. Reading more like a made-for-TV movie, this is a melodramatic story of heartbreak and joy.

467 James, P.D. **Innocent Blood**. New York: Scribner, 1980. 311pp. (OCLC 5942711)
Coming from a distant, uncommunicative adoptive family, Philippa has always had a fantasy of being the offspring of a aristocratic father and a now-dead mother. Instead she learns her mother, Mary, has been in prison for years for the murder of a young girl and will shortly be released. Still living a fantasy, for the two months prior to starting college, Philippa offers her birthmother shared lodging. Her birthmother accepts and the two live together as Mary resumes her outside life. In the meantime, the father of the slain young girl wants revenge and secretly plans to kills Mary. The book concentrates on the two parallel stories and Philippa's unsuspecting role in both. In a climatic scene, when Philippa finds her father in bed with another woman, she learns her birthmother gave her up before the murder of the young girl and not because of her prison sentence. Philippa feels betrayed by her birthmother, angrily confronts her and storms out of the flat. When she returns she finds the slain girl's father there planning to kill Mary who has already committed suicide leaving a note indicating this was her plan all along. A gothic murder mystery featuring an adoption angle, this is by the author of the renowned detective novels starring Adam Dalgliesh of Scotland Yard.

468 Jenkins, Robin. **A Love of Innocence**. London: J. Cape, 1963. 343pp. (OCLC 7987098)
Nine-year-old John and his brother, six-year-old Tom, are sent from the children's home in Glasgow to live with the McArthur family. Although no one knows if they remember, the boys are followed by the dreadful truth that in a fit of jealous rage, their birthfather murdered their birthmother. Wanting the family to know the truth, the case worker shares the secret with an older sister in the family, who then shares it with others so that it is no longer a secret. When the father learns of the news, he feels it is his Christian duty to return the boys to the home. He is met with significant resistance and the boys stay, but not until John relives the trauma when he sees what he thinks is a replay of the tragedy. John survives and the family is strengthened. In the meantime, the caseworker becomes involved with the boys' new uncle, who has the reputation for being a ladies' man, and another inhabitant of the island works towards the adoption of nine-year-old Jean, a good friend of the boys

at the home. The multiple plots and the Scottish dialect make this difficult to follow at times, but nonetheless is an exciting romantic thriller.

469   Johnston, Velda. **The Stone Maiden**. New York: Dodd, Mead, 1980. 228pp. (OCLC 6304626)
Twenty-eight-year-old Katherine Derwith learned in her mid-teens that she was adopted as an infant. Since that time it has become very important to her to discover who her birthparents so that she can make a good, informed decision about marriage and children. Her inquiry placed in a newspaper to seek information, is answered by Carl Dietrich who knows enough of Katherine's past he does not want her find out for fear his own life will be adversely affected. In the meantime, Katherine's birthfather has secretly kept track of her, following her life and success. He was a young accidental witness to a war crime in Italy which involved Carl's father. He abandoned her, after her mother's death, for her protection from Nazis who were still chasing him for information. Katherine eventually meets her birthfather on his deathbed and she and Carl go to Italy to verify and report the crime so they can continue their lives especially now that they are in love. This is a fascinating fast-paced story with many exciting subplots and characters of intrigue which add to a hard-to-put-down book.

470   Lawson, Will. **Gold in Their Hearts**. Sydney: Invincible Press, 1950. 256pp. (OCLC 11169178)
As he and his parents travel to their new home in a small New Zealand mining town, baby Christopher's father is thrown overboard and is drowned. He and his mother are taken to Mary Smith's hotel and reside with her. The baby's mother, in shock, fails to recognize Christopher and although her memory eventually returns, her feelings for the child do not. She remarries and leaves Christopher for Mary Smith to raise. The boy becomes the darling of the miners; they set up a trust fund for him and help guide him as he grows up. As an adult, Christopher tries to revive the dying mining community and bring honor to its name. Mary Smith remains his confidante until her death. Christopher discovers his true love, Nancy, has been waiting for him and the two marry and move to a more prosperous town. Set primarily in the late 1800s, this is an inside look at New Zealand frontier life. Later published as **Mary Smith's Hotel** (Sydney: Angus and Robertson, 1957).

471   Lewin, Michael Z. **And Baby Will Fall**. New York: William Morrow, 1988. 261pp. (OCLC 17439504)
Following the murder of a former agency worker, Adele Buffington, who heads a local private adoption agency, tries to help the police discover the agency's role and finds herself involved with Homer Proffitt, an ambitious detective with the police. While coping with her daughter's love life, general office politics and a boss who does not want bad publicity, Adele delves into the mystery, which is further complicated by a missing young mother and her twin Down's Syndrome daughters. Adele and Homer put clues together and find themselves at the mansion home of Anthony Bradberry where Adele discover a strange section of rooms, one of which has a collection of life-size inflatable female dolls, and a dead woman on the bottom of the pile. She escapes the gun-toting clutches of Bradberry, and runs to the nearest phone to call the

police. She and Homer learn they uncovered a ghastly baby-making adoption racket as well as the murder of the young mother and her two children. This is a fast-paced murder mystery with a grisly adoption twist. Readers may recognize Adele's boyfriend, Albert Samson, as the protagonist in other Lewin novels.

472   Lipman, Elinor. **Then She Found Me**. New York: Pocket Books, 1990. 307pp. (OCLC 20755588)
Thirty-six-year-old Latin teacher, April Epner, a single woman who grew up in the warm, secure adoptive home of two concentration camp survivors, is contacted by her birthmother who wants to meet her. Since her adoptive parents are now dead, April agrees to meet only to be surprised that her birthmother is a local celebrity, an excessive, flamboyant Boston talk show host, Bernice. April is at once both drawn to and repulsed by Bernice, but continues to see her even though she knows Bernice does not entirely approve of her lifestyle. When Bernice lets on that April's birthfather is the late Jack Kennedy, April seeks the research assistance of Dwight Willamee, the nerdy school librarian, who verifies the impossibility. April continues a relationship with Dwight as pushy Bernice tries to undermine April's adoptive parents and restructure her life. When her true birthfather, Jack, arrives on the scene, still legally married to Bernice, April finds herself fond of him. A judge refuses to grant Jack and Bernice a divorce, instead ordering counseling, and April and Dwight marry. This story with extreme personalities and characterization is a kindly love story set in a bizarre situation.

473   Magnuson, James, and Dorothea G. Petrie. **Orphan Train**. New York: Dial Press, 1978. 307pp. (OCLC 3843100)
Presenting a fictionalized account of the first orphan train, set in 1853, twenty seven homeless children are initially supervised by the Reverend Symns and his niece on their way to be adopted in the Midwest. When the Reverend becomes ill during the journey, Emma Symns carries on herself. Traveling in a box car from New York to Illinois, some of the children are taken at stops along the way, but most of them end up in one Illinois town. On the train Emma makes the acquaintance of Frank, a photographer who befriends and helps her. As the story progresses, they fall in love and she promises to wait for him until his current job is completed. The journey is dangerous, with one of the children drowning en route and the train having an accident over a river ravine. This is a fascinating story. For its qualities of warmth and spunk, it has been compared to **True Grit**. Orphan train stories for younger children include Nixon's **A Family Apart** (204) and Talbot's **An Orphan for Nebraska** (235). A nonfiction account of the orphan trains can be found in Patrick's **We Are Part of History** (396).

474   Maiden, Cecil. **Jonathan Found**. New York: Crowell, 1957. 185pp. (OCLC 1802125)
When Chinese terrorists menace and later kill his British missionary parents, seven-year-old Jonathan escapes with a old Chinese housemaid and is taken to the International Children's Aid (ICA) office in Hong Kong. He is adopted by Mr. Angus, a wealthy American businessman, after the death of his only child. Miss Lunt, an ICA employee, accompanies Jonathan to the United

States to meet his new parents at their home in Manhattan. Because their birth son, Robin, was killed in a school accident, Mrs. Angus will not allow Jonathan to be with other children. When a tutor tries to explain Jonathan's needs for peer interaction, Mrs. Angus' response is so violent it frightens Jonathan to run away where he finds comfort in a Chinese laundry until the police take him to Miss Lunt who has been made aware of the situation by the tutor. Mr. Angus is called back from a trip, Mrs. Angus is hospitalized for another breakdown and Jonathan and his father go home, both willing to start again to make a new family. A charming story of a curious, but confused young boy not knowing how to meet his new parents' expectations. This story also appeared in an abridged version in **The Ladies Home Journal**. The British title is **Image and Likeness** (London: J. Murray, 1957).

475   March, William. **The Bad Seed**. New York: Rinehart, 1954. 247pp. (OCLC 974385)
Eight-year-old Rhoda is an unusual child, looking somewhat old-fashioned, disliked by other children, but doted on by adults. Her mother, Christine, slowly realizes her odd unfeeling daughter has often been present during tragedies. Christine begins to worry as she discovers clues to Rhoda's involvement in so-called accidental deaths. Christine researches child murderers and shockingly learns her birthmother was a murderer who was executed in the electric chair, leaving Christine to be adopted. Realizing now the hereditary nature of Rhoda's attitude and behavior, Christine feels responsible and plans to rectify the situation. She gives Rhoda an overdose of sleeping pills, then kills herself with her husband's gun. A kind, but nosy neighbor finds them and seeks medical attention for Rhoda who survives. Her father returns and is consoled by Rhoda, although he is ignorant of the evil within her. Appearing as a cold calculating person, Rhoda is a fictionalized child without a conscience. This eerie story is the basis for the 1956 movie of the same name. Another child-killer thriller is Taylor's **Godsend** (494).

476   Maybury, Anne. **The Brides of Bellenmore and Falcon's Shadow**. Garden City, NY: Nelson Doubleday, 1964. 376pp. (OCLC 727455)
Twenty-four-year-old Loran Brant, the heroine of **Falcon's Shadow**, discovers she was adopted as an infant and leaves London to stay with Mrs. Cranmer, her father's friend who lives near where Loran was born. While there she is caught up in the mysterious disappearance of the wife of Sarne, owner of the farm on the manor and the father of three small children. Sarne's jealous seductive housekeeper, Deborah, is threatened by Loran's presence and unsuccessfully tries to scare her into leaving. When Loran follows a lead that Deborah's birthfather, Tom, may also be hers, Deborah tries to kill her father and blackmail Loran. During the struggle Deborah is arrested and charged with the death of Sarne's wife, Tom admits to Loran that he is her father and Loran and Sarne, who have grown fond of each other, are now free to pursue a romantic relationship. Here bound with **The Brides of Bellenmore**, **Falcon's Shadow**, an exciting gothic romance, was originally published under the pseudonym of Katherine Troy (London: Collins, 1964).

477   Miles, Judith M. **Journal From An Obscure Place**. Minneapolis: Bethany Fellowship, 1978. 140pp. (OCLC 4857451)

Written as if the narrator were an unborn child, this book is arranged in forty chapters each representing a week of pregnancy. The unborn child describes his physical development and responds to the world around him. In the ninth week the mother, Jill, a college student, goes against advice and does not have an abortion. A nurse talks to her about the ways of the Lord and Jill claims Christ, seeks forgiveness and chooses to continue her pregnancy with the intention of placing the child for adoption. At the end of the semester, Jill is sent to live with an aunt and uncle and while she initially felt rejected by her mother, she is happy to be in the safe, secure and supportive home of her Christian relatives. Jill's aunt helps her choose a Christian adoption agency and all necessary arrangements are made. She is well-supported by her parents, her aunt and uncle and the adoption worker who are with her for the birth. Using an interesting literary device, this book presents a decidedly anti-abortion message and promotes a Christian perspective.

478   Miller, Laura Owen. **The Place of Sapphires**. New York: John Day, 1956.
        319pp. (OCLC 599618)
Adopted as an infant, Anne Stacey Kendall is brought up by her wealthy doting adoptive father after the early death of her adoptive mother. She leads a sheltered, well-traveled, adult-oriented life and learns of her passion for painting through her art teacher. Thinking she will probably remain unmarried, she is swept off her feet by dashing Gil Weir and they marry. Devastated when Gil is killed in a car accident, she turns down his inheritance, is denounced by another beau and, seeking her heritage, she finds the cottage she was born in and discovers distant relatives are still there. She falls in love with her birthmother's now-deceased cousins's husband, Andrew, who has recently remarried. He speaks of divorce to marry Anne Stacey, however his young son, who reminds Anne Stacey so much of herself, despises her. Andrew helps to locate Anne Stacey's birthmother and she goes to Florida to visit her, but she doesn't learn much from her birthmother, who is ambivalent about seeing her. However, after her visit, her mother is taken to a sanitarium where she spends her days rocking a baby doll. Anne Stacey realizes the futility of a relationship with Andrew and makes plans to join her old art teacher in California to pursue painting, her true love. A long, involved story with many qualities of a soap opera.

479   Moen, Erna I. **Written in the Stars: The Story of Suki**. Seoul: Korean
        Consolidated Corporation, 1973. 215pp. (OCLC 9070237)
Born to a Korean woman and fathered by an American soldier, Un Sook (Suki) is a mixed-race child in Korea who lives the consequences of being a non-person. The story looks back on the lives of her grandmother and mother to put Suki's situation in perspective. After the death of her mother and grandmother, Suki is taken to an orphanage where she lives for two years until she is too old to remain there, seeing many children leave the orphanage to be adopted. All these years Suki has believed that her birthfather will rescue her and take her to his home, but now realizes he is never coming. Her hope replaced by anger, Suki is befriended by Don, an American GI who falls in love with her. He introduces Suki to a minister who works with mixed-race children and he helps her get to the States. In the meantime, Don contacts Suki's birthfather who is initially hostile, but when Don calls Suki to tell her

of her travel arrangements, he tells her he and her father will be at the airport to meet her. While not specifically an adoption story, there are similarities in the search for Suki's birthfather. In addition, this is an accurate account of the life of an Amerasian child in Korea, many of whom have been adopted by families in the States.

480   Morrison, Margaret. **The Cuckoo.** New York: Roy Publishers, [n.d.] 256pp.
       (OCLC 6871948)
       After twenty years of a childless marriage, James Peddle's plans to run off are changed when his wife, Maisie, announces she is pregnant. On Christmas 1900 Maisie gives birth to a dead baby girl, but while Maisie is in a drugged sleep, her husband and doctor secretly connive to replace the baby with a newborn infant from the local foundling home to aid Maisie's recovery. When she awakens, Maisie is overjoyed at her new little son whom they name Henry. In order to remove Henry from the immediate vicinity, the doctor advises they go on a long holiday for his health. When he grows, up Henry becomes an accomplished pianist and an internationally known opera singer who changes his name to Enrico Peddeli. After he marries, his parents return to England and Maisie accidentally learns of her son's real heritage. While momentarily feeling angered and betrayed, she instead makes arrangements to offer benefit funds to the foundling home and in her speech indicates a change in heart regarding illegitimate children. This is a long, involved story of keeping Henry's identity secret.

481   Neiderman, Andrew. **Bloodchild.** New York: Berkley, 1990. 268pp. (OCLC
       22333685)
       Shortly after Dana and Harlan Hamilton suffer the death of their infant child, they adopt a baby, Nikos, in hopes of passing him off as their birthchild. Dana's mother, Jillian, arrives to help the new family and sees Dana slowly undergo emotional and physical changes that the doctors believe is related to the trauma of the birthchild's death. Harlan's younger sister, Colleen, begins witnessing strange events concerning Jillian, her friend, Audra, and Nikos, who daily reveals remarkable physical changes. The story comes to a climax when Colleen discovers Nikos and his birthparents are vampires who intend to kill Dana. When Colleen tries to convince others, they do not believe her and her brother seeks psychiatric assistance for her. Colleen, taking the matter in her own hands, kills the adult vampires, as well as her friend, Audra, who is becoming one. Harlan then discovers the truth, gets Dana the help she needs and she recovers. The baby and the baby nurse disappear and by the end of the book, Dana is pregnant again. While good triumphs over evil in the story, neither adoption nor vampires are presented very knowledgeably.

482   O'Donnell, Lillian. **The Baby Merchants.** New York: Putnam, 1975. 185pp.
       (OCLC 1377537)
       Detective Norah Mulcahaney and her police lieutenant husband, Joe Capretto, wanting to have a child, turn to adoption, but when they are offered a child very quickly, without any investigation, they decline fearing it is illegal. Norah's father becomes a volunteer grandparent at a local agency and befriends Mark, an available adorable three-year-old and Joe and Norah contact the agency and begin proceedings to adopt him. In the meantime, Joe

is assigned to drug smuggling and murder cases and receives a threat regarding Mark. Joe and Norah, wanting to make sure Mark's adoption is legal, obtain the sealed record and discover the person who relinquished Mark is also the caseworker who placed him. They continue their investigation and learn the relationship between their new son and the murders and drugs. When Norah realizes that the completed investigation will result in Joe being responsible for the conviction of Mark's true birthmother, they sadly relinquishes Mark. One of several Norah Mulcahaney novels, this is an exciting murder mystery with adoption implications. Another mystery concerning an illegal adoption is Queen's **Inspector Queen's Own Case** (486).

483   Packer, Joy Petersen. **Veronica**. London: Eyre and Spottiswoode, 1970. 246pp. (OCLC 99942)
Set in South Africa, this is the story of Veronica, a fair-skinned black, her relationship with Derek, a British businessman, and the child, Lex, who appears white, born after they break off their illegal relationship. Learning of Lex prior to his marriage to Lindy, the daughter of long-established Afrikaners, Derek wants to keep this secret, arranging through his attorney a monthly stipend which will provide for Lex. When Lindy, who is unable to have children, learns about three-year-old Lex and Veronica, she agrees they will secretly adopt the child. Lex is later kidnapped by Veronica's cousin who had earlier acted as messenger and now he blackmails Derek. Lex is seriously injured and hospitalized. As he lies dying in the hospital, the adults in his life agonize over their part in his disaster. A powerful and moving story which illuminates the racial problems in South Africa, the chapters are narrated in first person by the different characters.

484   Paul, Phyllis. **Lion of Cooling Bay**. London: Heinemann, 1953. 243pp.
When she was five years old, Anne was adopted by Julian Rackenbury, one of five eccentric adult siblings who live together and are a curious institution among the literati. As a young teen, she is sent to live with the Laurents, family friends, for the summer and, years later, when Anne is twenty-two, she travels back to Sollas Sands to live with the Laurents' two daughters and they open a Christian boarding house where Anne serves as a maid in addition to her free-lance illustration work. Mrs. North, who works at the Laurents' boarding house and serves as the house monitor for the Rackenburys, wants to gain control of the house from the Laurents but needs Anne out of the way. She wants her son to be sweet and nice to Anne in hopes the younger Laurent girl will become jealous and send Anne away. Pryde, Mrs. North's driver, however, misunderstands her intentions and kills Anne. This is a very esoteric work, difficult to follow with several characters dealing in their own musings and having a bizarre plot.

485   Pullman, Philip. **The Ruby in the Smoke**. New York: Knopf, 1985. 230pp. (OCLC 14188953)
When Sally Lockhart's father dies in 1872, the sixteen-year-old girl never imagines how much her life will change. After receiving a message from Singapore, where her father died, Sally decides to investigate his death on her own. Through the use of opium, Sally reconstructs a recurring nightmare and discovers the truth about her past learning that as an infant she was traded for

a precious ruby and through this private arrangement became her father's daughter. Now an old woman, Mrs. Holland, believing the ruby is rightfully hers, wants it returned to her. Working with new-found friends, Jim, Frederick and Rosa, Sally finds the ruby and loses it again leading to Mrs. Holland's death. While a creative mystery/adventure story, this is not a very good adoption story. Sally's life is resumed six years later in the second book of the proposed trilogy, **The Shadow in the North** (New York: Knopf, 1988). A similar child-selling theme can be found in Andrews' **Heaven** (442).

486   Queen, Ellery. **Inspector Queen's Own Case: November Song**. New York:
            Simon and Schuster, 1956. 312pp. (OCLC 8990276)
        While visiting friends, Beck and Abe Pearl, a police chief, retired New York Police Department inspector Richard Queen, Ellery's father, gets in on a case involving the possible murder of a two-month-old infant adopted illegally by a multi-millionaire, Alton Humffrey, and his wife, Sarah. After the baby's death, Sarah suffers a nervous breakdown and is hospitalized. Joining forces with the baby's nurse, Jessie Sherwood, Queen, without the sanction of the police, pursues her certainty of the existence of a pillowslip, with a handprint, that was used to smother the baby. As Queen and Sherwood piece together the clues, they determine Humffrey is the birthfather, as well as the adoptive father, and pursue him as the murderer. When Queen and Sherwood trap him, Humffrey admits to the murders of a lawyer and the birthmother, but reveals Sarah killed the baby when she learned he was her husband's child by another woman. Queen and Sherwood, a single woman, grow close during the case and become engaged at the end of the story. Ellery is purposefully missing from this adventure as he is on a world tour. This is a typical, exciting Ellery Queen murder mystery combined with a little romance. Another mystery concerning an illegal adoption is O'Donnell's **The Baby Merchants** (482).

487   Reid Banks, Lynne. **Children At the Gate**. New York: Simon and Schuster,
            1968. 287pp. (OCLC 438603)
        Thirty-nine-year-old Gerda Shaffer, a half-Jewish Canadian woman living in Israel, is still reeling from the death of her only child and the subsequent break up of her marriage. She isolates herself allowing a dubious friendship with Kofi, a local painter who is a single father of a half-Jewish daughter, Hanna. Kofi convinces Gerda she needs to be responsible for someone else, that she should adopt a child. An orphaned half-Arab abused three-year-old girl, without benefit of law, becomes Gerda's daughter, Ella. Her older brother soon joins them and the little family makes it until Kofi warns Gerda the children's birthgrandmother wants them back. Gerda and the children leave the kibbutz and live in a small village, where the children are taken from her. When Kofi is wounded and dying from his defection attempt, Gerda visits him and he legally gives her custody of Hanna. Already hurt by three children taken from her, Gerda will not accept the responsibility of Hanna. After war breaks out, Gerda slowly warms and the book ends with her making plans to get Hanna. Some readers may object to the occasional references to sex in this heartbreaking story of a woman and her dashed desire to be a mother.

488   Robins, Denise. **Wait For Tomorrow**. Greenwich, CT: Fawcett, 1967. 160pp.
       (OCLC 9886362)
       While her parents are away in Paris, twenty-year-old Charlotte, at home in
       London, accidentally discovers she was adopted as an infant. She sets out to
       find her birthmother, but her best friend, Luke, a family friend twelve years
       her senior, is dubious of her plans. She confronts her parents, agreeing not to
       tell her brother. Charlotte hires a private detective and soon knows her
       birthmother's name and her maternal grandfather's name. She traces him to
       the south of France and Luke accompanies her on what turns out to be a
       disastrous meeting where she learns her birthmother's address. During this
       trip Luke expresses his love for Charlotte, but wrapped up in her search, she
       misunderstands his overtures. She eventually confronts her birthmother, who
       has since married a younger man, and the woman wants no relationship with
       her. Dejected, but wiser, the romantic Charlotte, returns to her now much
       more appreciated family where she is warmly welcomed. Knowing her heart
       better now, Charlotte finds Luke, expresses her love, but is initially rejected.
       The two reconcile and decide to marry. This is a light romance novel using
       the tragedy of an unknown adoption as its basis.

489   Savage, Thomas. **I Heard My Sister Speak My Name**. Boston: Little, Brown,
       1977. 242pp. (OCLC 30030000)
       Relating a fictionalized account of one woman's own adoption and life, this
       story is told by her younger birthbrother who had not been aware of her
       existence. Amy McKinney, born in 1912, searches for her birthparents after
       the death of her adoptive parents. Instead, she discovers her birthparents are
       also dead and is left with a disbelieving birthfamily that eventually realizes she
       is a blood relative. This is a somewhat cumbersome story as it provides much
       background on all sides of Amy's families. It is, perhaps, most noteworthy for
       the perspective of the narrator. Instead of being told by an adoptee, it is told
       by a sought-out member of the birthfamily.

490   Slosberg, Mike. **The August Strangers**. New York: Dial Press, 1977. 234pp.
       (OCLC 2680809)
       When he still shows signs of illness after a strep infection clears up, eleven-
       year-old David August is diagnosed with pending kidney failure and is in need
       of a transplant. While a relative donation would be best, Mike and Mandy
       August have never told David and his nine-year-old sister, Ellen, they are
       adopted. Mike searches for and finds David's birthfather who angrily refuses
       to be a donor. The birthmother is later turned down due to her fragile health,
       but she offers their retarded nine-year-old daughter, Paula, without the
       knowledge of her husband. She plans for Mike to kidnap the girl, substituting
       her for Ellen who is scheduled to be the donor. When the birthfather storms
       into the hospital and sees David for the first time, he relents and becomes the
       kidney donor. David successfully recovers and the children are told of their
       adoptions. Although the ending may be too convenient, this is an exciting
       story told by a doting, but frantic father. Another story about the immediate
       need to locate birthparents for medical reasons is found in Hulse's **Jody** (371).

491   Stroud, John. **On The Loose**. London: Longmans, 1961. 191pp. (OCLC
       15735095)

Obviously unloved and unwanted, Royston's presence during his summer vacation is a burden on his busy, social parents so he runs away only to be returned by the police. Royston takes up with Tod, a youthful hoodlum, and learns about birth certificates. He goes home to find his own to learn something about his past and discovers he was adopted as an infant. When Royston runs away again, his exasperated parents cannot be bothered any longer and he is taken into custody by juvenile authorities. He does well at the children's home, until he meets up with Tod again. Miss Mole, a spinster woman who reported Royston's attempted breaking and entering, agrees to serve as his foster mother, but before long she feels used and beaten and Royston runs away from her. He searches for his birthmother in hopes perhaps she wants him, but he is very disappointed when he finds her. Royston becomes involved with an illegal operation of Tod's, but after thoughtful deliberation, he withdraws himself, returns to Miss Mole and decides to invest himself in her care. Involving multiple rejections, this story demonstrates the struggle between differing value systems.

492   Supervielle, Jules. **The Colonel's Children**. Trans. of **Le Voleur d'Enfants** by Alan Pryce-Jones. London: Secker and Warburg, 1950. 150pp. (OCLC 2343739)
Seven-year-old Antoine is separated from his nanny in a crowded Paris street and is taken home by kindly South American colonel Philemon Bigua, who, he learns from the several other children, has stolen them all. Bigua's wife, Desposoria, kindly goes along with her husband's urges to take children. Bigua finds himself attracted to teenage Marcelle and at the same time is aware of teenage Joseph's attraction to her. He controls himself, but even the locks he has installed do not keep the young lovers apart. Soon, Marcelle is pregnant and Joseph is thrown out of the house. Marcelle suffers a miscarriage just before Bigua decides it is time for his "family" to sail back home to South America and they meet again with Joseph who is a sailor on the boat. The two young lovers become engaged and unable to do anything else, Bigua throws himself overboard only to discover he accidentally kept his will with him. The sequel, **The Survivor** (trans. from the French **Survivent** by John Russell, London: Secker and Warburg, 1951) continues the adventures of the family after Bigua gets back on the boat. While quite unbelievable, this is a humorous story presenting an unfavorable view of adoptive parents.

493   Swinnerton, Frank. **A Flower for Catherine**. London: Hutchinson, 1950. 295pp. (OCLC 7533079)
Catherine Barter, the only married sister of three close sisters, is wife to nervous Bob and mother to fun-loving, twenty-two-year-old Andy. When Catherine and her older sister, Madeleine, learn that Celia, their younger sister, has died, they discover Celia has a ten-year-old daughter, Rosie, they never knew about. Catherine, who has always wanted a daughter, and Bob agree to adopt Rosie who will live with them and attend school locally. Catherine is very taken with Rosie and the two get on well until Rosie accidentally slips and calls Bob "Daddy". Catherine then realizes Rosie is really Bob's daughter by Celia. Hurt and shaken, Catherine wants rid of Bob and Rosie, who knows she has spoiled her chance. Catherine is injured and with a variety of visitors has a change of heart and mind agreeing to stay with

Bob and to continue with their plans to adopt a much-relieved Rosie. This is sometimes difficult to follow and rather melodramatic.

494   Taylor, Bernard. **The Godsend**. New York: St. Martin's Press, 1976. 208pp. (OCLC 2034814)
Under unusual circumstances, Alan and Kate Marlowe, already the parents of four small children, adopt newborn, Bonnie. Not long after her arrival, one morning one of the other children is dead, suffocated by his bedding. Over the next several years, the other children are mysteriously killed and Alan becomes suspicious fearing Bonnie is the cause of the other children's "accidents." With only Lucy, their oldest child, alive, he fears for her life, but Kate cannot accept such ideas about Bonnie. Alan kidnaps Lucy to keep her safe, but returns when Kate is hospitalized from a fall in which she lost the baby she had not yet told Alan she was carrying. Now convinced of Bonnie's evil nature, Alan unsuccessfully tries to have the authorities remove Bonnie from their home. When Kate discovers he took this action without her knowledge, she goes to his workplace to ask for a divorce. Alan becomes furious to learn Kate left Lucy home alone with Bonnie and becomes more anxious when Lucy calls complaining about Bonnie. They rush home to find Lucy falling out a window to her death. Still denying the possibility, a dazed Kate prepares to leave Alan taking Bonnie with her. This is a chiller thriller similar to **The Bad Seed** (475).

495   Tevis, Walter S. **The Queen's Gambit**. New York: Random House, 1983. 243pp. (OCLC 8708429)
Prior to her adoption at age thirteen, loner Beth learned to play chess at the orphanage. Her new parents separate when she arrives and Beth continues her love of chess, winning the state competition without her new mother's knowledge. When money gets tight, Mrs. Wheatley and Beth turn to Beth's chess tournaments as a source of income. Ever aloof, Beth continues playing and winning tournaments becoming the co-champion of the U.S. Open at age sixteen. During Beth's first international tournament in Mexico City, she loses to the world champion, Mrs. Wheatley dies and Mr. Wheatley turns the house and belongings over to Beth. Beth continues playing more substantial tournaments and becomes nationally recognized. Experiencing slumps, episodes of overuse of alcohol and drugs, followed by periods of great energy when she studies with former champions, Beth prepares for a major competition in Moscow and at age nineteen she wins, paving the way for her to become the World Champion. Written by the same author who wrote **The Hustler**, the exciting pool story, this is definitely a chess story which uses the orphan and adoption angle to promote a sense of isolation and aloofness. This book contains drug and sexual references.

496   Timperley, Rosemary. **House of Secrets**. London: Hale, 1971. 174pp. (OCLC 16195914)
Jeannie Gentian, a doctor's receptionist, invites widowed Anna Lake, a medical center waitress, to visit her family on the weekend. Obliging, Anna spends the day with Gentian family which includes Sean, the carpet salesman husband, adopted fifteen-year-old Angela and an elderly, sickly grandfather. During their visit, a Mrs. Langley, Angela's unknown birthmother, arrives

unannounced and although somewhat daunted, Angela establishes a relationship with her to the disappointment of her adoptive mother. Wanting to maintain truthfulness, Jeannie and Sean confess their own extramarital affairs and agree to call them off. Anna begins to spends weekends at the Gentian home becoming a helpful member of the household. Mrs. Langley introduces Angela to her birthfather who agrees Angela has significant musical talent. He agrees to pay for Angela's musical training and arrangements are made for her to move in with Mrs. Langley. The family is distraught after the death of the grandfather and Anna helps by filling in at Jeannie's job so she can have a holiday. Once Angela is settled, her adoptive parents decide to return to Ireland to live and Anna takes over Jeannie's job. This is a multifaceted story which exposes its characters' secrets as well as their consequences.

497   Tutton, Diana. **The Young Ones**. London: Davies, 1959. 247pp. (OCLC 13413936)
When Charlotte was fifteen and her brother, Ned, was five their recently widowed mother adopted an infant daughter, Julie. Now grown, Julie has been set up in a flower shop by her godmother, Ned is a photographer and widowed Charlotte works in a doctor's office. Ned becomes engaged to Sylvia, a friend of Julie's, but the engagement is short as it becomes evident Ned loves Julie. Rationalizing that Julie's adoption means they are not really related, the two become engaged much to the dismay of their older sister. When her godmother finds out the plans, she contacts Charlotte and reveals to her that Julie is really their half-sister. Charlotte relates the news to Ned and Julie who do not heed the advice and get married anyway. Within a year the relationship falls apart and Ned and Julie split up when his conscience makes the situation unbearable. In the meantime, Charlotte also has occasional romantic adventures. This is a romance that involves an adoption which is not really an adoption.

498   **The Two Brothers of Different Sex: A Story from the Chinese**. Trans. of **Tse-Hiong-Hiong-Ti** from the French of Stanislas Julien by Frances Hume. Illus. by Edy Legrand. London: Rodale Press, 1955. 51pp. (OCLC 2762266)
Innkeepers Lieou-te and his wife are both sixty years old and childless. When a visitor dies, they adopt his twelve-year-old son, Chin-eul. A few years later they nurse a twenty-year-old shipwreck victim and as Lieou-ki recovers he becomes as fond of the family as they are of him, taking a special liking to Chin-eul whom he tutors. When he finds his village destroyed, he returns to Lieou-te and his wife and they adopt him as well. The parents grow old, but are happy now they have sons to carry out the family business and manage the land. After the death of their parents, twenty-two-year-old Lieou-ki cannot understand his seventeen-year-old brother's balking at the notion of their marriages to provide their own posterity. They write each other notes about their feelings and plans and it becomes clear that Chin-eul loves Lieou-ki. Soon Chin-eul reveals to Lieou-ki that he is really a girl who had assumed the role of son for her own protection while traveling with her birthfather and has never been able to drop the disguise. Now, she loves her brother and wants to marry him. Although surprised, Lieou-ki agrees and the two marry, have many children and live well and happily. A charming Chinese folktale,

illustrated by occasional full-color plates of disguises, tradition and good fortune.

499　Vining, Elizabeth Gray. **I, Roberta**. Philadelphia: Lippincott, 1967. 224pp.
(OCLC 688288)

In 1895, a few years after her husband leaves her penniless, Roberta Morelli and her five-year-old son, Kent, are visited by a woman who claims to have been married to the same man. The woman, Grace Morelli, found Roberta's address among her now-dead husband's belongings and traced her only to learn of her husband's bigamist relationship. In her grief over Tony, her lost husband, Grace proposes to Roberta that she allow her to adopt and raise Kent as he was Tony's child. In her grief and panic, Roberta, who had been controlled by her now-dead mother, realizes she has to count on herself to make this major decision. Roberta writes journal entries to help herself sort out her feelings and at one point comes close to allowing Kent's adoption, but changes her mind to control her own life. She keeps Kent, applies for a job a postmistress to support them and begins her new life. There is much tension in this work that walks the reader through one woman's examination of her life.

500　Whalley-Tooker, Dorothea Caroline. **Son By Adoption**. London: Faber and Faber, 1955. 254pp.

Orphaned when he is three years old, Laurence is adopted by a distant childless cousin and her husband. Set in England, Edith Everard is delighted and much taken with her new son. While her husband, Duncan, is supportive, he remains cool toward the child but relieved to have an heir. Arriving from India, Edith's cousin, Owen Arbuthnot, who has always loved Edith, is also smitten with the child she loves so much. Three years later, to everyone's surprise, Edith gives birth to a son, Arthur, and Laurence's position as first-born heir is in jeopardy. When he is ten and away at school, Laurence's mother is killed in a horse and carriage accident. Shocked, but supported by Owen's encouragement, Laurence resumes his life without the person who loved him most. After his schooling is completed, Laurence goes to India with Owen to learn his tea business. Feeling he is no longer part of the family, he is called back home following the death of twenty-one-year-old Arthur who dies in a horse accident. Laurence's father reconciles with him, he once again becomes the heir, makes arrangements to stay in England and plans to marry his childhood sweetheart. The relationship between Laurence and his mother is strong and purposeful, however, the theme of adoption as second-best is pervasive.

501　White, Robin. **Elephant Hill**. New York: Harper and Brothers, 1959. 245pp. (OCLC 1153130)

Thirty-five-year old Beth Sumner travels to India to visit her sister, Agnes and her medical missionary husband, George and their three children, one of whom is an Indian child. While on the train to their city, she meets Mr. Alagarsami, a charming widower who insists on showing her the sights of their shared destination. Upon describing him to Agnes and George, they recognize him as the meddling birthfather of their child, Mutthu, which causes Beth better to understand Mr. Alagarsami's coolness once he learned where she was going. George and Agnes fear he wants to regain custody of Mutthu, but Beth learns he only want to know the boy. Beth, who finds herself attracted to Mr. Alagarsami, takes it upon herself to help these people understand their misunderstandings and come to a mutual agreement. The two sides eventually get together, Mutthu is told of Mr. Alagarsami's identity, the families find a way to cooperate and, after yet another misunderstanding, Mr. Alagarsami, or Mani, and Beth get together. Although seemingly unrealistic, this story nicely presents the cultural differences when East meets West.

502   Whitney, Phyllis A. **The Golden Unicorn**. Garden City, NY: Doubleday, 1976. 279pp. (OCLC 2090894)
Courtney Marsh, a journalist in her mid-twenties, seeks out her birthfamily by falsely arranging an interview with Judith Rhodes, a recluse artist whom Courtney believes may be her birthmother. As Courtney is pulled into the strange people and problems of the Rhodes family, Judith's daughter, Stacia, who resents the intrusion on her inheritance of the family estate she plans to sell away from her parents, is the first to realize Courtney's real mission. Apparently, years ago Judith's brother-in-law John Rhodes' wife and infant daughter were to have died in a boating accident. Courtney learns she is the supposedly dead baby and through many dangerous events learns of the role John Rhodes played in his wife's death and now in the attempt on her life. Courtney discovers that while Judith is not her birthmother, her husband, Herndon is her birthfather. In the meantime, Courtney falls in love with Evan, Judith's son-in-law, and they decide to remain together. This is a fast-paced gothic romance with an unusual adoption.

503   Whitney, Phyllis A. **Woman Without a Past**. New York: Doubleday, 1991. (OCLC 21973077)
When mystery writer, thirty-year-old Molly Hurst, who had grown up with her adoptive family, discovers her birthmother and twin birthsister with the assistance of a handsome stranger, she also uncovers a background of kidnapping and murder. Another offering from a prolific author, this book was unavailable for personal review.

Appendix A:
Selected Resources
for Further Reading

The Adoption Directory. Detroit: Gale Research, 1989.

Adoption Factbook. Washington, DC: National Committee for Adoption, 1989.

Andersen, Robert S. "The Nature of Adoptee Search: Adventure, Cure or Growth?" **Child Welfare** 68 (November-December 1989): 623-32.

Baskin, Barbara and Karen H. Harris. **More Notes From a Different Drummer: A Guide to Juvenile Fiction Portraying the Disabled**. New York: Bowker, 1984.

Berger, Louisa and Ellen G. Satre. **Books on Adoption for Children and Youth**. Philadelphia: National Adoption Center, 1986.

Bernstein, Joanne E. **Books to Help Children Cope With Separation and Loss**. 2nd ed. New York: Bowker, 1983.

Bibliotherapy Sourcebook. Rhea Joyce Rubin, editor. Phoenix, AZ: Oryx Press, 1978.

Booth, Marion. **Recommended Books to Use With Adopted Children**. Walnut Creek, CA: Post Adoption Center for Education and Research, 1982.

Bothun, Linda. **When Friends Ask About Adoption: Question and Answer Guide for Non-Adoptive Parents and Other Caring Adults**. Chevy Chase, MD: Swan Publications, 1987.

Bunin, Sherry. "Essential Reading if You're Planning to Adopt." **Parents** 60 (March 1985): 42-48.

Bunin, Sherry. "Up With Adoption: An Adoptive Mother Challenges Society's Attitudes About Adopted Children." **Parents' Magazine** 65 (January 1990): 78-80.

Canape, Charlene. **Adoption: Parenthood Without Pregnancy**. New York: Holt, 1986.

Carlin, Margaret F. **Understanding Abilities, Disabilities and Capabilities: A Guide to Children's Literature**. Englewood, CO: Libraries Unlimited, 1991.

Cianciolo, Patricia Jean. "Children's Literature Can Affect Coping Behavior." **Personnel and Guidance Journal** 43 (May 1965): 897-903.

Cochran-Smith, Marilyn. **What is Real? An Adoptive Parent's Guide to Children's Books**. Unpublished bibliography, 1983.

Cole, Elizabeth S. **National Adoption Directory**. Washington, DC: National Adoption Information Clearinghouse, 1989.

Coleman, Marilyn. **Bibliotherapy With Stepchildren**. Springfield, IL: Charles C. Thomas, 1988.

Cuddigan, Maureen and Mary Beth Hansen. **Growing Pains: Helping Children Deal With Everyday Problems Through Reading**. Chicago: American Library Association, 1988.

De Hartog, Jan. **Adopted Children**. New York: Adama Books, 1987.

Donelson, Kenneth L. and Alleen Pace Nilsen. **Literature for Today's Young Adults**. 3rd ed. Glenview, IL: Scott, Foresman, 1989.

Dreyer, Sharon Spredemann. **Bookfinder: A Guide to Children's Literature About the Needs and Problems of Youth Aged Two and Up**. Circle Pines, MN: American Guidance Service, 1977-1989.

Fassler, David. **Changing Families: A Guide for Kids and Grown-ups**. Burlington, VT: Waterfront Books, 1988.

Fassler, Joan. **Helping Children Cope: Mastering Stress Through Books and Stories**. New York: The Free Press, 1978.

Garry, V.V. "Books About Kids With Special Needs." **Instructor** 88 (November 1978): 113-16.

Gillis, Ruth J. **Children's Books for Times of Stress**. Bloomington: Indiana University Press, 1978.

Gilman, Lois. **The Adoption Resource Book**. New York: Harper and Row, 1984.

Grossman, Lenore. "From Infertility to Adoption." **Parents' Magazine** 64 (March 1989): 96-99.

Hamm, Wilfred. **Self-Awareness, Self-Selection and Success: A Parent Preparation Guidebook for Special Needs Adoptions**. Washington, DC: North American Council on Adoptable Children, 1985.

Handbook for Single Adoptive Parents. Chevy Chase, MD: Committee for Single Adoptive Parents, 1987.

Hendrickson, Linda B. "The 'Right' Book for the Right Child in Distress." **School Library Journal** 34 (April 1988): 40-41.

Hirsch, Elisabeth S. **Problems of Early Childhood: An Annotated Bibliography and Guide**. New York: Garland, 1983.

Huck, Charlotte S. **Children's Literature in the Elementary School**. 4th ed. New York: Holt, Rinehart, 1987.

Jewett, Claudia. **Adopting the Older Child**. Harvard, MA: Harvard Common Press, 1978.

Johnston, Patricia. **An Adopter's Advocate**. Fort Wayne, IN: Perspectives Press, 1984.

Koh, Frances M. **Oriental Children in American Homes**. Minneapolis, MN: East-West Press, 1981.

Komar, Miriam. **Communicating With the Adopted Child**. New York: Walker, 1991.

Ladner, Joyce. **Mixed Families: Adoption Across Racial Boundaries**. Garden City, NY: Anchor Books/Doubleday, 1977.

LeClercq, Patricia A. "Children's Fiction Dealing With Self-Esteem." **Catholic Library World** 48 (December 1977): 209-13.

Lindsay, Jeanne Warren. **Adoption Awareness: A Guide for Teachers, Counselors, Nurses and Caring Others**. Buena Park, CA: Morning Glory Press, 1989.

Long, Margo Alexandre. "The Interracial Family in Children's Literature." **Language Arts** 55 (April 1978): 489-97.

McInnis, Kathleen M. "Bibliotherapy: Adjunct to Traditional Counseling with Children of Stepfamilies." **Child Welfare** 61 (March 1982): 153-60.

McNamara, Joan. **The Adoption Advisor**. New York: Hawthorn Books, 1975.

McNamara, Joan. **Tangled Feelings: Sexual Abuse and Adoption**. Greensboro, NC: Family Resources, 1988.

Materials of Interest to Interracial Families. Washington, DC: Interracial Family Circle, 1989.

Meezan, William. **Care and Commitment: Foster Parent Adoption Decisions.** Albany: State University of New York Press, 1985.

Melina, Lois R. **Adoption: An Annotated Bibliography and Guide.** New York: Garland, 1987.

Melina, Lois R. **Making Sense of Adoption: A Parent's Guide.** New York: Harper and Row, 1989.

Miles, Susan G. "Periodicals for Adoptive Families." **Serials Review** 11 (Fall 1985): 21-29.

Olsen, Henry D. "Bibliotherapy to Help Children Solve Problems." **Elementary School Journal** 75 (April 1975): 422-429.

Oppenheim, Joanne. **Choosing Books For Kids: How to Choose the Right Book For the Right Child at the Right Time.** New York: Ballantine Books, 1986.

Pardeck, Jean A. and John T. **Young People With Problems: A Guide to Bibliotherapy.** Westport, CT: Greenwood Press, 1984.

Pardeck, John T. and Jean A. "Bibliotherapy for Children in Foster Care and Adoption." **Child Welfare** 66 (May-June 1987): 269-78.

Pardeck, John T. and Jean A. "Bibliotherapy for Your Adopted Child." **OURS** (March-April 1988): 30-32.

Pardeck, John T. and Jean A. "Helping Children Adjust to Adoption Through the Bibliotherapeutic Approach." **Early Child Development and Care** 44 (March 1989): 31-37.

Pasner, Julia L. **The Adoption Resource Guide: A National Directory of Licensed Agencies.** 2nd ed. Washington, DC: Child Welfare League of America, 1990.

Powers, Douglas. "Of Time, Place, and Person: **The Great Gilly Hopkins** and Problems of Story for Adopted Children." **Children's Literature in Education** 15 (Winter 1984): 211-19.

Prater, Gwendolyn S. and Lula T. King. "Experiences of Black Families as Adoptive Parents." **Social Work** 33 (November-December 1988): 543-45.

Pufki, Peter M. "Silly Questions and Straight Answers About Adoption." **Children Today** 12 (July-August 1983): 11-14.

Purdy, A. Jane. **He Will Never Remember: Caring For the Victims of Child Abuse.** Atlanta, GA: S. Hunter, 1989.

Roles, Patricia. **Saying Goodbye to a Baby.** Washington, DC: Child Welfare League of America, 1989.

Rudman, Masha Kabakow. **Children's Literature: An Issues Approach.** 2nd ed. New York: Longman, 1984.

Sadker, Myra P. and David M. **Now Upon a Time: A Contemporary View of Children's Literature.** New York: Harper and Row, 1977.

Schaffer, Judith and Christina Lindstrom. **How to Raise an Adopted Child.** New York: Crown Publishers, 1989.

Schneider, Phyllis. "What It's Like to Adopt." **Parents' Magazine** 62 (November 1987): 167-168+.

Sharkey, Paulette Bochnig. "Adoption in Fiction for Teens and Preteens: Best of the 1980s." **OURS** 24 (March-April 1991): 32-34.

Sharkey, Paulette Bochnig. "Being Adopted: Books to Help Children Understand." **Emergency Librarian** 17 (May-June 1990): 23-26.

Sharp, Pat Tipton. "Adoption Books Over Two Decades." **Top of the News** 38 (Winter 1982): 151-154.

Siegel, Stephanie. **Parenting Your Adopted Child.** New York: Prentice Hall, 1989.

Smith, Charles A. **From Wonder to Wisdom: Using Stories to Help Children Grow.** New York: New American Library, 1989.

Van Why, Elizabeth Wharton. **Adoption Bibliography and Multi-Ethnic Sourcebook.** Hartford, CT: Open Door Society of Connecticut, 1977.

Ward, Margaret. "The Special Needs of the Adopted Child." **Parents' Magazine** 47 (December 1972): 42-43, 67-68.

Watson, Jerry J. "Bibliotherapy for Abused Children." **The School Counselor** 27 (January 1980): 204-208.

Whitehead, Robert J. **A Guide to Selecting Books for Children.** Metuchen, NJ: Scarecrow Press, 1984.

Wilkinson, Hei Sook Park. **Birth Is More Than Once: The Inner World of Adopted Korean Children.** Bloomfield Hills, MI: Sunrise Ventures, 1985.

Williams, Dennis A. "Black Family Adoption: Making Homes for Our Own." **Essence** 18 (May 1987): 87-91.

Appendix B:
Directory of Adoption-related Organizations

AASK America Adoption Exchange
Aid to Adoption of Special Kids
595 Market St.
San Francisco, CA 94105
(special needs information and child referral organization)

AASK Midwest
400 Holland A-5
Maumee, OH 43537
(special needs information and child referral organization)

ALMA Society (Adoptees' Liberty Movement Association)
P.O. Box 154
Washington Bridge Station
New York, NY 10033
(search information and support group)

Adopted Child
c/o Lois R. Melina
P.O. Box 9362
Moscow, ID 83843
(newsletter)

Adoptee-Birthparent Support Network
P.O. Box 23674
L'Enfant Plaza Station
Washington, DC 20026
(search support group)

Adoptive Families of America (formerly OURS)
3333 Highway 100 North
Minneapolis, MN 55422
(national adoptive parent support group)

AdoptNet
P.O. Box 50514
Palo Alto, CA 94303-9998
(newsletter)

Adoptees' Liberty Movement Association, see ALMA

Adoptive Parents for Open Records, Inc.
P.O. Box 193
Long Valley, NJ 07853
(adoption reform group)

American Adoption Congress
Cherokee Station
P.O. Box 20137
New York, NY 10028-0051
(service organization)

American Foster Care Resources
P.O. Box 271
King George, VA 22485
(research about and resources for foster families)

Attachment Disorder Parents Network
P.O. Box 12127
Boulder, CO 80303
(information and support organization with newsletter)

Committee for Single Adoptive Parents
P.O. Box 15084
Chevy Chase, MD 20815
(support group for single adoptive parents)

Concerned Persons for Adoption
P.O. Box 179
Whippany, NJ 07981
(adoptive parent support group)

Concerned United Birthparents (CUB)
2000 Walker St.
Des Moines, IA 50317
(birthparent support group)

Down Syndrome Parents' Group, Inc.
6350 Laurel Canyon Blvd. #429
North Hollywood, CA 91606
(information and support organization)

Families Adopting Children Everywhere (FACE)
P.O. Box 28058

Northwood Station
Baltimore, MD 21239
(adoptive parent support group)

Families for Private Adoption
P.O. Box 6375
Washington, DC 20015
(information, referral and support organization)

Fetal Alcohol Syndrome Resource Coalition
7802 SE Taylor
Portland, OR 97215
(support and information group)

Four D Information Systems
1720 L. Los Angeles Ave.
Suite 2368
Simi Valley, CA 93065
(**The Adoption Life Cycle** game)

Heritage Key
10116 Scoville Ave.
Sunland, CA 91041
(mail-order house for adoption and multicultural items)

Homes for Black Children
2340 Calvert
Detroit, MI 48206
(placement resource for black children)

International Concerns Committee for Children (ICCC)
911 Cypress Dr.
Boulder, CO 80303
(annual **Report on Foreign Adoption**)

Hope Cottage Adoption Center
4209 McKinney Ave.
Suite 200
Dallas, TX 72505
(publishes "Adoption Therapist" newsletter)

Jan Elsberry Designs
8000 60th Ave. N.
New Hope, MN 55428
(adoption items, stationary, etc.)

Latin American Parents Association
P.O. Box 72
Seaford, NY 11783
(support group for families adopting from Latin America)

Mary Sue Originals
N105 W. 16806 Old Farm Rd.
Germantown, WI 53022
(adoption and multicultural stationary and announcements)

Michigan Association for Openness in Adoption
P.O. Box 5117
Traverse City, MI 49685
(organization promoting open adoption)

Moms in Celebration of Adoption
P.O. Box 1018
Melville, NY 11747
(stationary and unique gifts for the adoptive family)

National Adoption Center
1218 Chestnut St.
Philadelphia, PA 19107
(information and child referral organization)

National Adoption Information Clearinghouse
1400 Eye St., N.W.
Suite 600
Washington, DC 20005
(information referral organization)

National Coalition to End Racism in America's Child Care System
22075 Koths
Taylor, MI 48180
(lobbying organization)

National Committee for Adoption
1930 17th St., N.W.
Washington, DC 20009
(lobbying organization)

National Foster Parents Association
226 Kilts Dr.
Houston, TX 77024
(information and support organization)

National Information Center for Children and Youth With Handicaps
P.O. Box 1492
Washington, DC 20013
(information and referral agency)

National Resource Center for Special Needs Adoption
P.O. Box 337
Chelsea, MI 48118
(information, training and referral organization)

Operation Identity
13101 Blackstone Rd., N.E.
Albuquerque, NM 87111
(search support)

Orphan Voyage
2141 Rd. 2300
Cedaredge, CO 814413
(search support)

Our Special Family
Davar Publishing Co.
P.O. Box 32382
Baltimore, MD 21208-8382
(newsletter about alternative forms of family building)

OURS, see Adoptive Families of America

Perspectives Press
P.O. Box 90318
Indianapolis, IN 46290-0318
(publisher of books about adoption, foster care and infertility)

Post Adoption Center for Education and Research (PACER)
2255 Ignacio Valley Rd.
Suite L
Walnut Creek, CA 94598
(education and research supporting post-adoption)

RESOLVE, Inc.
5 Water St.
Arlington, MA 02174
(infertility support group)

Stars of David
9 Hampton St.
Cranford, NJ 07016
(Jewish adoption support group)

Stepfamily Association of America
215 Centennial Mall South
Suite 212
Lincoln, NE 68508
(stepfamily support group)

Wallmark Associates
P.O. Box 173
Ringoes, NJ 08551
(mail-order adoption books)

Author and Illustrator Index

Numbers refer to entry, not page, numbers in the bibiography

Adam, Ruth, 441
Adams, Adrienne, 92
Adler, C.S., 120, 268
Agre, Patricia, 117
Aks, Patricia, 269
Alcock, Gudrun, 121
Allen, Elizabeth B., 334
Althea, 24
Ames, Mildred, 122
Ancona, George, 19
Anderson, Ann K., 335
Anderson, C. W., 25
Anderson, Deborah, 26
Anderson, Margaret K., 88
Anderson, Rachel, 336
Andrews, V.C., 442
Angel, Ann, 123
Angell, Judie, 124
Angelo, Valenti, 270
Anthony, Joseph, 337
Armer, Alberta, 271
Arms, Suzanne, 338
Arthur, Ruth M., 272
Auch, Mary J., 125, 126
Averill, Esther H., 27

Bain, Barnard E., 340
Baker, Josephine, 339
Baker, Margaret J., 127
Ball, Zachary, 273
Barley, Ann L., 341
Barnett, Moneta, 200

Barton, Byron, 37
Bates, Betty, 128, 129
Battelle, Phyllis, 403
Bauer, J.B., 174
Bauer, Marion D., 274
Bawden, Nina, 28, 130, 275, 443
Beachy, Sara, 77
Becker, John T., 342
Becker, Kayla M., 249
Becker, Stanli K., 342
Beckwith, Lillian, 276
Begley, Vincent J., 343
Bell, Harry, 344
Benary-Isbert, Margot, 277
Bennett, Richard, 178
Berckman, Evelyn, 278
Berman, Claire, 104, 345
Bilow, Pat, 346
Bishop, Sheila, 444
Blackmore, Jane, 445
Blank, Joseph P., 347
Blass, Jacqueline, 56
Bloom, Suzanne, 29
Blue, Rose, 30, 131
Blume, Judy, 132
Bontrager, Rhoda, 77
Bonzon, Paul J., 133
Booth, Nyla, 348
Bornstein, Ruth L., 69
Bouillon, Jo, 339
Bowring, Joanne, 46, 123
Bradbury, Bianca, 279

Braenne, Berit, 134
Bragdon, Elspeth, 135
Braithwaite, E.R., 349
Brandon, Sandra, 31
Branscum, Robbie, 136
Brodzinsky, Anne B., 32
Brooks, Terry, 446
Brown, Christine, 350
Brown, Irene B., 280
Brown, Linda P., 368
Buchwald, Ann, 351
Buck, Pearl S., 1, 137
Budbill, David, 138
Bulla, Clyde R., 33, 34
Bunin, Catherine, 2
Bunin, Sherry, 2
Bunting, Eve, 281
Burch, Robert, 139
Byars, Betsy, 140
Byrd, Elizabeth, 447

Caddell, Foster, 146
Cady, Frank, 352
Caines, Jeannette F., 35
Cameron, Eleanor, 141
Campbell, Hope, 282
Caplan, Lincoln, 353
Carey, Helen H., 52
Carlson, Natalie S., 142, 143
Carney, Ann, 354
Carney, Christina S., 67
Carter, Mary A., 448, 449
Cassedy, Sylvia, 144
Caudill, Rebecca, 145
Cecil, Henry, 450
Chapman, Noralee, 36
Charlton, Michael, 65
Chatterton, Ruth, 451
Cheatham, K. Follis, 283
Cheng, Judith, 86
Cherne, Jacqolyn, 355
Chinnock, Frank W., 356
Christenson, Larry, 3
Christopher, Matt, 146
Clark, Margaret G., 147
Claus, M.A. and W.A.J., 198
Clayton, Robert, 121
Cleaver, Vera, 148
Clewes, Dorothy, 284
Coalson, Glo, 96

Cober, Alan E., 195
Cohen, Shari, 250
Coleman, Pauline H., 285
Collins, Heather, 68, 300
Colman, Hila, 149
Connor, Grace, 358
Conover, Chris, 223
Converse, James, 233
Conway, Laura, 452
Corbett, Suzanne, 21
Corbin, William, 286
Covington, Vicki, 453
Craven, Linda, 251
Crawford, Christina, 359
Cray, Dorothy, 454
Crook, Marion, 252
Cross, Gilbert, 150
Cuffari, Richard, 172
Cunningham, Julia, 151
Cutrell, Pauline, 97

Dahl, Judy, 360
Dalgliesh, Alice, 152
Dalton, Ann, 187
Daringer, Helen F., 153
Dauer, Rosamond, 37
Day, Betsy, 102
De Vries, Peter, 456
Deal, L. Kate, 243
Deland, Margaret, 455
Dellinger, Annetta E., 38
Dennis, Muriel B., 357
Derby, Pat, 287
Doane, Pelagie, 154
Dolce, Ellen, 83
Dorris, Michael, 361
Doss, Helen G., 4, 105, 155, 362
Downes, Mary, 156
Drescher, Joan E., 5
Drummond, June, 457
Dubkin, Lois, 39
Duling, Gretchen A., 363
Duncan, Lois, 289
Dunlop, Eileen, 157
Dunn, Linda, 332
DuPrau, Jeanne, 253
Dusky, Lorraine, 364
Dwyer-Joyce, A., 458

Eber, Christine E., 40

Edwards, Lenora F., 459
Ehrlich, Henry, 427
Eisenberg, Eleanor, 41
Eitz, Maria, 365
Endres, Helen, 31
Enright, Elizabeth, 158
Epp, Margaret A., 290
Epstein, Judith, 18
Erichsen, Jean, 6
Erickson, Barbara, 131
Etchinson, Birdie, 393
Evans, Dale, 408, 409
Evans, Graci, 78
Evernden, Margery, 159
Eyerly, Jeannette, 291, 292

Fairbank, Anna, 42
Fairclough, Chris, 95
Fall, Thomas, 43
Falstad, Lisa, 14
Feelings, Tom, 30
Fenner, Peggy, 72
First, Julia, 160
Fisher, Dorothy C., 161
Fisher, Florence, 366
Fisher, Iris L., 44
Fitzgerald, John D., 162
Fitzgerald, Tom, 460
Fletcher, Karen, 75
Floethe, Richard, 231
Floyd, Gareth, 209
Forrai, Maria S., 7
Fortnum, Peggy, 232
Fredkove, Ann, 106
Freudberg, Judy, 45
Friedman, Judith, 48
Funai, Mamoru, 137
Furan, Paul, 182

Gabel, Susan L., 46, 107
Galdone, Paul, 181
Garfield, Leon, 293
Garling, Gloria, 47
Gates, Doris, 163
Gay, Kathlyn, 254, 367
Gediman, Judith S., 368
Geeg, Charles, 207
Geiss, Tony, 45
George, Stephen R., 461
Giddens, Lynn, 369

Gili, Phillida, 28
Gill, Margery, 63
Girard, Linda W., 48, 49
Glassman, Bruce, 255
Goldberg, Pat, 9
Gordon, Shirley, 50
Goudge, Elizabeth, 294
Goudy, Rosemary, 8
Graber, Esther R., 166
Green, Phyllis, 51, 164
Greenberg, Judith E., 52
Gritter, James, L., 333
Gruber, Ruth, 389
Guy, Anne, 53

Haag, Peg R., 76
Haas, Alan D., 1
Hafner, Marylin, 89
Hale, Arlene, 295
Hale, James G., 91
Hall, Lynn, 165
Hall, Tom, 81
Hamilton, Dorothy, 166
Hansen, Joyce, 167
Harden, Laurie, 234
Hark, Mildred, 168
Harvey, Paul, 93
Harwood, Pearl A., 54
Hausherr, Rosemarie, 71
Haywood, Carolyn, 55
Heckert, Connie K., 249
Helprin, Mark, 462
Hermes, Patricia, 169
Herne, Jack, 145
Hess, Edith, 56
Hill, Grace L., 463
Hoffman, Louise, 464
Holt, Bertha, 370
Holtan, Barbara, 425
Holz, Loretta, 108
Howard, Ellen, 170
Hughes, Shirley, 62
Hull, Helen S., 36
Hulse, Jerry, 371
Hutchins, Pat, 57
Hutton, Malcolm, 465
Hyams, Joe, 404
Hyde, Margaret O., 256
Hyde, Robert, 372

Ireland, Jill, 373
Irwin, Hadley, 296

Jacob, Naomi, 466
Jaeger, Elinor, 217
James, P.D., 467
Jenkins, Jerry B., 171
Jenkins, Robin, 468
Jenness, Aylette, 110
Jennings, John E., 297
Jensen, Henning B., 54
Jeruchim, Simon, 133
Jeschke, Susan, 58
Johnson, Doris, 59
Johnson, Jean M., 374
Johnson, Joyce, 375
Johnston, Patricia I., 398
Johnston, Velda, 469
Jones, Adrienne, 172
Jones, Rebecca C., 173
Joy, Deborah B., 174

Kalil, Kathleen M., 257
Keller, Holly, 60
Kellogg, Steven, 35
Kirk, Barbara, 52
Kiser, Martha G., 175
Kjelgaard, Jim, 298
Klass, Sheila S., 299
Klein, Norma, 176
Knapp, Audrie L., 4
Koch, Janice, 9
Koehler, Phoebe, 61
Koons, Carolyn A., 376
Kornheiser, Tony, 377
Kornitzer, Margaret, 62, 63
Korschunow, Irina, 64
Kramer, Betty, 428
Kravik, Patricia J., 332
Kremenztz, Jill, 258
Kropp, Paul, 300
Kruck, Gerald, 82
Krush, Beth, 141
Krush, Joe, 141
Kuklin, Susan, 10
Kulin, Kathy, 227

Lambo, Don, 199
Lampman, Evelyn S., 177, 178
Landau, Elaine, 259, 260

Lapsley, Susan, 65
Lasker, Joe, 22
Lattimore, Eleanor, 179
Launders, Michele, 375
Laurie, 84
Lawrence, John, 293
Lawrence, Mildred, 180, 181
Lawson, Will, 470
Lazare, Jerry, 186
Le Shan, Eda J., 261
Leach, Christopher, 301
Leder, Dora, 23
Lee, Joanna, 302
Legrand, Edy, 498
Leitch, David, 378
L'Engle, Madeleine, 303
Levinson, Nancy S., 182
Lewin, Michael Z., 471
Lewin, Ted, 147
Lewis, Mark, 183
Lifton, Betty J., 304, 379, 380
Lindbergh, Anne, 184
Lindeman, Bard, 381
Lindgren, Astrid, 185
Lindsay, Jeanne W., 382, 383
Lipman, Elinor, 472
Little, Jean, 186
Lively, Penelope, 187
Livingston, Carole, 111
Lobel, Arnold, 103
Lonette, Reisie, 224
Long, Carol, 66
Lowe, Darla, 67
Lowe, Patricia T., 188
Lowry, Lois, 305
Luks, Peggy, 51
Lumn, Peter, 205
Lund, Doris H., 384

McCloskey, Robert, 219
McDonald, Joyce, 189
McGuire, Paula, 262
McHugh, Elisabet, 190
MacKay, Jed, 68
MacLachlan, Patricia, 69
McMillon, Doris, 385
McNamara, Joan, 11, 112
McNamara, Bernard, 112
McQueen, Noel, 168
McTaggart, Lynne, 386

Magnuson, James, 473
Magorian, Michelle, 306
Maiden, Cecil, 474
Mall, E. Jane, 387
March, William, 475
Marchesi, Stephen, 113
Marcus, Clare, 388
Marden, Priscilla, 100
Margolies, Marjorie, 389
Martchenko, Michael, 73, 74
Martin, Ann M., 70, 191, 192, 193
Mathieu, Joe, 45
Mattozzi, Patricia, 38
Maxtone-Graham, Katrina, 390, 391
May, Julian, 12
Maybury, Anne, 476
Mayer, Mercer, 162
Mayhar, Ardath, 194
Mayle, Peter, 111
Mays, Victor, 244
Means, Florence C., 307
Meredith, Judith C., 13
Michaels, Ruth, 18
Michl, Reinhard, 64
Miles, Judith, 477
Miles, Miska, 195
Milgram, Mary, 71
Miller, Laura O., 478
Mills, Claudia, 196
Milton, Joyce, 113
Miner, Jane C., 197
Miquelle, Jean B., 72
Moen, Erna I., 479
Montgomery, L(ucy) M., 198
Moon, Ivan, 226
Morrill, Leslie, 218
Morrison, Margaret, 480
Mulcahy, Lucille, 199
Munsch, Robert N., 73, 74
Murphy, Frances S., 200, 201
Musser, Sandra K., 392
Myers, Walter D., 202, 308, 309
Myers, Bill, 90

Nason, Diane, 393
Neiderman, Andrew, 481
Neilsen, Shelly, 203
Nelson, Sara, 17
Nerlove, Evelyn, 310
Nerlove, Miriam, 310

Neufeld, John, 311
Nickman, Steven L., 263
Nixon, Joan L., 204
Norris, Faith, 205
Nystrom, Carolyn, 206, 357

O'Brien, Bev, 394
O'Donnell, Lillian, 482
O'Sullivan, Tom, 18
Oistad, Georgia, 47
Okimoto, Jean D., 312
Opel, Joanne, 11
Oppenheimer, Joan L., 313
Osborn, Pamela, 13
Owens, Carolyn, 14

Packer, Joy P., 483
Palmer, Frances, 395
Palmer, Juliette, 39
Palmquist, Eric, 185
Paradis, Marjorie B., 207
Parker, Richard, 208, 209
Parrish-Benson, Barbara, 75
Partridge, Jackie, 15
Paschal, Nancy, 326
Pate, Rodney, 202
Paterson, Katherine, 210
Patrick, Michael, 396
Patterson, Eleanora, 16
Patterson, Robert, 155
Paul, Phyllis, 484
Paull, Grace, 177
Payson, Dale, 142
Pearce, Isabel, 24
Pedersen, Maia, 397
Peebles, Katherine, 264
Peipenbrink, Ruth, 399
Peister, Ruby L., 400
Perl, Lila, 211
Petrie, Dorothea G., 473
Pfeffer, Susan B., 212, 314
Piepgras, Ruth, 76
Platt, Kin, 213
Pogrebin, Letty C., 2
Pointer, Priscilla, 53
Powell, John Y., 401
Powledge, Fred, 265
Prentice, Carol S., 402
Prey, Barbara Ernst, 16
Price, Christine, 246

Prohaska, Ray, 43
Pullman, Philip, 485
Pursell, Margaret S., 7

Queen, Ellery, 486
Quinlan, Joseph and Julia, 403
Quinn, Barbara, 114

Rabe, Berniece, 214
Rankin, Carrol W., 215
Read, Elfreida, 315
Reagan, Michael, 404
Redmond, Wendie, 405
Reeder, Red, 216
Register, Cheri, 406
Reid Banks, Lynne, 487
Rhoda, 77
Rich, Louise D., 217
Rigert, Joe, 407
Rippey, Carol, 17
Rivera, Geraldo, 266
Roberts, Luann, 240
Roberts, Willo D., 218
Robins, Arthur, 111
Robins, Denise, 488
Robinson, Charles, 50
Robinson, Thomas P., 219
Rogers, Dale E., 408, 409
Ron-Feder, Galilah, 220
Rondell, Florence, 18
Rose, Anna P., 410, 411
Rose, Phyllis, 339
Rosenberg, Maxine B., 19, 115
Rosenhouse, Irwin, 220
Roth, Arthur J., 316
Row, Gavin, 208
Rowe, Viola, 317
Rud, Borghild, 134
Ryan, Marguerite, 413
Ryan, Kristapher, 412

Sachs, Marilyn, 221
Salkman, Victoria, 414
Sanders, Patricial, 415
Sandness, Grace L., 416
Sanford, Doris, 78
Sass, Norma J., 79
Saunders, Lowell, 80
Savage, Thomas, 489
Scarboro, Elizabeth, 222

Schaefer, Carol, 417
Schaer, Miriam, 44
Schaffer, Patricia, 20, 21
Schindel, Ronnie L., 81
Schnitter, Jane T., 82
Schwartzbaum, Avraham, 418
Schwartz-Nobel, Loretta, 436
Scott, Ann, 348
Scott, Elaine, 116
Seale, Clem, 239
Seredy, Kate, 153
Seregny, Julie, 107
Seuling, Barbara, 83
Sewall, Marcia, 34
Sheehy, Gail, 419
Shinn, Florence S., 215
Shute, Linda, 49
Shyer, Marlene F., 318
Sibley, Don, 139
Silber, Kathleen, 420
Silman, Roberta, 223
Silverman, Helen, 84
Simon, Norma, 22, 23
Simon, Shirley, 224
Sitterly, Nancy, 415
Sleightholm, Sherry, 405
Slosberg, Mike, 490
Sly, Kathleen O., 85
Sly, Leland D., 85
Smith, Doris B., 225
Smith, Doris D., 421
Smulcer, Jan, 66
Sobol, Harriet L., 117
Sommer, Susan, 226
Spanfeller, James, 151
Speedlin, Phylis, 419
Spilka, Arnold, 168
Spring, Beth, 439
Stahl, Hilda, 227, 228, 229, 319
Standiford, Debi, 422
Stanek, Muriel, 86
Stanford, James, 118
Stanley, Carol, 230
Stanley, Diana L., 32, 398
Stein, Sara B., 87
Steven, Hugh, 423
Stevens, Mary, 180
Stewart, Gail, 119
Stingley, James, 424
Storr, Catherine, 320

Strang, Celia, 321
Strassberger, Laurel, 425
Streatfeild, Noel, 231, 232
Stroud, John, 491
Summers, James L., 322
Supervielle, Jules, 492
Swartley, David W., 233
Swetnam, Evelyn, 234
Swofford, Jeanette, 26
Sykes, Jo, 323

Taber, Barbara G., 88
Talarczyk, June, 80
Talbert, Marc, 324
Talbot, Charlene J., 235, 236
Tang, Susan, 70
Tate Eleanora E., 237
Tax, Meredith, 89
Taylor, Bernard, 494
Taylor, Theodore, 238
Tennant, Kylie, 239
Terris, Susan, 325
Tevis, Walter S., 495
Thomas, Pamela, 438
Thompson, Jean, 90, 426
Timperly, Rosemary, 496
Tomei, Lorna, 212
Tomes, Jacqueline, 317
Torrey, Marjorie, 163
Towles, Ed., 167
Tripp, Valerie, 240
Troy, Katherine, 476
Trotter, Grace, 326
Turner, Ann, 91
Tutton, Diana 497

Udry, Janice M., 92
Unwin, Nora S., 127
Urfer, Robert F., 85

Valenti, Laura L., 429
Van Stockum, Hilda, 241
Van Woerkom, Dorothy, 93
Viglucci, Pat C., 327
Viguers, Susan T., 430
Vining, Elizabeth G., 499
Vista III Design, 197
Voigt, Cynthia, 328
Vonnegut, Edith, 266

Waber, Bernard, 94
Wagstaff, Sue, 95
Wahl, Richard, 171
Walker, Leslie, 431
Walles, Dwight, 3
Walter, Paul, 104, 111
Ward, Jeannette W., 242
Warner, Gertrude C., 243
Warren, Betsy, 41
Warren, Mary P., 244
Wasson, Valentina P., 96
Watson, Wendy, 33
Waybill, Marjorie A., 97
Weaver, Stella, 329
Weinman, Fred L., 365
Weisgard, Leonard, 59
Weiss, Emil, 248
Welch, Sheila K., 245
West, Helen L., 432
Weston, Martha, 42
Wexler, Susan S., 433
Weyn, Suzanne, 98
Whalley-Tooker, Dorothea C., 500
Wheeler, Kathryn, 343
White, Robin, 501
White, William L., 435
Whitehead, Mary B., 436
Whitney, Phyllis A., 502, 503
Whitt, Anne H., 437
Wickstrom, Lois, 100
Wier, Ester, 246
Wiese, Kurt, 205
Wilkin, Eloise, 175
Williams, Garth, 143
Williams, Jett, 438
Williams, Jill, 439
Williams, Pat, 439
Williams, Vera B., 101
Williamson, Ada C., 161
Wilson, Dick, 104
Windsor, Patricia, 330
Winter, Marjorie, 440
Winthrop, Elizabeth, 247
Woodbury, Mabel J., 201
Woodcock-Clarke, Sylvia, 118
Woodward, Hildegard, 152
Woolfolk, Dorothy, 331
Wright, Betty R., 102

Youd, Pauline, 267

Young, Jan, 248
Young, Miriam, 103

Title Index

Numbers refer to entry, not page, numbers in the bibliography

A is for Adoption, 47
Aaron's Door, 195
Abby, 35
About David, 314
Adopted, 52
Adopted and Loved Forever, 38
Adopted Child Looks at Adoption, 402
Adopted Daughter, 284
Adopted Family, 18
Adopted for a Purpose, 267
Adopted Four and Had One More, 432
Adopted Jane, 153
Adopted One, 87
Adopted Woman, 390
Adopting Baby Brother, 88
Adopting Children With Special Needs, 332
Adopting Joe: A Black Vietnamese Child, 363
Adopting of Rosa Marie, 215
Adoption, 116, 119, 253
Adoption: A Hand Full of Hope, 338
Adoption and Foster Care, 254
Adoption is for Always, 48
Adoption Experience, 263
Adoption: Let's Talk, 257
Adoption Story: A Son is Given, 413
Adoption Without Fear, 333
Advice for Adopted Kids, 106
African Library, 156
Ain't Nothing as Sweet as My Baby, 438

Alden Family Mysteries, 243
All Blood is Red--All Shadows are Dark, 342
All Kinds of Families, 22
All the Children of the World, 4
All the Proud Tribesmen, 239
All Together: An Unusual American Family, 407
And Baby Will Fall, 471
And Four to Grow On, 395
And I'm Stuck With Joseph, 226
And Now We Are a Family, 13
And Now We Are Four, 346
And With the Gift Came Laughter, 335
Andy's Big Question: Where Do I Belong?, 206
Ann Aurelia and Dorothy, 142
Annabelle Starr, E.S.P., 211
Anne of Avonlea, 198
Anne of Green Gables, 198
Anne of Ingleside, 198
Anne of the Island, 198
Anne of Windy Poplars, 198
Anne's House of Dreams, 198
Answering Miss Roberts, 301
Are Those Kids Yours?, 406
At Sixes and Sevens, 397
August Strangers, 490
Austin Family Trilogy, 303
Awakening of Helena Ritchie, 455

Baby Brokers, 386

Baby Chase, 377
Baby for Betsy, 53
Baby Merchants, 482
Baby-Sitters Club series, 191, 192
Baby-Sitters Little Sisters series, 70
Bad Seed, 475
Bakers' Dozen, 98
Ballet Shoes, 231
Bamboo Cradle, 418
Barney and the UFO, 147
Barney in Space, 147
Barney on Mars, 147
Becky's Special Family, 85
Beginnings, 416
Behind the Attic Wall, 144
Being Adopted, 19
Believers, 173
Benjamin Bear Gets a New Family, 174
Big Little Island, 270
Big Secret, 68
Birthbond, 368
Birthmark, 364
Black Fawn, 298
Black Market Adoption and the Sale of
    Children, 259
Blind Girl's Bluff, 278
Bloodchild, 481
Blue Marshmallow Mountains, 199
Blue Teapot, 152
Boardwalk With Hotel, 196
Bones on Black Spruce Mountain, 138
Bounces of Cynthiann', 177
Boxcar Children, 243
Boy Who Wanted a Family, 50
Boy Without a Name, 187
Bradford Family Adventures, 171
Brian Was Adopted, 78
Brides of Bellenmore, 476
Brimming Over, 416
Broken Cord, 361
Brother for the Orphelines, 143
Brother the Size of Me, 155
Brothers Are All the Same, 71
Brothers By Choice, 315
Bugs in Your Ears, 128
Bullfrog and Gertrude Go Camping, 37

Carrots and Miggle, 194
Carry It On, 428
Cassandra Robbins, Esq., 327

Cat That Was Left Behind, 120
Caught in the Act, 204
Celebration Family, 393
Chag Sameach! Happy Holiday, 20
Changes for Samantha, 240
Children at the Gate, 487
Children of Open Adoption, 420
Chinese Daughter, 179
Chinese Egg, 320
Chinese Eyes, 97
Chloris and the Creeps, 213
Chocolate Charlie, 460
Chocolate Charlie Comes Home, 460
Chosen Baby, 96
Chosen Children, 357
Christmas for Holly, 166
City of Bells, 294
Charlotte's Web, 143
Claudia and the Great Search, 191
Clint Lane in Korea, 216
Colonel's Children, 492
Color Me Loved, 14
Commitment, 416
Coping With Being Adopted, 250
Coping With Stepfamilies, 250
Cuckoo, 480

Dandelion Cottage, 215
Daniel's Big Surprise, 171
Dark Angel, 442
Dark Rice, 365
David's Father, 73
Day We Met You, 61
Dead Birds Singing, 324
Dear Birthmother, 420
Dearest Debbie, 408
December Tale, 221
Dicey's Song, 328
Different One, 285
Different Ones, 188
Do You Know What Adoption Means?,
    17
Don't Call Her Lisa, 375
Don't Call Me Marda, 245
Don't Disturb Daddy, 358
Dorp Dead, 151
Duffy, 121

Eddie and the Fairy Godpuppy, 218
Eddie No-Name, 43

Edgar Allan, 311
Elder Brother, 178
Elephant Hill, 501
Elf-Stones of Shannara, 446
Elizabeth Gail and the Terrifying News, 227
Elizabeth Gail series, 227
Escape From Yesterday, 454
Eternal Inspirations, 369
Europe on Eight Kids a Day, 407
Everything You Need to Know About Stepfamilies, 255

Face in the Mirror, 252
Faces of Adoption, 369
Falcon's Shadow, 476
Fallen Hearts, 442
Familiar Passions, 443
Families, 89
Families: A Celebration of Diversity, 110
Families: A Coloring Book for Families to Share, 11
Families Grow in Different Ways, 75
Family Apart, 204
Family for Jamie, 29
Family Nobody Wanted, 362
Family Secrets, 378
Family That Grew, 18
Family That Grew and Grew, 127
Fathers in Law, 450
Fifteen Most Asked Questions About Adoption, 429
Filling in the Blanks, 107
Find a Stranger, Say Goodbye, 305
Finding, 275
Firerose, 58
Flower for Catherine, 493
Follett Family Life Education Program, 12
For Love of Martha, 440
For the Love of a Child, 400
For the Love of Sang, 336
Forever Family, 399
Forgive Me If I'm Frayed Around the Edges, 357
Foster Child, 108, 274
Foster Care and Adoption, 256
Foster Mary, 321
Foundling Fox, 64

Fox Farm, 157
Freckled and Fourteen, 317
From We to Just Me, 412

Gates of Paradise, 442
Gathering Home, 453
Gentle House, 410
Gift-Giver, 167
Girl Like Cathy, 284
Girl Like Me, 291
God Gives Me a Family, 77
God Stand Up for Bastards, 378
Godsend, 494
Gold in Their Hearts, 470
Golden Eagle, 297
Golden Unicorn, 502
Good Night, Mr. Tom, 306
Goodbye Patrick, 350
Grandma's Little Darling, 461
Grandmother for the Orphelines, 143
Grandmother Orphan, 164
Great Brain, 162
Great Gilly Hopkins, 210
Greg Louganis: Diving for Gold, 113
Growing Up Adopted, 115

Happy Orpheline, 143
Happy Birthday, Samantha, 240
Heaven, 442
Her Own Song, 170
Here's a Penny, 55
He's My Baby Now, 292
Holly's New Year, 166
Hollywell Family, 62
Home for Penny, 168
Home From Far, 186
Home to Hawaii, 282
Homecoming, 328
Homeward Borne, 451
Horace, 60
House of Secrets, 496
House of Tomorrow, 426
How Babies and Families Are Made, 21
How It Feels to Be Adopted, 258

I Am Adopted, 65, 79
I Am Jungle Soup, 81
I Have a Question, God, 242

I Heard My Sister Speak My Name, 489

I, Rebekah, Take You, the Lawrences, 160

I, Roberta, 499

I Want to Keep My Baby, 302

I Will Make Darkness Light, 423

I Wish You Didn't Know My Name, 375

I Would Have Searched Forever, 392

I Would Rather be a Turnip, 148

I'm Going to Run Away, 90

I'm Still Me, 304

Image and Likeness, 474

In Our House Scott is My Brother, 268

In Our Neighborhood series, 78

In the Face of Danger, 204

Innocent Blood, 467

Inspector Queen's Own Case, 486

Iron Doors Between, 322

Iron Woman, 455

Is That Your Sister?, 2

It Must've Been the Fish Sticks, 129

It Won't Happen to Me, 262

It's Fun to Be Me, 66

It's Me, Christy, 164

It's Neat to be Adopted, 72

It's Only FAIR: A Child's View of Adoption, 109

Jane is Adopted, 24

Jason's Story: Going to a Foster Home, 26

Jazz Cleopatra: Josephine Baker in her Time, 339

Jellyfoot, 248

Jenny's Adopted Brothers, 27

Jody, 371

Jonathan Found, 474

Jo's Search, 300

Josephine, 339

Journal From an Obscure Place, 477

Journey for Margaret, 435

Just an Overnight Guest, 237

Just Another Gorgeous Guy, 280

Just as Long as We're Together, 132

Just Between Us, 212

Just Mama and Me, 40

Kaliban's Christmas, 183

Karen and Vicki, 190

Karen Ann: The Quinlans Tell Their Story, 403

Karen's Little Sister, 70

Karen's Sister, 190

Katie-Bo: An Adoption Story, 44

Kate's Story, 301

Kayla O'Brien and the Dangerous Journey, 228

Kep, 273

Kim: A Gift From Vietnam, 356

Kim/Kimi, 296

Kim of Korea, 205

Kitten Who Was Different, 80

Kristy and the Mother's Day Surprise, 192

Laurie, 279

Libby's Step-Family, 224

Life Lines, 373

Life on a Cool Plastic Ice Floe, 283

Limb of Your Tree, 421

Lion of Cooling Bay, 484

Little House on the Prairie, 143

Little Sister Tai Mi, 134

Liza's Story: Neglect and the Police, 26

Loner, 246

Lonesome Little Colt, 25

Long Way Home, 277

Look at Adoption, 7

Lost and Found; The Adoption Experience, 379

Love of Innocence, 468

Loving River, 416

Lucky Me! An Adoption Story, 42

Lyle Finds His Mother, 94

Lyncoya, 159

Mad Martin, 330

Mail-Order Kid, 189

Make Room for Patty, 98

Mama One, Mama Two, 69

Man and Woman, 12

Marathon Miranda, 247

Margaret's Story: Sexual Abuse and Going to Court, 26

Mario's Big Question: Where Do I Belong?, 206

Mary Smith's Hotel, 470

Matthew, Mark, Luke and John, 137

Me and My Little Brain, 162
Me, Mop, and the Moondance Kid, 202
Meet Samantha, 240
Meet the Austins, 303
Member of the Family, 448
Michael's Story: Emotional Abuse and
    Working With a Counselor, 26
Miracle of Time: Adopting a Sister, 197
Miss Suzy's Birthday, 103
Miss Suzy's Easter Surprise, 103
Missing Links, 343
Mr. Fairweather and His Family, 63
Mixed Blessing, 385
Molly By Any Other Name, 312
Mom I'm---Pregnant, 394
Moment of Truth, 452
Mommie Dearest, 359
Moon by Night, 303
Moonshadow of Cherry Mountain, 225
More, More More Said the Baby, 101
Mother, Can You Hear Me?, 334
Mother, How Could You!, 281
Mother, Mother, 424
Mother, Where Are You?, 331
Mother's Story, 436
Mrs. Portree's Pony, 165
Mulberry Bird: Story of an Adoption,
    32
Murmel, Murmel, Murmel, 74
My Brother, the Thief, 318
My Friend, My Brother, 233
My Journey Home From Colombia, 6
My Journey Home From Korea, 15
My Journey Home From Vietnam, 8
My Little Foster Sister, 86
My Name is Mike Trumsky, 76
My New Mom and Me, 102
My One Hundred Children, 340
Mystery at Loon Lake, 150

Natural Curiosity: Taffy's Search for
    Self, 264
Need to Know Library, 255
New Mother for Martha, 51
Nickel for Alice, 201
Nineteen Steps Up the Mountain, 347
No More Here and There, 354
Nobody's Orphan, 184
Nothing But a Stranger, 295

Oliver, 100
On the Loose, 491
On the Outside Looking In, 404
Once Removed, 405
Only Child, 288
Open Adoption, 353
Open Adoption: A Caring Option, 382
Open Adoption: My Story of Love and
    Laughter, 335
Open the Door and See all the People,
    33
Ordinary Miracle, 112
Orphan for Nebraska, 235
Orphan Train, 473
Orphan Train Quartet, 204
Orphans, 214
Orphans of Simitra, 133
Orphelines in the Enchanted Castle,
    143
Other Mother, 417
Other Room, 445
Our Adopted Baby: How You Came
    Into Our World, 9
Our Baby: A Birth and Adoption
    Story, 9
Our Baby is Best, 57
Outside Child, 130
Outstretched Arms, 370

P.S. I Love You, 387
Paid Servant, 349
Partners, 463
Passages, 419
Patchwork Clan, 384
Pathfinders, 419
Patrick Calls Me Mother, 341
Paul and Etta, 208
Peachtree Island, 180
Pegeen, 241
Penny and Peter, 55
Penny Goes to Camp, 55
Perspectives on a Grafted Tree, 398
Pet for the Orphelines, 143
Peter and Susie Find a Family, 56
Pick of the Litter, 125
Pinballs, 140
Pippi Longstocking, 185
Place for Jeremy, 169
Place of Sapphires, 478
Place to Belong, 204

Poor Boy, Rich Boy, 34
Poppy in the Corn, 329
Por Que Me Adoptaron?, 111
Prairie Youth Adventure Series, 229
Pregnant By Mistake: The Stories of
    Seventeen Women, 391
Pregnant Too Soon: Adoption is an
    Option, 383
Pretty House That Found Happiness,
    41
Princess Alice, 28

Queen's Gambit, 495
Quiet Passion, 464
Quiet Place, 30
Quiet Street, 39

Rainbow Effect: Interracial Families,
    367
Raising Mother Isn't Easy, 190
Rascal and the Pilgrim, 337
Rasmus and the Vagabond, 185
Reach for the Shadows, 458
Ready-Made Family, 200
Real For Sure Sister, 123
Really Real Family, 105
Refiner's Fire, 462
Relief's Rocker, 152
Requiem for a Princess, 272
Ring of Endless Light, 303
River of Promise, 360
Robin's Story: Physical Abuse and See-
    ing the Doctor, 26
Room for One More, 348, 411
Roundup series, 182
Ruby in the Smoke, 485
Runaway Alice, 201

Sadie Rose and the Cottonwood Creek
    Orphan, 229
Salute to Sandy, 409
Samantha, An American Girl, 240
Samantha Learns a Lesson, 240
Samantha Saves the Day, 240
Samantha's Surprise, 240
Search Aftermath and Adjustments, 415
Search for Anna Fisher, 366
Search for Maggie Hare, 447
Searching Heart, 269
Second Best Sister, 230

Second-hand Family, 209
Secret Language of the SB, 222
Secret Lover of Elmtree, 316
Seed From the East, 370
Seems Like Yesterday, 351
Sensible Kate, 163
Seven Years From Home, 131
Shadow in the North, 485
Shrine of Rainbows, 276
Sign of the Tumbling T, 290
Silent Fear, 182
Six More at Sixty, 372
Skinny, 139
Smoke, 286
So, Nothing is Forever, 172
So Sweet a Changeling, 441
So You're Adopted, 118, 261, 265
Somebody Else's Child, 223
Somebody Go and Bang a Drum, 145
Somebody That Nobody Knows, 459
Something to Crow About, 93
Son by Adoption, 500
Son of Fortune, 156
Song of the Heart, 326
Sons From Afar, 328
Sound of Coaches, 293
Speaking Likeness, 444
Special Kind of Courage, 266
Special You: A Story of Adoption, 84
Spell is Cast, 141
Spirit of Survival, 419
Star Island Boy, 217
Step-Families: New Patterns in Harmo-
    ny, 251
Stone Maiden, 469
Stories for Free Children, 2
Story of Adoption: Why Do I Look Dif-
    ferent?, 67
Story of Barbara, 36
Story of Sandy, 433
Strange Beginning, 466
Stranger With My Face, 289
Stuart Little, 143
Su An, 59
Sudden Change of Family, 126
Sudden Family, 422
Sudden Fury, 431
Suitcases, 437
Sunshine for Merrily, 175
Surrogate Mothers, 260

Surrogate Sister, 281
Survivor, 492
Susan and Gordon Adopt a Baby, 45
Sweet Illusions, 308
Sword of Shannara, 446

Tallie, 181
Tanya, 434
Tara, 465
Teddy Jo and the Missing Family, 319
Teddy Jo series, 319
Teenagers Talk About Adoption, 252
Tell Me My Name, 449
Tell Me No Lies, 149
Terror Train!, 150
That Jud!. 135
Then and Now, Victoria, 203
Then She Found Me, 472
Then There Were Five, 158
Theodore's Parents, 92
There is a Child for You, 414
They Became Part of Us, 425
They Came to Stay, 389
This Encircling Chain, 355
Thoughts on Adoption, 374
Through Moon and Stars and Night
    Skies, 91
Thursday's Child, 232, 457
Time to Search, 427
Tina Gogo, 124
To Keera With Love, 249
To Love and Let Go, 338
To My Son, 408
To Myself, 220
To See My Mother Dance, 299
To Sir With Love, 349
Toby, Granny, and George, 136
Tomas Takes Charge, 236
Tony: Our Journey Together, 376
Too Many Fathers, 207
Touchdown for Tommy, 146
Trigger John's Son, 219
Trina Finds a Brother, 134
Trouble Creek, 323
Trouble With Tuck, 238
Troublemaker, 271
True Grit, 473
Tuck Triumphant, 238
Tunnel of Love, 456
Twelve-Part Harmony, 439

Twice Born: Memoirs of an Adopted
    Daughter, 380
Twice-Upon-a-Time: Born and Adopt-
    ed, 16
Twins Who Found Each Other, 381
Two Brothers of Different Sex, 498

Unbroken Circle, 428
Understanding Kim, 154
Understood Betsy, 161
Us Maltbys, 307

Veronica, 483
Vicky, 320
Visiting Miss Pierce, 287

Wait for Tomorrow, 488
Walk in My Moccasins, 244
Wayne is Adopted, 95
We Adopted a Daughter, 344
We Adopted Three, 352
We Adopted You, Benjamin Koo, 49
We Are a Part of History, 396
We Don't Look Like Our Mom and
    Dad, 117
We Take This Child, 345
Web of Dreams, 442
Welcome Child, 1
We're a Family, 31
Were You Adopted?, 114
What Am I Doing in a Stepfamily?, 104
What If They Knew?, 169
What It's All About, 176
What Kind of Family is This?: A Book
    About Stepfamilies, 83
What Kind of Love is This, 392
What Lisa Knew, 375
When I See My Doctor, 10
Where Did I Come From, 111
Where the Sun Kisses the Sea, 46
Which Mother is Mine?, 313
Whirling Rainbows, 325
Who is David, 310
Who Is My Mother?, 388
Who Wants to Adopt Billy the Brave
    Bunny, 99
Who Wants to Adopt Georgie the Bold
    Baby Goose, 99
Who Wants to Adopt Paddy the Playful
    Puppy, 99

Who Wants to Adopt Willy the Wan-
     dering Kitten, 99
Whose Child am I?, 401
Why Am I Different?, 23
Why Was I Adopted?, 111
Widdles, 54
William is My Brother, 82
Wishsong of Shannara, 446
With Child, 430
Without Hats, Who Can Tell the Good
     Guys?, 122
Woman at the Well, 408
Woman Without a Past, 503
Wonderful Way Babies Are Made, 3
Won't Know Till I Get There, 309
Written in the Stars, 479

Yes, My Darling Daughter, 234
You and Your Child, 18
Young Ones, 497
Your Family, My Family, 5
Yours Turly, Shirley, 193

Subject Index

Numbers refer to entry, not page, numbers in the bibliography

Abuse, see Child abuse
Acting-out behavior, 142, 144, 162, 164, 195, 197, 206, 213, 226, 234, 237, 248, 271, 318, 322, 369, 372, 410, 491
Activity books, see Workbooks
Adolescent adoption (ages 12-18), 120, 158, 188, 216, 273, 309, 313, 329, 334, 416, 422, 461, 495
Adoption, explanation of, see Explanation of adoption
Adoption, legalization of, see Finalization
Adoptive parents, 61, 92, 106, 114, 119, 250, 315, 333, 344, 352, 406, 418, 425, 428, 435, 445
Adoptive parent as birthparent, 278, 424, 443, 456, 483, 486, 493, 497
Adult adoptees, 115, 252, 334, 364, 366, 369, 371, 378, 379, 380, 381, 388, 396, 401, 402, 421, 423, 424, 427
Africa, 156
Age at adoption, see Infant adoption, Preschooler adoption, Older child adoption, Adolescent adoption
Alcoholism, 108, 268, 373
Amerasians (see also Biracial, and Transracial adoption), 1, 137, 349, 363, 365, 408, 416, 479
Anger, 48, 83, 87, 102, 120, 122, 124, 131, 140, 144, 160, 164, 195, 213, 271, 300, 301, 310, 324

Animal stories (see also Fantasy stories), 25, 27, 32, 37, 60, 64, 80, 93, 94, 99, 100, 103, 174
Animals, 120, 151, 165, 218, 225, 248, 286, 298
Apprenticeship, 151, 187
Arrival stories, 16, 17, 18, 24, 29, 35, 36, 41, 42, 44, 45, 56 46, 47, 49, 59, 61, 67, 78, 81, 91, 96, 105, 242, 341, 406
Artificial insemination, 21
Astral projection, 289, 461
Attachment, see Bonding
Australia, 239

Baby M, 260, 436
Babysitting, 191, 192
Baseball, 202
Biblical characters, 38, 267
Biracial (see also Amerasians, and Transracial adoption), 113, 289, 325, 385
Birthmother, 32, 85, 94, 108, 124, 129, 136, 142, 210, 227, 249, 284, 299, 313, 334, 338, 353, 392, 412, 413, 417, 420, 436, 441. 449
Birthfather, 28, 128, 130, 208, 292, 296, 316, 450, 453, 454, 490, 501
Birthparents (see also Birthmother, and Birthfather), 48, 206, 250, 287, 368, 445, 448, 464, 472
Black family, 30, 35, 45, 237, 309, 385

Black market adoption (see also Child selling), 259, 377, 386, 440, 471, 482, 486, 487

Bonding, 25, 51, 83, 120, 128, 138, 140, 149, 154, 157, 200, 201, 209, 210, 213, 217, 219, 224, 225, 226, 234, 244, 246, 248, 261, 273, 277, 322, 354, 356, 363, 395, 455

Buchwald, Art, 351

Cambodia, 419

Canada, 152, 198, 252, 290, 300, 312, 388, 405, 412

Celebrity adoption, 351, 359, 373, 404, 408, 409, 438

Chess, 495

Child abuse, 106, 174, 182, 221, 233, 264, 274, 306, 359, 375, 385, 442

Child selling (see also Black market adoption), 170, 259, 442, 485

Children as authors, 2, 106, 109

Children's homes, see Orphanages

China, 179, 498

Chinese family, 178

Christian perspective, 3, 4, 14, 31, 36, 38, 77, 78, 203, 206, 227, 228, 229, 233, 242, 267, 290, 319, 335, 346, 348, 357, 360, 387, 394, 395, 399, 408, 409, 422, 423, 439, 463, 477

Colombia (for adoption of Colombian children, see Intercountry adoption - Colombian), 6, 428

Counseling, 106, 107

Crawford, Joan, 359

Deafness, 238

Death, 25, 51, 64, 102, 146, 186, 188, 199, 214, 273, 276, 284, 286, 290, 301, 314, 319, 323, 324, 331, 375, 403, 408, 409, 448, 468, 470, 474, 478, 480, 481, 499, 500

Differences, 4, 5, 11, 19, 22, 23, 31, 38, 49, 58, 67, 73, 74, 78, 79, 82, 89, 97, 110, 117, 153, 163, 179, 184, 188, 191, 193, 196, 206, 230, 233, 239, 245, 247, 285, 288, 309, 317, 325, 326, 330, 342, 414

Disability, mental, 245, 332, 357, 361, 393, 433

Disability, physical, 80, 238, 266, 332, 347, 348, 357, 393, 411, 416, 422, 423, 434

Dolls, 33

Dyslexia, 193

Edna Gladney Center, 400

Elderly, 287, 309

England, 24, 28, 62, 63, 95, 118, 209, 284, 293, 294, 301, 306, 320, 329, 349, 435, 441, 444, 445, 450, 454, 458, 466, 476, 480, 488, 494, 500

Evans, Dale, 408, 409

Explanation of adoption, 2, 3, 4, 6, 7, 8, 9, 11, 13, 14, 15, 16, 17, 18, 19, 21, 24, 32, 36, 38, 47, 48, 49, 52, 63, 65, 66, 67, 72, 77, 79, 87, 88, 109, 111, 112, 114, 115, 116, 118, 119, 223, 250, 252, 253, 254, 256, 258, 263, 265, 345, 374, 388, 401, 405, 425, 429

Extended family, 52, 56, 127, 136, 144, 148, 172, 280, 288, 296, 325

Family, concept of, 5, 11, 13, 17, 18, 22, 23, 33, 34, 37, 40, 42, 64, 65, 68, 77, 79, 83, 85, 89, 90, 92, 95, 110, 112, 117, 131, 138, 152, 175, 200, 201, 203, 209, 229, 246, 257, 261, 271, 279, 298, 321

Family, extended, see Extended family

Family trees, 269, 304

Fantasies, 78, 122, 128, 129, 139, 149, 157, 184, 210, 211, 218, 221, 269, 280, 299, 300, 305, 316, 467

Fantasy stories (see also Animal stories), 58, 73, 74, 90, 92,, 144, 147, 151, 183, 446

Feelings about adoption (see also Anger), 106, 109, 111, 258

Fertility problems, see Infertility

Fetal alcohol syndrome, 361

Finalization, 44, 50, 63, 78, 95, 128

Foreign adoption, see Intercountry adoption

Foster care, 17, 26, 30, 69, 76, 86, 95, 105, 108, 120, 121, 122, 124, 140, 142, 146, 157, 165, 166, 167, 174, 182, 200, 201, 208, 209, 210, 217, 220, 221, 222, 248, 254, 256, 264,

271, 274, 283, 307, 313, 319, 320,
   322, 324, 330, 334, 346, 349, 411,
   437, 491
Foster parent adoption, 146, 166, 181,
   227, 241, 346
France, 143, 351, 492
Friends, 2, 55, 73, 75,76, 93, 103, 132,
   135, 142, 154, 167, 185, 211, 212,
   215, 223, 247, 308, 320

Gay/lesbian parents, 110, 360, 453
Germany, 385, 387
Greece, 133
Guardianship, 141, 337, 433, 451

Hispanic family, 199
Historical fiction, 153, 159, 170, 177,
   178, 187, 198, 204, 215, 235, 240,
   272, 285, 293, 294, 297, 447, 455,
   470, 473, 499
Holt Adoption Program, 370
Homosexuals as parents, see
   Gay/lesbian parents
Hong Kong, 474
Horror stories, 289, 461, 475, 481, 494

Identity, 49, 60, 67, 78, 107, 239, 269,
   283, 327, 342, 406, 414
Independent adoption, 375, 448
Independence, 135, 136, 138, 158, 161
India (for adoption of Indian children,
   see Intercountry adoption - Indian,
   East), 501
Infant adoption (ages 0-2), 2, 18, 24, 29,
   36, 42, 44, 45, 52, 53, 56, 57, 61, 62,
   63, 66, 67, 70, 72, 75, 78, 79, 84, 85,
   88, 96, 123, 231, 293, 295, 302, 311,
   335, 338, 341, 344, 350, 352, 360,
   363, 365, 413, 416, 430, 432, 444,
   445, 447, 456, 457, 463, 466, 481, 494
Infertility, 29, 62, 314, 335, 352, 377,
   387, 430, 447, 450, 457, 482
Intercountry adoption (for adoption in
   foreign country, see name of country; see also Transracial adoption)
   -General, 31, 145, 239, 348, 360, 363,
   406
   -African, 28, 134
   -Arabic, 339
   -Asian, non-specific, 10, 46, 91

-Brazilian, 49, 393
-Cambodian, 419
-Chinese, 54, 178
-Colombian, 6, 72, 169, 384, 428, 430
-El Salvadoran, 393
-English, 435
-French, 277, 341, 351
-German, 277, 385, 387
-Indian, East, 19, 79, 339, 393, 501
-Irish, 351
-Italian, 277
-Japanese, 54, 339
-Korean, 1, 15, 19, 44, 49, 59, 67, 72,
   78, 81, 97, 106, 117, 134, 137, 154,
   189, 190, 205, 216, 238, 277, 339,
   347, 370, 389, 408, 416, 423, 428,
   431, 439
-Latvian, 410
-Mexican, 123, 376
-Norwegian, 339
-Philippine, 439
-Polish, 451
-Puerto Rican, 54
-Spanish, 351
-Taiwan, 222, 418
-Venezuelan, 339
-Vietnamese, 8, 70, 150, 176, 191,
   192, 193, 197, 266, 347, 356, 363,
   365, 384, 389, 393, 422, 428
Interracial families (see also Trans-
   racial adoption, and Intercountry
   adoption), 2, 20, 28, 37, 54, 98, 101,
   145, 155, 172, 206, 307, 339, 342, 367
Ireland, 458
Ireland, Jill, 373
Israel, 462, 487

Jackson, Andrew, 159
Japanese family, 191, 296, 312
Jealousy, 125, 168, 186, 193, 196, 289
Journalists, 173, 350, 371, 377, 378, 379,
   380, 385, 386, 389, 407, 419, 424,
   435, 463, 502
Judaism, 20, 325, 418, 451

Kidnapping, 492
Korea (for adoption of Korean chil-
   dren, see Intercountry adoption -
   Korean), 15, 59, 67, 81, 106, 117,

137, 205, 216, 337, 370, 389, 423, 428, 479

Large families (5 or more children), 28, 95, 98, 105, 145, 155, 158, 206, 244, 282, 285, 303, 307, 317, 330, 339, 347, 348, 350, 357, 362, 370, 372, 373, 384, 393, 397, 399, 407, 411, 416, 432, 439, 492, 494
Legalization of adoption, see Finalization
Louganis, Greg, 113

Maternity home, 302, 426
Mennonite, 77, 226, 233
Mental illness, 69, 76, 274, 410
Mexico, 376
Migrant workers, 246, 321, 372
Multi-racial families, see Interracial families
Murder, 314, 431, 471, 475, 486, 494, 502
Mystery stories, 141, 150, 199, 272, 275, 278, 290, 294, 315, 323, 331, 447, 458, 464, 467, 468, 469, 471, 475, 482, 484, 485, 486, 502, 503

Native American family, 283, 361
New Zealand, 470
Neglect, 174, 237, 264, 271, 330, 375, 399, 409, 410, 432, 440, 442
Norway, 134

Older child adoption (ages 6-11), 43, 46, 50, 55, 59, 68, 81, 98, 123, 127, 137, 138, 141, 146, 147, 152, 153, 160, 163, 168, 173, 181, 183, 193, 195, 198, 202, 205, 209, 218, 219, 225, 227, 234, 238, 241, 276, 306, 324, 358, 376, 389, 395, 396, 399, 416, 423, 431, 434, 440, 447, 455, 466, 474, 493, 498
Open adoption, 85, 249, 333, 335, 338, 353, 379, 382, 412, 420
Orphan train, 204, 228, 235, 240, 396, 473
Orphanages, 43, 46, 81, 139, 143, 153, 160, 168, 171, 183, 185, 202, 205, 218, 232, 340, 400, 437

Parents, see Adoptive parents, and Birthparents
Personal narratives, 105, 109, 115, 332, 333, 335, 337, 339, 341, 343, 346, 347, 348, 350, 351, 352, 356, 358, 359, 360, 361, 362, 363, 364, 365, 366, 369, 370, 372, 376, 377, 378, 380, 385, 387, 390, 392, 393, 394, 397, 399, 402, 403, 404, 407, 408, 409, 410, 411, 412, 413, 414, 416, 417, 418, 419, 421, 422, 423, 425, 426, 428, 430, 434, 436, 437, 438, 439, 440
Poetry, 47, 84, 355, 398
Pregnancy (see also Unwed mothers), 125, 249, 262, 291, 292, 308, 383, 391, 394, 426, 477, 480
Prejudice, 97, 148, 170, 172, 244, 245, 311, 342, 451, 483
Preschooler adoption (ages 3-5), 1, 2, 56, 65, 91, 147, 159, 162, 176, 190, 191, 226, 352, 354, 358, 361, 389, 399, 416, 432, 435, 460, 483, 500
Personal identity, see Identity
Private adoption, see Independent adoption
Private arrangement, 135, 139
Puerto Rican family, 236

Quinlan, Karen Ann, 403

Racial identity, see Identity
Reagan, Ronald, 404
Refugees, 133, 277, 419, 451, 462
Relative adoption, 34, 130, 161, 172, 178, 180, 194, 199, 211, 232, 237, 243, 270, 282, 294, 303, 328, 329, 493
Religious fanatics, 173, 274
Reunion with birthfamily, 94, 126, 149, 264, 269, 290, 291, 295, 296, 300, 304, 305, 312, 316, 331, 334, 343, 364, 366, 368, 369, 371, 378, 379, 380, 381, 390, 392, 415, 417, 421, 424, 427, 438, 442, 444, 447, 449, 453, 464, 465, 467, 469, 472, 476, 478, 488, 489, 490, 491, 496, 501, 502, 503
Rogers, Roy, 408, 409
Romance stories, 280, 313, 326, 452, 463, 464, 466, 468, 472, 488

Running away, 90, 99, 201, 217, 322, 491

School, 269, 287, 304
Scotland, 118, 157, 276, 350, 447, 467, 468
Search for birthfamily, 94, 126, 131, 149, 253, 264, 269, 278, 279, 291, 295, 300, 304, 305, 310, 312, 320, 331, 334, 343, 364, 366, 369, 371, 378, 379, 380, 381, 388, 390, 392, 415, 417, 421, 424, 427, 438, 442, 443, 447, 453, 458, 459, 465, 467, 469, 476, 478, 479, 488, 489, 490, 491, 503
Secrecy about adoption, 126, 184, 191, 207, 212, 247, 272, 289, 295, 296, 317, 326, 449, 452, 454, 458, 459, 465, 469, 476, 480, 481, 483, 488, 490, 491, 496, 497
Self-acceptance, 23, 58, 60, 66, 80, 89, 97, 107, 118, 140, 144, 169, 220, 279, 285, 285, 291, 310, 498
Self-reliance, 161, 163, 167, 168, 180, 182, 188, 194, 198, 236, 243, 246, 281, 328, 329, 457, 478, 499
Sesame Street, 45
Sex education, 3, 9, 12, 16, 21, 36
Sibling adoption, 65, 103, 105, 147, 152, 175, 186, 195, 202, 228, 229, 240, 264, 319, 372, 395, 396, 399, 422, 439, 468
Sibling rivalry, 27, 83, 86, 105, 125, 128, 186, 189, 193, 196, 208, 224, 230, 242, 245, 288, 315, 326
Siblings, 27, 35, 39,52, 57, 70, 71, 72, 75, 82, 86, 88, 114, 117, 122, 123, 130, 131, 133, 151, 154, 155, 157, 158, 169, 171, 174, 177, 181, 188, 197, 200, 204, 206, 214, 226, 231, 236, 243, 282, 303, 309, 437, 489, 497
Single parent adoption, 40, 50, 93, 127, 175, 190, 214, 276, 306, 341, 360, 365, 376, 460
South Africa, 483
Soto, Hernando de, 297
Special needs, see Disability, and Mental illness
Stealing, 164, 271, 318, 322

Stepfamilies/stepparents, 21, 51, 70, 83, 102, 104, 121, 176, 224, 251, 255, 268, 286, 299, 301, 323
Stepparent adoption, 128, 129, 149, 212, 213, 296, 318, 466
Support groups, 310, 312
Surrogate parenting, 259, 260, 281, 436

Teasing, 43, 97
Teenage pregnancy, see Pregnancy
Transracial adoption (see also Intercountry adoption, and Interracial families)
  -General, 60, 145, 155, 336, 362, 367, 393
  -Asian child, 132, 179, 312, 387, 407, 430
  -Black/biracial child, 2, 19, 62, 71, 88, 95, 123, 132, 311, 327, 347, 350, 384, 393, 407, 414, 416, 460, 483
  -Hispanic child, 171, 413
  -Native American child, 159, 244, 283, 289, 297, 325, 407
Twins, 53, 54, 152, 214, 289, 371, 381, 397, 421, 439, 503

Unwed mothers (see also Pregnancy), 249, 262, 291, 302, 308, 383, 391, 394, 412, 413, 426, 444, 445, 457, 477

Vampires, 481
Vietnam (for adoption of Vietnamese children, see Intercountry adoption - Vietnamese), 8, 266, 356, 384, 389, 409, 428

Williams, Hank, 438
Workbooks, 6, 8, 11, 14, 15, 66, 107, 257

About the Author

SUSAN G. MILES, reference librarian and associate professor at Central Michigan University, is a parent of eight adopted children. Professor Miles is the author of two books on computer technology in library science, as well as many professional articles.